'So That You Might Know Each Other'

FAITH AND CULTURE IN ISLAM

COLLECTIONS FROM THE VATICAN *ANIMA MUNDI* MUSEUM, THE SHARJAH MUSEUMS AUTHORITY AND THE NATIONAL MUSEUM OF AUSTRALIA

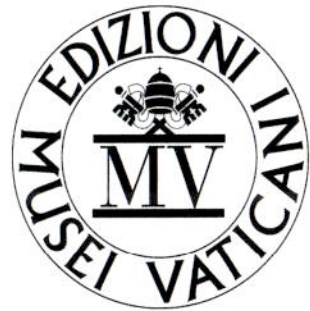

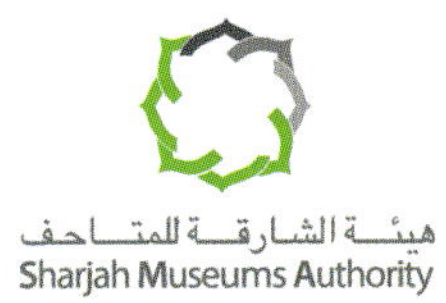

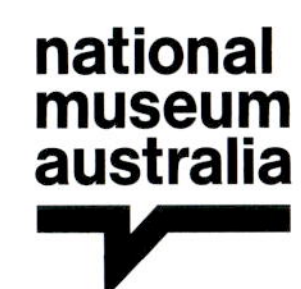

First edition

Editorial direction	**Ulrike Al-Khamis, Fr Nicola Mapelli**
Texts	**Katherine Aigner, Nadia Fiussello, Ulrike Al-Khamis**
Vatican research support	**Claudia Di Fede, Alessandra Ceccarelli**
Scientific and editorial coordinator	**Ulrike Al-Khamis**
Translation and editing	**Mamdouh Khodir**
Translation of research texts	**Fr William Skudlarek OSB**
Arabic proofreading	**Abdul Motalib Al Saab**
Catalogue design concept	**Yellow Designs, www.tyduae.com**
Map design	**Bassant Mamdouh Abu Ali**
Vatican photography	**Pietro Zigrossi, Alessandro Bracchetti, Luigi Giordano**
Additional photography	**Eric Stoner, Matteo Carnevali (assisted by Alessandra Rocco)**
Vatican photographic research	**Rosanna Di Pinto, Filippo Petrignani, Paola Di Giammaria**
Vatican Museums Publishing Office	**Federico Di Cesare, Carla Cecilia**

Second edition

Additional texts	**Huda Alteneiji, Carol Cooper**
Sharjah object research	**Huda Alteneiji, Muna Al Ali, Amanda Snyder, Ulrike Al-Khamis**
Sharjah photography	**Abdul Hanaan, Pankaj Shah**
Lead curator	**Carol Cooper**
Curatorial assistance	**Katherine Aigner, Mona Soleymani**
Exhibition project management	**Vicki Northey, Kate Bruxner**
Registration	**Sara Kelly, Louise Palmer**
Conservation	**Tania Riviere**
Research librarians	**Noellen Newton, Naomi Newton**
Publisher's editors	**Thérèse Osborne, Julie Simpkin**
Additional copyediting	**Federico Di Cesare, Carla Cecilia, Cristina D'Andrea**
Design	**Po Sung**
Copyright and image delivery	**Denis French, Almaz Berhe, Hermini Rohmursanto**
Australian object photography	**Brendan Bell, George Serras, unless otherwise credited**

First published 2014

Second edition April 2018

Cover image: *Taqsireh* (lady's festive jacket), Vatican *Anima Mundi* Museum, inv. 112314, p. 88

A catalogue record for this book is available from the National Library of Australia.
ISBN: 9781921953323 (paperback)

National Museum of Australia Press
GPO Box 1901 Canberra ACT 2601 Australia
Telephone +61 2 6208 5000
nma.gov.au

Print: Australian Book Connection, Hong Kong
Typeset in Mrs Eaves and Sero Pro

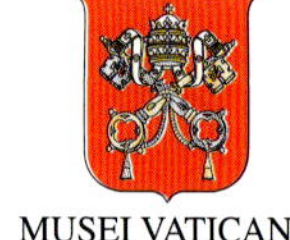

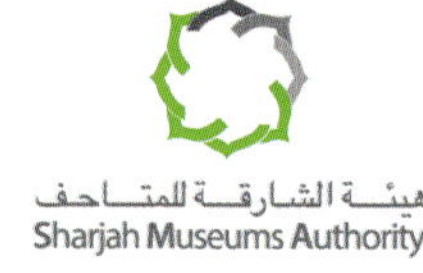

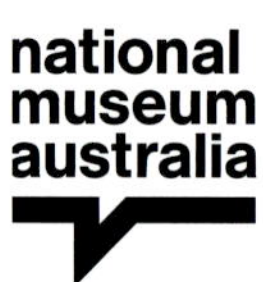

Note
In this catalogue, the term 'Middle East' refers to countries in south-west Asia including Turkey, Iran, Iraq, Lebanon, Oman, Palestine, Saudi Arabia, Syria and the United Arab Emirates. It does not include North African countries such as Egypt, Libya, Tunisia, Algeria or Morocco. The country ascribed to an object is judged to be where its most significant use occurred, if it differs from the country of manufacture.

Contents

Acknowledgements

The National Museum of Australia warmly thanks the Vatican *Anima Mundi* Museum of World Arts and Cultures, Vatican City State, and the Sharjah Museums Authority, Emirate of Sharjah, our international partners in delivering '*So That You Might Know Each Other': Faith and Culture in Islam* in Australia.

Our respect and gratitude goes to Fr Nicola Mapelli, Director of the Vatican *Anima Mundi* Museum, who has worked tirelessly to bring the museum's collections to wider public access and recognition. We also thank curators Katherine Aigner and Nadia Fiussello; the head of the Laboratorio Polimaterico, Stefania Pandozy, and her team of restorers; Exhibition Assistant Isabella Leone; Dr Rosanna Di Pinto, Head of the Images and Rights Office; and Federico Di Cesare, Head of the Editorial Office. We thank Dr Barbara Jatta, Director of the Vatican Museums, its Administrative Delegate, Monsignor Paolo Nicolini; and its Scientific Delegate, Dr Guido Cornini.

We pay tribute to Hazelle Anne Page, Collections Manager for the Sharjah Museums Authority. Ms Page and her colleagues have demonstrated a commitment to sharing with Australian audiences their precious objects, as well as their deep understanding and appreciation of other cultures. We also acknowledge from the Sharjah Museums Authority the contributions made by Ulrike Al-Khamis, former Senior Strategic Advisor; Curator Entisar Muean Al Obaidili; Director of Executive Affairs Aisha Rashid Deemas; and Historical Researcher Huda Alteneiji.

Within Australia, we have enjoyed the support, advice and co-operation of other cultural institutions. Our gratitude goes to the Islamic Museum of Australia, Melbourne, in particular Head Curator Jake Carter and Director of Education Sherene Hassan. The Islamic Museum of Australia has been inspirational for our Canberra exhibition, and has willingly provided information and expertise to help shape the exhibition for Australian audiences. From the Casula Powerhouse Arts Centre, Curator Adam Porter and Registrar Semi Ozacardi contributed valuable assistance in relation to the Islamic community in Western Sydney.

Other Australian collecting institutions have loaned significant historical objects for the exhibition and provided advice about their collections. Our thanks to Senior Curator Philip Jones and Senior Collections

Manager Alice Beale of the South Australian Museum, Adelaide; Registrar Poppy Searle and Collections Officer Samantha Lillie of the Northern Territory Museum and Art Gallery, Darwin; and Margaret Simpson, Transport Curator at the Museum of Applied Arts and Sciences, Sydney.

We thank the exceptional individuals who have shared their skills and insights in the process of developing the Australian stories in the exhibition. Kuranda Seyit, Executive Director of Whirling Dervish Media, and Bejah Dervish's grandson William Bejah have given freely of their knowledge of this famous Muslim cameleer. The National Museum has also benefited from the specialised expertise of Professor Campbell Macknight and independent curator and art historian Susan Scollay.

The Museum also recognises the contributions of its own staff in the development of this exhibition, and thanks them all for their tireless dedication and commitment.

Finally, our thanks to the peoples represented in this catalogue, for sharing with us their faith and culture.

Carol Cooper

Senior Curator, National Museum of Australia

Foreword

It is a great honour for the National Museum of Australia to join with the Vatican *Anima Mundi* Museum, Rome, and the Sharjah Museums Authority, Emirate of Sharjah, to present cherished cultural objects from the world of Islam to an Australian audience. Similarly, I am delighted that the Museum has sourced — from its own collection and those of other Australian museums and galleries — objects that illustrate the ongoing contribution of people of Islamic faith to Australian history.

The exhibition '*So That You Might Know Each Other*' celebrates the continuing relationship of the National Museum of Australia with the Vatican *Anima Mundi* Museum and its enlightened director, Fr Nicola Mapelli. In 2010 Fr Mapelli re-opened the ethnological collections for the Vatican Museums with *Rituals of Life*, an exhibition dedicated to the spirituality and culture of Indigenous Australians. Co-curated by staff from the National Museum, this exhibition sought to give voice to Australian Aboriginal people, a fundamental aspiration of our own institution.

The original '*So That You Might Know Each Other*' exhibition was held at the Museum of Islamic Civilization, Sharjah, during Sharjah's celebrations as ISESCO Capital of Islamic Culture in 2014. It displayed Islamic objects from the Vatican Museums, mostly obtained as gifts to Pope Pius XI in 1925. It continued the Vatican's efforts to promote dialogue and peaceful co-existence, as well as recognition and respect for world cultures. Furthermore, the exhibition was highly commended as reflecting the wise vision and conviction of His Highness Sheikh Dr Sultan bin Mohammed Al Qasimi, Member of the Supreme Council of the United Arab Emirates and Ruler of Sharjah.

Objects and artworks in museum collections can serve as ambassadors for the people and cultures of whom they are an expression. As custodians of cultural collections, the National Museum of Australia and its international partners jointly strive to acknowledge and appreciate these objects' beauty and individual brilliance, and endeavour to make them accessible to the widest audience. I warmly thank our partners in Rome and Sharjah for their foresight and generosity in bringing their precious objects from across the Islamic world to Australia. They come with the spirit to extend the network of global relationships that allows people of different cultures to share a love of art, design and craftsmanship, and help to get to know and appreciate each other.

My thanks to all of the teams across the three institutions who have contributed their creativity and commitment to produce this highly significant exhibition.

Dr Mathew Trinca
Director, National Museum of Australia

Foreword

It is a source of joy for me to introduce this catalogue, published on the occasion of the exhibition, '*So That You Might Know Each Other*', at the National Museum of Australia in Canberra. In an unprecedented collaboration, the Vatican Museums, the Sharjah Museums Authority and the National Museum of Australia worked together to organise an exhibition to show arts from the world of Islam from Africa to Asia, and Australia.

In the Vatican Museums, Islamic artefacts are held in the *Anima Mundi* Museum, the section of the Vatican Museums that hosts art and religious objects from all over the world. A selection of these objects has been sent to Australia for the exhibition, giving testimony to the fruitful, cultural and artistic exchange that has taken place between Islam and Christianity over the centuries. These precious works of art have come to the Vatican Museums from many different parts of the world: Morocco to Indonesia, Zanzibar to China, Palestine to Iraq, the Ivory Coast to the Philippines. Many of them were sent as gifts to Pope Pius XI on the occasion of a major exhibition held at the Vatican in 1925. They have all been carefully preserved as a cherished inheritance from the past and a treasure for future generations.

I find it significant that this exhibition, along with the catalogue that accompanies it, is taking place during the pontificate of Pope Francis. Mutual understanding and dialogue between cultures are clearly among the priorities of his ministry.

This catalogue is the fruit of a collaboration between prestigious cultural institutions from three continents. May it deepen the friendship that already exists and strengthen mutual respect and harmony.

Giuseppe Cardinal Bertello
President of the Governorate of Vatican City State

Foreword

In 2014 the Vatican Museums organised a major exhibition in Sharjah, United Arab Emirates, in collaboration with the Sharjah Museum of Islamic Civilization. It was the first time in the 500-year history of the Vatican Museums that their unseen treasures of Islamic art and cultures were put on display in an Islamic country.

The success of the event was such that, only a few months after its closing, Fr Nicola Mapelli, head of the section of the Vatican Museums where the Islamic art is held, and curator Katherine Aigner, during a research trip to Australia, met Mathew Trinca, now Director of the National Museum of Australia, and proposed to have a similar Islamic exhibit for the Australian public. Dr Trinca gladly saw the beauty of such an idea.

In the following years the project was developed until it reached the present form: a unique collaboration among three museums — the Vatican Museums, the Sharjah Museums Authority, and the National Museum of Australia — with the aim of showing parts of the world of Islam from Africa and Asia to Australia through their own collections.

I have only recently become Director of the Vatican Museums, and it's always a pleasure for me to learn something new about their vast collections. As I followed the preparation of this exhibition, I was sincerely struck not only by the dedication of our team to the project, but also by the beauty and sophistication of the Islamic world. I saw firsthand, through the objects in our museum, the refined productions of people living in a vast area stretching from Africa to Australia.

I wish to commend Fr Nicola Mapelli, his collaborators Katherine Aigner and Nadia Fiussello, and the team of restorers led by Stefania Pandozy for all they have done over the past four years to prepare this exhibition. At the same time, I wish to thank our colleagues in Australia and Sharjah for their enthusiastic collaboration on this project which, I am sure, will contribute to fostering a fruitful dialogue of peace between Islam and Christianity not only in Australia but also in the rest of the world.

Barbara Jatta
Director of the Vatican Museums

Foreword

Building upon a unique and unprecedented collaboration of friendship between the Sharjah Museums Authority and the Vatican *Anima Mundi* Museum, we are delighted with the result of an exciting new partnership with the National Museum of Australia in Canberra, to present a groundbreaking exhibition showcasing collections from all three prestigious institutions. '*So That You Might Know Each Other*' is an exhibition devised to give a glimpse of the diverse ways of life of Muslims all over the world, their customs and cultural traditions, and the fascinating stories that lie behind some of the objects they made and used. At the same time it is intended to increase intercultural dialogue and promote tolerance and peace — among Muslims the world over and between Islam and other religions.

We are extremely pleased to collaborate once again with the Vatican Museums to re-create the '*So That You Might Know Each Other*' exhibition, which was originally designed to coincide with the official launch of Sharjah's year-long celebrations as Capital of Islamic Culture in 2014. This exhibition profoundly reflects the vision of His Highness Sheikh Dr Sultan bin Mohammed Al Qasimi, Member of the Supreme Council of the United Arab Emirates and Ruler of Sharjah, in showcasing Sharjah as the region's foremost beacon of Islamic culture, art and education.

Manal Ataya
Director General, Sharjah Museums Authority

Introduction

Fr Nicola Mapelli
Director of the Vatican Anima Mundi *Museum of World Arts and Cultures*

Ulrike Al-Khamis
Former Senior Strategic Adviser, Sharjah Museums Authority

Carol Cooper
Senior Curator, National Museum of Australia

This exhibition of Islamic art and material culture has been many years in the making. It builds on a previous exhibition held in Sharjah, in the United Arab Emirates, in 2014, which evolved from the Vatican's wish to make its Islamic collection more widely known within the Muslim world and beyond. His Highness Sheikh Dr Sultan bin Mohammed Al Qasimi, Member of the Supreme Council of the United Arab Emirates and Ruler of Sharjah, wholeheartedly supported the idea, enabling the Vatican *Anima Mundi* Museum and the Sharjah Museum of Islamic Civilization to co-curate the exhibition, hand in hand.

Later, a similar project was proposed to the National Museum of Australia for a Canberra exhibition, and so a three-way collaboration commenced to bring this bold idea to fruition. Over the years, we have jointly discussed, selected, researched and prepared the objects for the show — a process that has established a lasting trust and warm friendship between colleagues on three continents.

The resulting exhibition keeps the same title as its 2014 counterpart: '*So That You Might Know Each Other*'. Inspired by a verse within the Holy Qur'an, it invites us all to reach out across religions and cultures in a spirit of positive curiosity, creativity, friendship, tolerance and peace. More specifically, from the Vatican's viewpoint, the exhibition demonstrates its respect for and appreciation of the Islamic world, not least by its efforts to preserve and cherish within its walls an extensive collection of Islamic art and material culture, which it treats with the same dedication extended to the masterpieces of Michelangelo, Raphael and Leonardo Da Vinci also in its care.

The experience of developing this exhibition has been a positive and creative one for all those involved, in the Vatican, in Sharjah and in Australia. We hope that this spirit of friendship and mutual commitment will shine through to all who visit the exhibition.

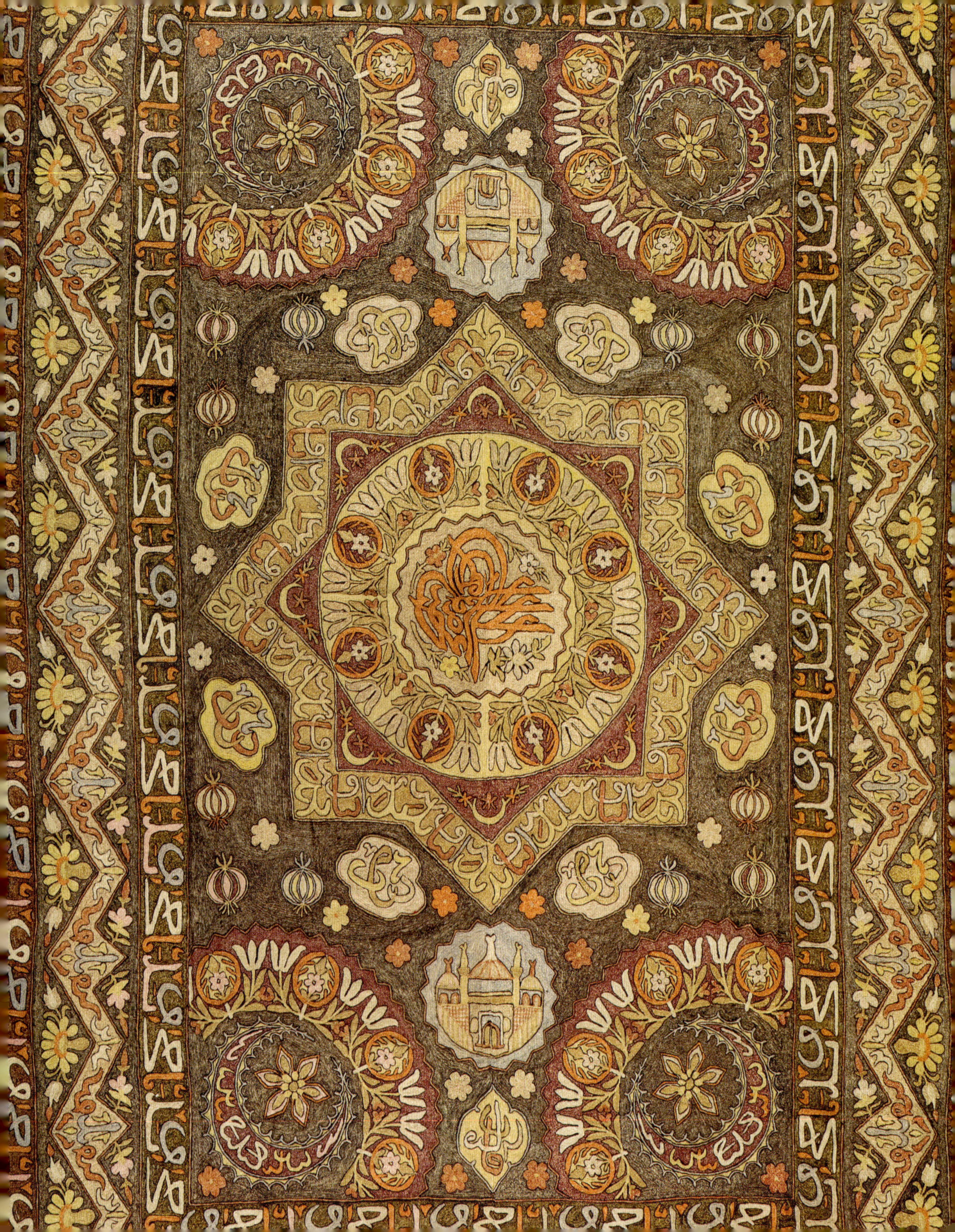

The ethnography of Islam

From the African collection of the Vatican *Anima Mundi* Museum

KATHERINE AIGNER

The African collection of the Vatican *Anima Mundi* Museum (formerly the Vatican Ethnological Museum) comprises approximately 10,000 objects; inventory records indicate that about 2000 of them come from 'North Africa'. Most of the museum's artefacts that represent the African Muslim world come from this area.[1]

The African Muslim objects can be grouped into two main categories. The first is made up of historical-archaeological or art-historical items, such as ceramic shards (Fig. 2; inv. 100696) or artefacts that give evidence of various Islamic metalwork traditions (Fig. 3; inv. 100760, p. 14).

The second group consists of ethnographic pieces dating mainly from the late 19th to early 20th centuries. This larger sector of the collection boasts many interesting, visually fascinating and unusual objects that represent the rich and diverse ethnographic material culture of the Islamic world of North Africa. To these, a smaller number of other ethnographic items is added, which testify to the spread of the Islamic world to other parts of Africa, such as Ghana and Zanzibar. Taken together, all these artefacts show that the Islamic world is not a monolithic civilisation, but includes a plurality of expressions that reflect the different cultural contexts in which they are embodied.

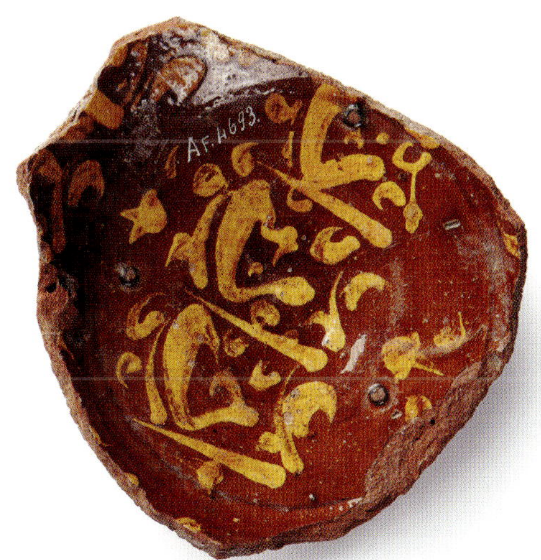

Figure 2

This paper focuses on this second category of artefacts, the Islamic African ethnographic collection. It grants us but one window into the extraordinary creativity found throughout the Islamic world.

Figure 1: Metal-thread embroidered textile (detail), inv. 112414, p. 56

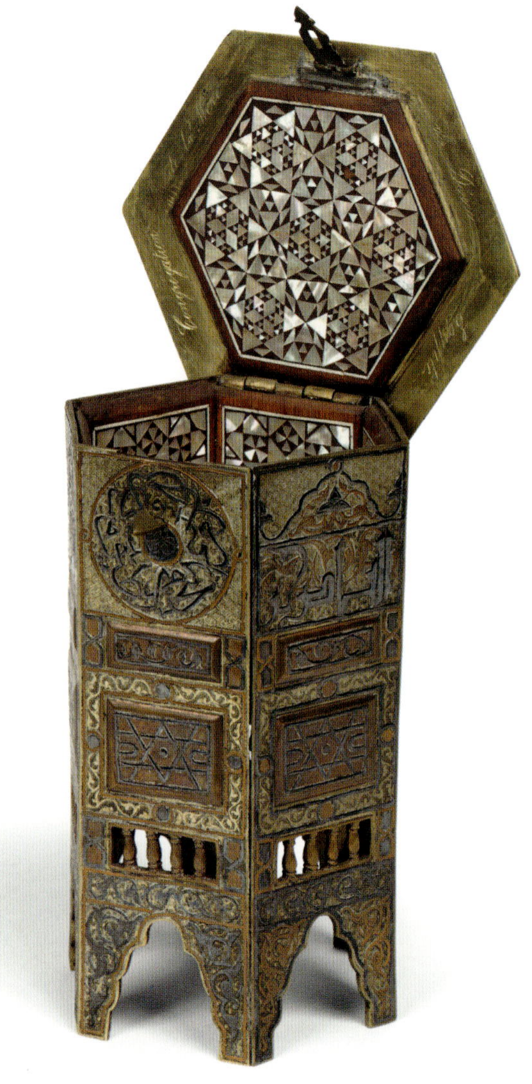

Figure 3

THE BORGIA COLLECTION

The beginnings of the African collection can be traced back to the collections of Cardinal Stefano Borgia (1731–1804; Fig. 4).

Cardinal Borgia was a scholar and collector of works of art and objects from all over the world, which in his day were regarded as 'curiosities'. His collections included African objects that he had purchased or received as gifts. His interest in collecting such works was helped by the fact that for a long time he worked at the highest levels of the Congregation of Propaganda Fide, the department of the Catholic Church charged with overlooking its affairs in non-European countries. Eventually he became the head of this Congregation. In this position, he met travellers and guests from all over the world, who often brought with them gifts from distant lands.

When the Cardinal died in 1804, most of his collection was transferred to the Palazzo di Propaganda Fide near the Piazza di Spagna in Rome and placed in a special area called the Borgia Museum. The collection remained there until the late 1920s, when Pope Pius XI ordered it to be transferred to the Vatican Ethnological Museum, which he had officially established in 1926.

According to an undated list that gives a general inventory of the works transferred from the Borgia Museum to the Vatican Ethnological Museum at that time, there were 113 North African objects among those works.[2] This list, however, gives only the total number of objects from some major areas or specific groups and does not go into detail about individual pieces. Furthermore, the only source of reliable information on the Borgia Museum, Angelo Colini's *Collezioni Etnografiche del Museo Borgiano* (1885), does not dedicate much space to African and Islamic ethnography.[3] Therefore, identifying these objects among today's collections has required considerable archival work as well as careful evaluation of the actual contents of the collection, which is still ongoing.

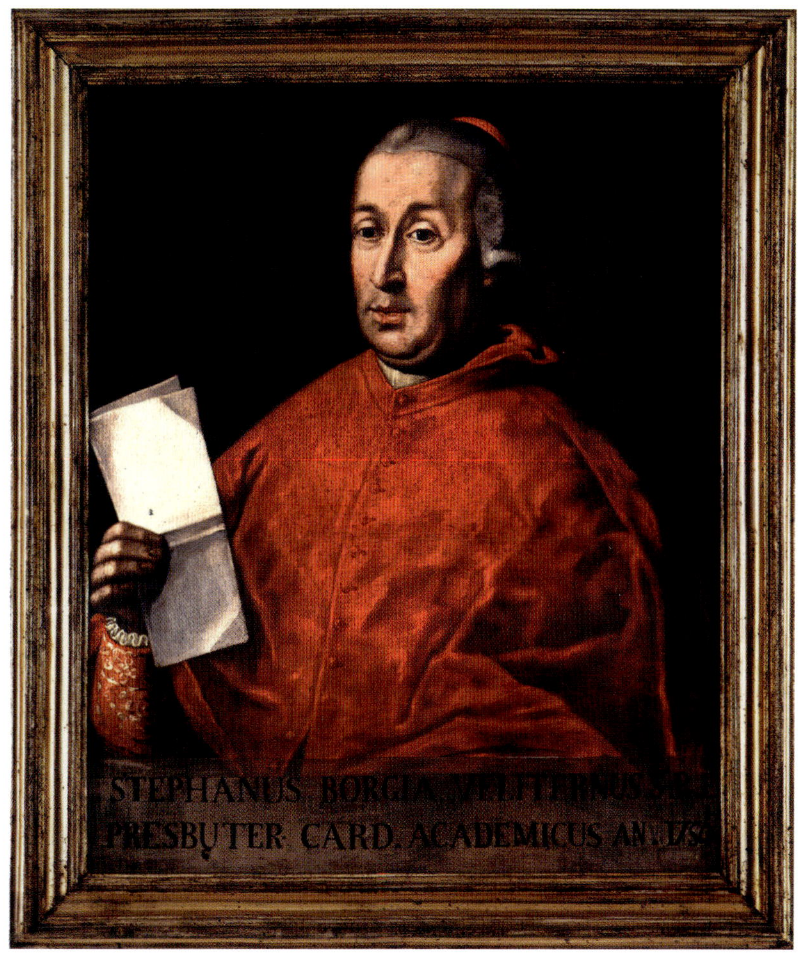

Figure 4

The artefacts that make up the largest group on the list (28 items) are called 'Kabyli(e?)' after a culture from the area of what is now Algeria. Four of the artefacts in this group have been identified among the current holdings of the museum: three necklaces (inv. 100747; 100759; 100769) and a tray (inv. 100750). Six items on the list are generically identified as coming from the 'Sahara', of which two have been identified as Tuareg saddlecloths (inv. 112240, p. 58; 112241). Another generic classification is 'North Africa' (29 items), of which so far only a pair of sandals (inv. 111998.2, p. 100) could be identified. Finally, two other areas are listed more specifically: Somalia (14 items) and Zanzibar (12 items). Two objects from these countries have been identified: a Somalian shield (inv. 100762) and a hat (inv. 115359) from Zanzibar.

The artefacts above are among the oldest Islamic African ethnographic objects conserved in the Vatican *Anima Mundi* Museum. It is not possible with the present state of research to determine with certainty whether these objects were already part of the Cardinal Borgia collection and therefore dating from the late 18th century, or if they were acquired after 1804, when his collection was moved to the Palazzo di Propaganda Fide in Rome, where it remained throughout the 19th century and continued to be enriched by donations.

THE UNIVERSAL EXPOSITION OF 1925

The majority of ethnographic objects relating to the African Islamic world came to the Vatican between 1924 and 1925. The occasion was a great Universal Exposition that Pope Pius XI wanted to hold in the Vatican to demonstrate the attention, respect and openness of the Catholic world towards the arts, culture and religions of the peoples of the world. The exhibition was officially opened on 21 December 1924. More than 100,000 items from around the world arrived and were exhibited in 26 halls in various areas of the Vatican. When the exhibition closed, 60 per cent of the objects were returned to their place of origin.

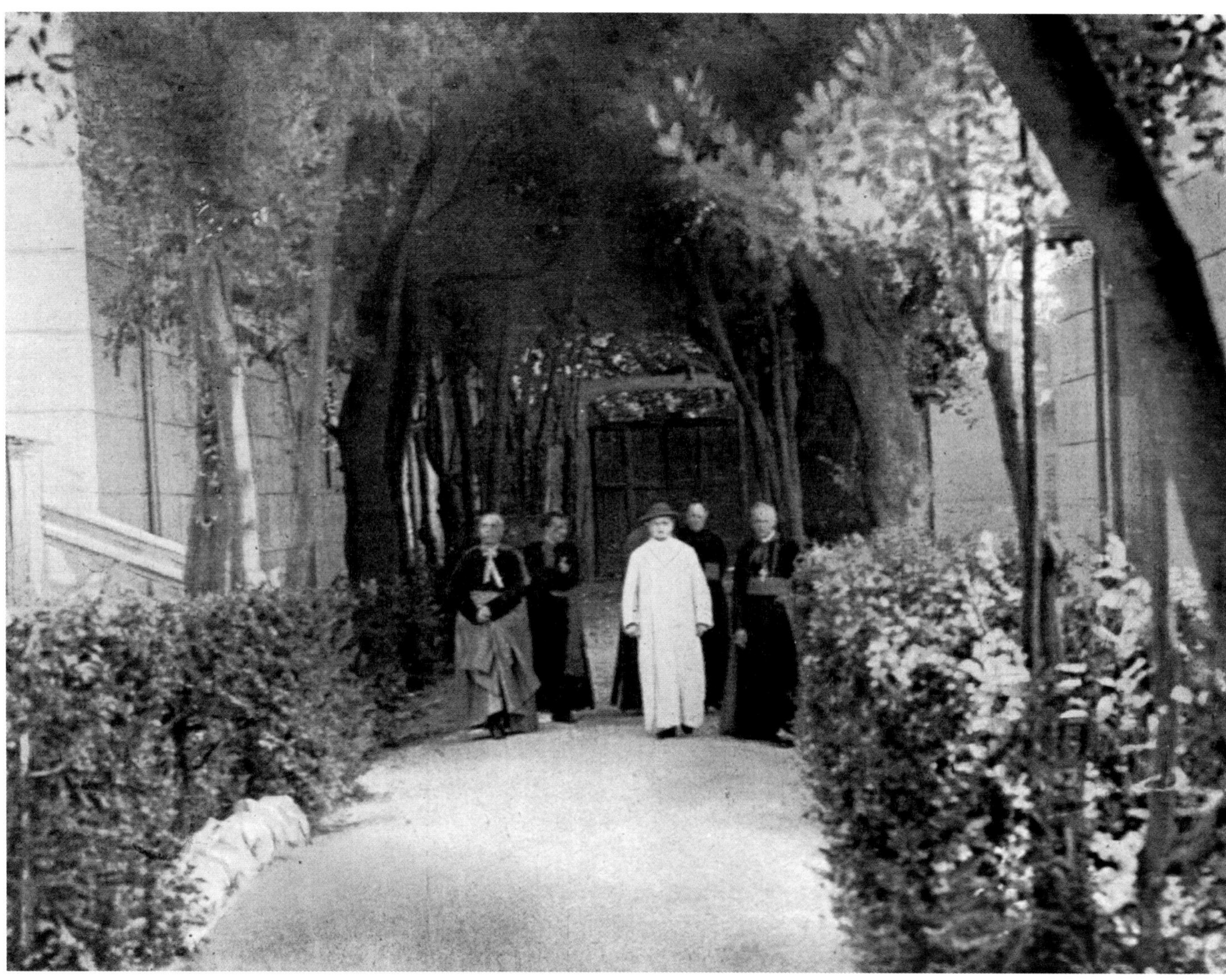

Figure 5: Pope Pius XI in the avenue leading to the Africa Pavilion

Six halls were constructed in the Vatican Gardens, and one of these, Pavilion XIX, was dedicated to North and Central Africa. This is where the majority of ethnographic objects sent from Islamic Africa to the Vatican were exhibited. Wherever possible, instead of simply being put in display cases or placed on shelves, these objects were used to re-create the environment and cultural context from which they came. A life-sized exhibit of an Islamic Sudanese family dressed in traditional clothing, drinking tea next to a Bedouin tent was especially popular. Unfortunately, no photograph of this interesting diorama has been located.

It seems the attention of photographers was captured by other events. One of these was the visit of Pope Pius XI to the halls of the exhibition on 11 August 1925. The *Rivista Illustrata*, the official publication of the Exposition, describes his arrival as follows: 'At about half past four in the afternoon, the Pope, accompanied by his chamberlain, Bishop Confalonieri, stepped out of his carriage in the Vatican Gardens and entered the area of the exhibition by the door at the end of one of the great avenues of the so-called Boschetto, specifically at the end of the avenue that runs between the pavilions of Japan and those of Oceania and Africa'.[4] The article states that 'the exhibit had been closed to the public on this occasion', and goes on to describe the various stages of the visit. It concludes: 'Finally, as a kind of crowning touch, he entered the African pavillion' (Fig. 5; RI 1925 581), where many objects showing the daily life of the people, as well as beautiful Islamic handicraft, were on display. A magnificent example of the latter was a pair of riding boots from the Sahara (inv. 122932.2).

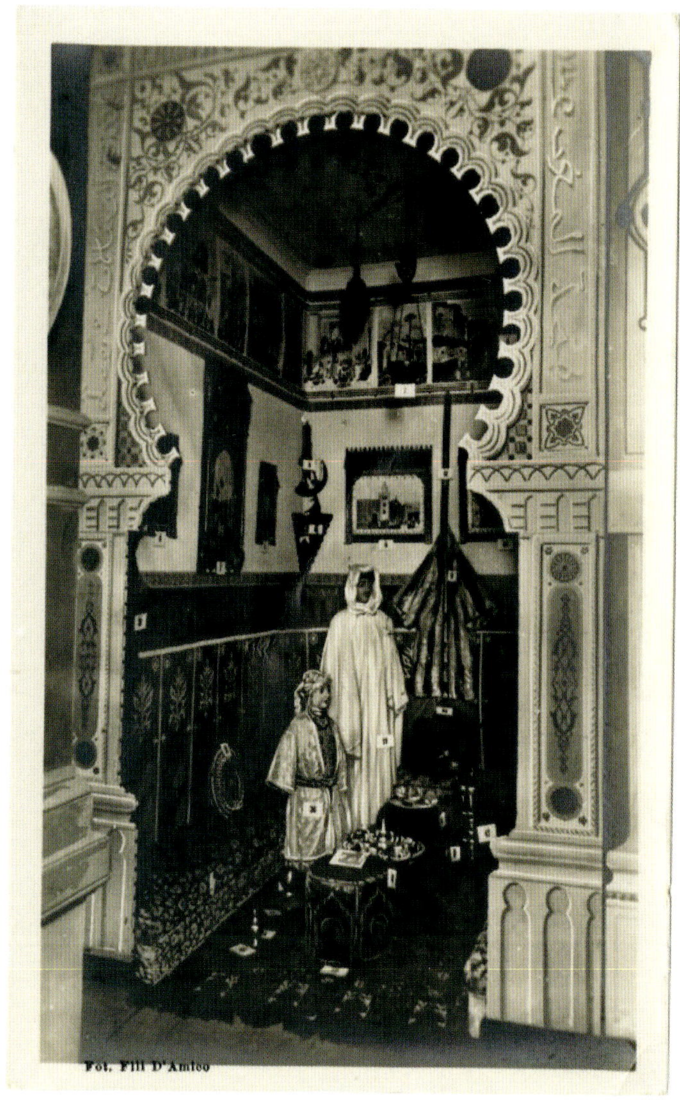

Figure 6

The Universal Exposition was an extremely important event, especially because of when it took place. In 1925, European powers were engaged in colonial policy, and Fascism and Nazism were on the rise. Pope Pius XI wanted to organise an exhibition at the centre of Catholicism to demonstrate the dignity and the value of non-European artistic and religious expressions. Exhibiting Islamic traditions was an excellent way to do that. This display of tolerance and mutual understanding lasted an entire year and was visited by over a million people. It is no wonder that when the Exposition was officially closed on 10 January 1926, the Pope declared: '*Omnium expectationem exitus superavit*' ('Its success exceeded all expectations') and for this reason part of that collection soon provided the foundations of a new, permanent museum.

THE LATERAN ETHNOLOGICAL MUSEUM

Not all 100,000 items sent for the exhibition would become part of the new museum. A special commission, headed by the most well-known Catholic ethnologist of the time, Fr Wilhelm Schmidt (1868-1954), of the Vienna School, selected what were considered to be the best works. The African Islamic artefacts that are still present in the museum are the result of that selection. Along with 40,000 other objects chosen from around the world, they were transferred to the new home of the Ethnological Museum.

The new venue was the prestigious Lateran Palace, which had been the official residence of the popes for centuries. The new museum, sometimes called the Lateran Ethnological Museum from the name of the historic building where it was housed, was officially opened on 21 December 1927, exactly three years after the opening of the Universal Exposition. The design layout was the work of the same Fr Schmidt, assisted by Fr Michael Schulien (1888–1968), an Africanist, who in 1939 would succeed Schmidt as director.

The new Lateran Ethnological Museum broadly followed the same arrangement as the exhibition of 1925. Instead of 26 halls, there were 26 rooms located on two floors of the historic Roman building. The rooms were arranged geographically, and the ethnographic artefacts of African Islam were housed on the second floor. The main attraction, as at the exhibition of 1925, was a diorama, but now it featured a reconstruction of a Moroccan living room rather than a nomadic Bedouin tent (Fig. 6).

The early years of the Lateran Ethnological Museum were also those of the rise and consolidation of Fascism in Italy and Nazism in Germany, but the museum continued its mission of presenting peoples and their religions with equal dignity and without racist overtones. An attempt was made to introduce little-known aspects of the cultures of North Africa, for example, by exhibiting a Moroccan lute (inv. 112083, p. 60) to show the refined musical life of North Africa. Two objects that are still conserved in the museum, however, are an expression of the climate of the time. Even if they were never exhibited, they bear witness to the colonial expansion of Italy in East Africa and Libya. The first object is a dagger with scabbard (inv. 112105.2) of the Benadiri people of Somalia. The dagger has an engraved wooden hilt and a metal blade with decorative engravings. The leather scabbard is also decorated. The object was donated to the museum in 1939. In that same year, the museum was bequeathed an Arab necklace (inv. 112705, p. 57) that had been worn by a lady from Cyrenaica. This eastern region of Libya was occupied by Italy during the Italo-Turkish war and administered by it from 1927 to 1943. Called Barqa by the Arabs, the region has always been distinguished by its complex jigsaw puzzle of tribal peoples, united in the 19th century under the leadership of the Sufi Sanusi order, established by Muhammad ibn Ali al-Sanusi (1787–1859). Omar al-Mukhtar, the famous 19th-century freedom fighter against the Italian occupation, was a senior member of the Sanusi order.

All in all, during the time the Ethnological Museum was housed in the Lateran Palace, donations remained very few. The last came in the 1960s and consisted of some objects from North Africa and the Middle East that were part of a collection donated by Countess Marina Gauttieri in 1962 and 1967.[5] Among these gifts was a pair of finely embroidered boots from Senegal (inv. 111984, p. 64).

THE VATICAN ETHNOLOGICAL MUSEUM

The Ethnological Museum remained in the Lateran Palace until 1963, when Pope John XXIII decided to make the palace the seat of the diocese of Rome. The ethnological collections were removed from their exhibition spaces, carefully packed and stored for about 10 years in the Palace of San Callisto in Rome's Trastevere quarter. Plans were made and construction started on new quarters for the ethnological collection. It would be conserved within the Vatican Museums, the same place that houses the masterpieces of Raphael and Michelangelo. Construction was completed in the early years of the 1970s, and the new space was officially opened in April 1973.

Schulien, weakened by age and illness, was assisted in his final years by Fr Joseph Penkowski (1927–2006). The year after Schulien's death in 1968, Penkowski became the director of the new Vatican Ethnological Museum. The museum he oversaw encompassed a total area inside the Vatican Museums of over 7000 square metres, with displays extended along a distance of approximately 700 metres. It was divided into 25 sections, each corresponding to a geo-cultural area of the non-Western world. The North African area was situated at the far end of the museum. The fact that the layout followed a geographical course meant that the section devoted to North Africa came after the one dedicated to Australia and near a 'communal hut' from Papua, New Guinea. The section devoted to North Africa began with some Egyptian statuettes, continued with Christian artefacts, and then, in a room all by itself, there was a throne donated to Pope Pius XI by the Egyptian Government. After that came the section devoted to Islamic ethnography.

Here, Penkowski was able to fulfill his desire to create a museum of religions that would demonstrate, as he put it, 'man's eternal search for the Divine'.[6] His agenda explained the choice of some objects at the expense of those that were considered to be less interesting and more related to daily life. These were relegated to the so-called 'secondary path', that is, the area of the museum where conserved objects could be studied by researchers on request. In the 'main path', the one intended for the public, a privileged place was given to religious objects, such as amulets with verses from the Qur'an of the Marabouts, wandering Muslim holy men of Ghana (inv. 100765, p. 65; 122325), or a flask used by the Muslims of Eritrea for ablutions before prayer (inv. 100753, p. 69). The principal showcase also contained objects that were representative of particular Islamic African handcrafted goods, such as a miniature door (inv. 100775, p. 68) from

Zanzibar. However, it was the religious world that attracted the attention of Penkowski. Right in the centre of the showcase, he quite intentionally placed the figure of an imam calling the faithful to prayer.

For a variety of issues related to conservation, the Ethnological Museum was closed to the public at the end of the 1990s. For about 10 years, the Ethnological Materials Restoration Laboratory (Laboratorio Polimaterico) of the Vatican Museums, coordinated by Stefania Pandozy, put into place a program for safeguarding all the assets of the Ethnological Museum, including its Islamic holdings.

In 2010, on the occasion of an exhibition devoted to Aboriginal Australians, the Ethnological Museum was reopened to the public. Under the direction of Fr Nicola Mapelli, a program has been put in place to evaluate all the holdings of the museum and to reconnect them with the communities which sent them to the Vatican long ago. I have worked with Fr Mapelli in this process, and the 2014 Sharjah exhibition *'So That You Might Know Each Other': The World of Islam from North Africa to China and Beyond from the Collections of the Vatican Ethnological Museum*, and its latest incarnation in the National Museum of Australia in 2018 dedicated to the ethnography of Islam, is one of many steps taken not only to 'rediscover' the time-honoured collections and reveal their beauty, but also to promote a dialogue between cultures and religions aimed at respect and mutual knowledge.

Notes

1 The non-Islamic works classified under the generic heading 'North Africa', totalling around 2000 items in all, are concerned with expressions of Coptic and Ethiopian Christianity as well as expressions of ancient civilisations (e.g. Egyptian and Roman) once present in these areas of Africa (such as inv. AS 10661, from Leptis Magna in present-day Libya).

2 Ethnological Museum Archives.

3 GA Colini, *Collezioni Etnografiche del Museo Borgiano, Memoria*, Rome, 1885, pp. 13-18.

4 *Rivista Illustrata* (RI) 1925, Anno II, n. 18, 31 agosto 1925, pp. 580-581.

5 For more on the Gauttieri collection, see the essays of Nadia Fiussello and Ulrike Al-Khamis in this catalogue.

6 J Penkowski, 'Pontificio Museo Etnologico', in *The Vatican Collections; The Papacy and Art*, The Metropolitan Museum of Art, New York, Harry N. Abrams Inc. Publishers, New York, 1983, p. 227.

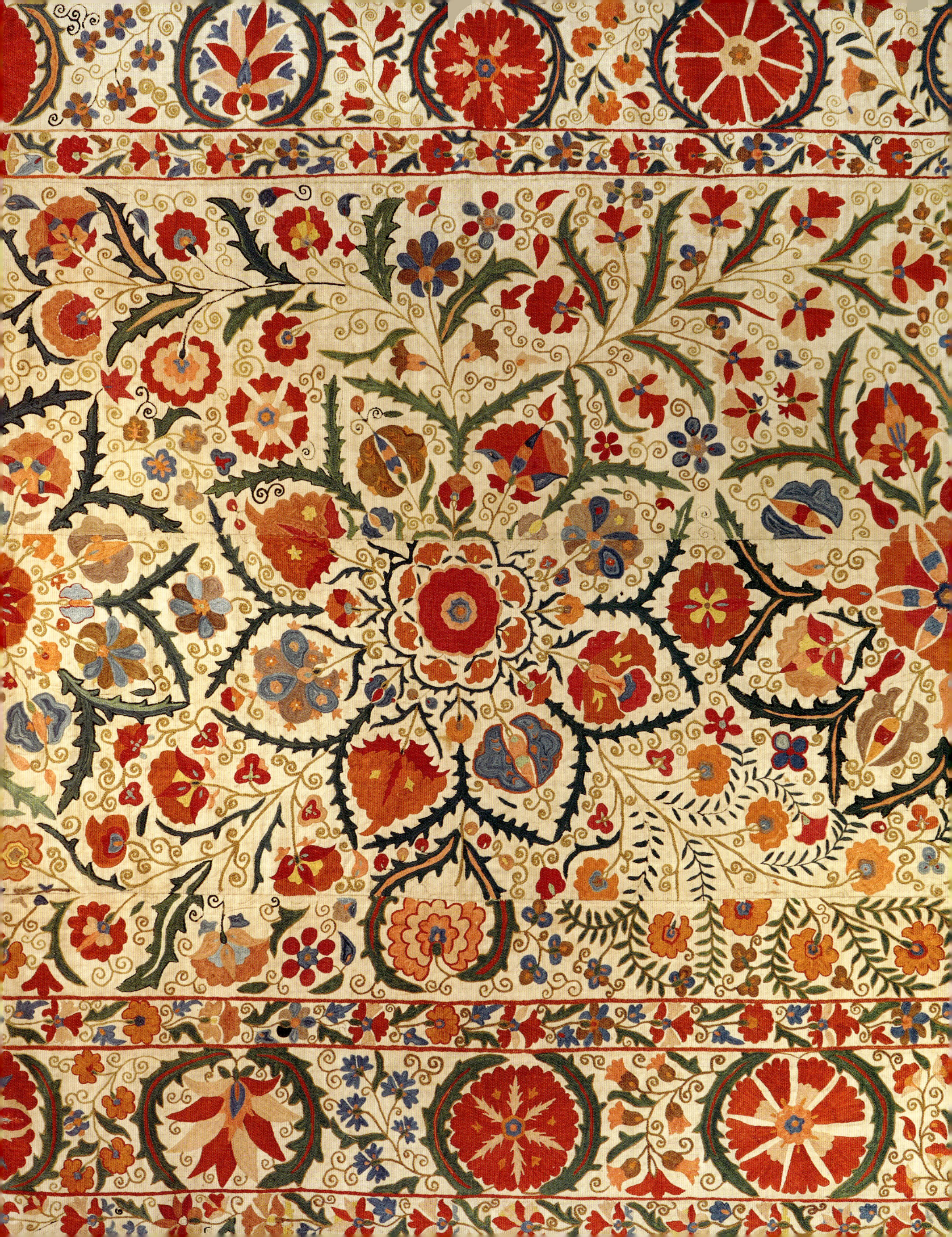

Following the path of Islam in Asia

NADIA FIUSSELLO

Before analysing the story of those objects from East Asian Muslim cultures kept in the Vatican *Anima Mundi* Museum, we will recall the historical events that led to the presence of Islamic art and material culture in countries that at first glance do not seem to belong to the Islamic religious and cultural sphere. In fact, with regard to the Eurasian continent, the spread of Islam has been one of the major events both from a historical and cultural point of view. Over the centuries, it subsequently interacted and merged with the indigenous cultures of peoples and countries across the region, while at the same time itself introducing ethnicities and cultures. All this contributed to the evolution of what we now call Islamic art and culture.

The momentous Islamic expansion began in the seventh century from the Arabian Peninsula, favoured by the decline of the Roman and Persian empires. From the year 622 (commonly regarded as the beginning of Islamic expansion, when Muhammad emigrated from Makkah to Yathrib (Madinah)) to 632 (the year of his death), the foundations for the future expansion and spread of the Islamic religion were laid. The first caliph, Abu Bakr, completed the conquest of the Arabian Peninsula, and then the expansion reached Palestine and Damascus. After the year 636 it progressed eastwards into Sassanid Iraq, Persia, Baluchistan and Armenia and further east, right to the borders of India.

By the time the second caliph, Omar, died in 644, Egypt, Cyprus, Crete and Rhodes had already been conquered. The expansion continued to reach Andalusia (Spain) in the West and China in the East, reaching its climax in 1258 when Baghdad eventually fell to the Mongols. Subsequently, in 1299, the Ottoman Empire, a Turkish and Muslim state that was to expand consistently until 1697, conquered and ruled over most of the territories previously dominated by the Arabs, as well as new countries such as Hungary, Serbia and Crete. From the 15th century onwards, with the great Islamic empires of Safavid Persia and Mughal India on the Ottomans' eastern flank, the presence of Islamic culture continued to strengthen in Eastern Europe, the Arabian World and across Asia.

In Iran, Safavids of Turkish origin moved from Persian Kurdistan to present Azerbaijan and ruled Persia (now Iran) between 1501 and 1736.

The history of the Indian Mughal Empire (1526–1707) meanwhile began with the deeds of Babur (who reigned from 1526–1530). Babur was the descendant of the great Turkish-Mongol conqueror Tamerlane, who ruled from Samarkand, a city in Transoxiana (present Uzbekistan). Babur invaded India and, during his reign, his empire expanded from Afghanistan to Bengal. He favoured the Turkish migration from Central Asia to India and at the same time fostered the dissemination of the Islamic religion. The Mughal Empire's expansion reached

Figure 1: Suzani *(embroidered textile hanging) (detail), inv. 112536, p. 97*

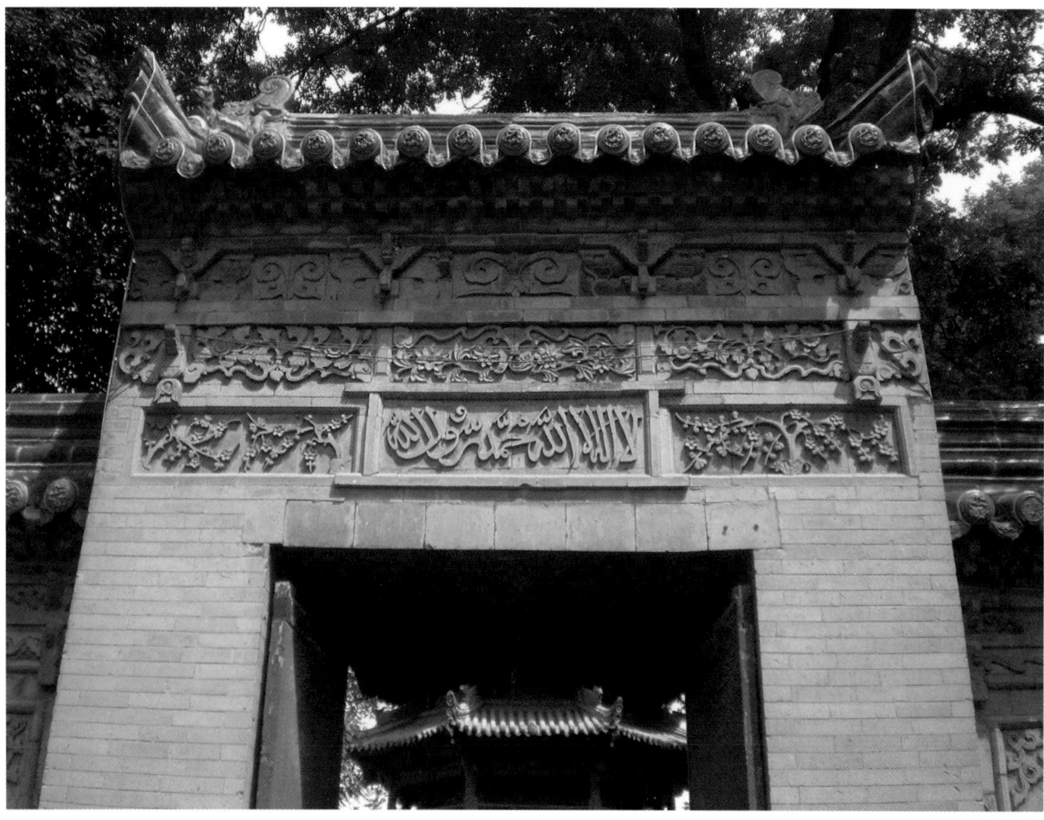

Figure 2

its apogee with the third ruler, Akbar (1556–1605), who tried to give life to a new syncretic Hindu–Islamic religion. Towards the end of the Mughal Empire, Aurangzeb (1658–1707) found himself engaged in continuous struggle in defence of Islam. When he died, the empire had completely disintegrated and subsequently saw defeat and eventual conquest by the British in 1859.

Throughout the Islamic world, politics and military enterprises were accompanied by an ever wider commercial expansion, leading to a consistent spread of people, ideas and artistic traditions and giving rise to new forms of artistic and cultural syncretism. Knowledge about the histories of many nations and people with their different languages, religions and customs were narrated along the intercontinental caravan routes and waterways along the Silk Road, and knowledge travelled to and fro with the people and goods exchanged between the Arabian Peninsula and India. Indeed, it was not least the merchants who created diverse, international networks of communication across the Islamic world, aided by the language common to Muslims everywhere: Arabic.

Across the vast expanses of Asia, there were many countries and peoples that Islam penetrated in the wake of commercial contacts without ever having undergone political and territorial conquest. Among those are the Philippines, where Islamisation can be linked directly to the development of trade from the Arabian Peninsula to the archipelago through Malaysia, Borneo and Sulu. According to various Chinese sources, the Philippines provided an important maritime stopover and trading centre for Chinese and Muslim merchants from as early as the 10th century.

In 1390 the arrival of Rajah Baguinda, still remembered as the founder of Islam in the Philippines, saw the spread of the Islamic religion and a subsequent mass conversion. The subsequent flowering of Muslim culture in the Philippines and the material culture of its people, the so-called Moros, are represented in the Vatican collection by a distinctive Moro male suit of armour with helmet (inv. 123358; 123514, p. 109) and female filigree ornaments such as the two bracelets and buttons (inv. 100143; 100145; 100154.2, p. 110), elaborately decorated with floral motifs.

Trade was also at the heart of Islam's spread into China. Although never politically conquered by a Muslim power, China has witnessed a considerable presence of Muslims since the 8th century, when Persian and Arab traders first arrived and settled along the southern coasts as well as in the territory of today's Xi'an (the ancient Chang'an), the arrival and departure point of the Silk Road where trading caravans unloaded their goods. As early as 651, Emperor Gaozong (ruled 649–683) of the Tang Dynasty officially allowed the practising of the Islamic religion in his lands, and Chang'an became the first Chinese

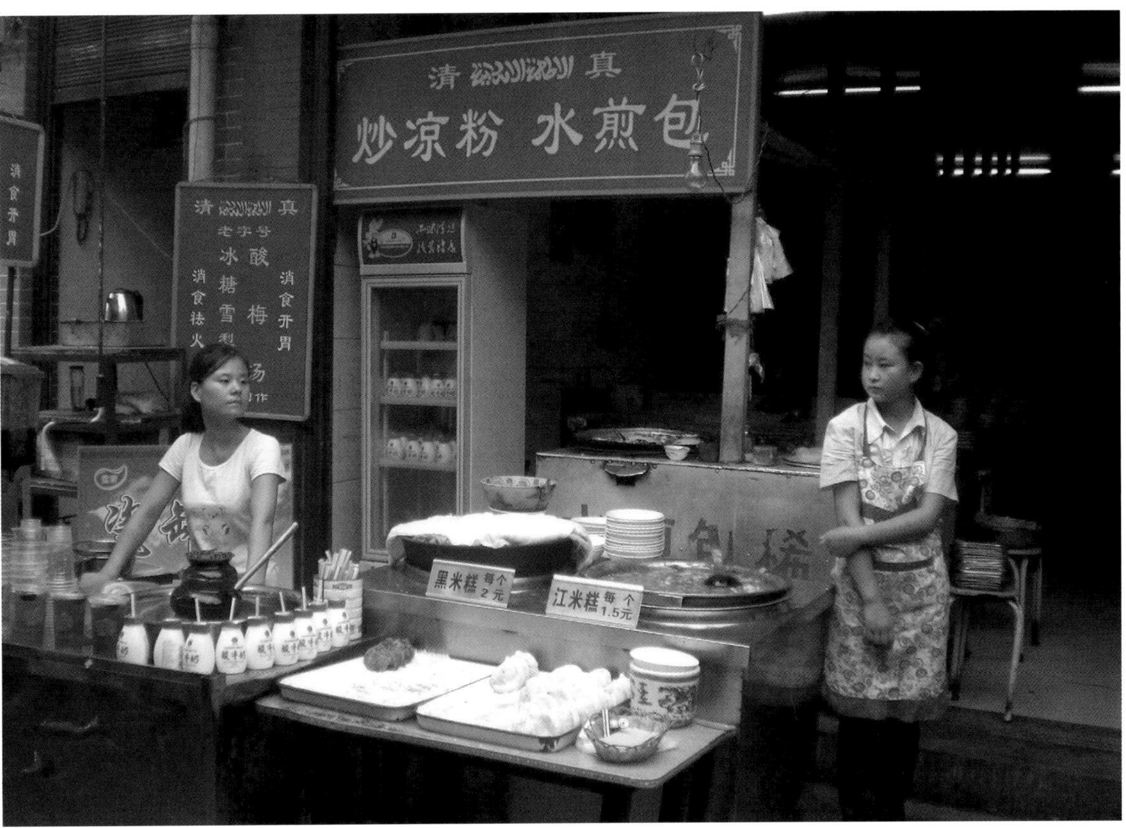

Figure 3

city where Islam was officially introduced. Today, there are seven mosques in Xi'an. The oldest and most famous is the Qingzhen Dasi or Great Mosque, originally built in 742 with the structures seen today dating from the late Ming dynasty (14th century, Fig. 2). A second massive wave of Muslim immigrants arrived between the 12th and 14th centuries during the Mongol Yuan dynasty (1279–1368) when Muslim soldiers, bureaucrats and businessmen were preferred as employees to Han Chinese. In 1274, the city of Dali in Yunnan Province was even ruled by a Muslim government.

The Chinese Muslims living in the territory of present China are identified as the so-called Hui minority (Fig. 3). Meanwhile, when talking about Tungans or Dungan people, the term 'Hui' refers to those who migrated in the 1780s from China to Kyrgyzstan and Kazakhstan and are at present located in Russia, Uzbekistan, Ukraine, Tajikistan and Mongolia. The term also refers to the Dungan language that is similar to Mandarin Chinese as well as to the Zhongyuan dialect spoken in some Chinese regions.

Wherever in the world Islamic faith and culture have mingled with indigenous cultures and ways of life, the resulting material cultures and artistic creations bear witness to a fusion of ideas and religio-philosophical speculations as well as an ongoing dialogue that reflects the desire to represent the many people living side by side around the world. The selected objects aim to give a taste of the fascinating interplay between Islamic and indigenous cultures across the world, since each one has been chosen to tell a story about how Islamic artistic and cultural traditions mingled with the most diverse and fascinating influences flowing from local arts, costumes and beliefs.

The coffee set (inv. 102439; 120440.2; 102441.2, p. 92) sent to the Vatican in 1925 on the occasion of the Vatican Mission Exposition by the Augustinian Frs of Kütahya, Turkey, represents a beautiful fusion between West and East in its style and decoration. A centre of colourful ceramic production in the 19th century, Kütahya produced many wares that combined Western shapes with traditional Islamic patterns. The function of the service also reflects the interaction of different cultures. Originally discovered in Ethiopia, coffee was first used in Yemen. From there, it soon travelled to Ottoman Turkey, where it became a cultural phenomenon. By the 17th century, coffee had reached Europe, and today the whole world shares in the enjoyment of coffee and the cafe.

Kütahya ceramics are famous for their polychrome palette, but one of the most groundbreaking colour schemes developed in the Islamic world as early as the ninth century was in fact 'blue on white'.

First developed in Abbasid Iraq, the blue-and-white aesthetic soon travelled east. It subsequently proved one

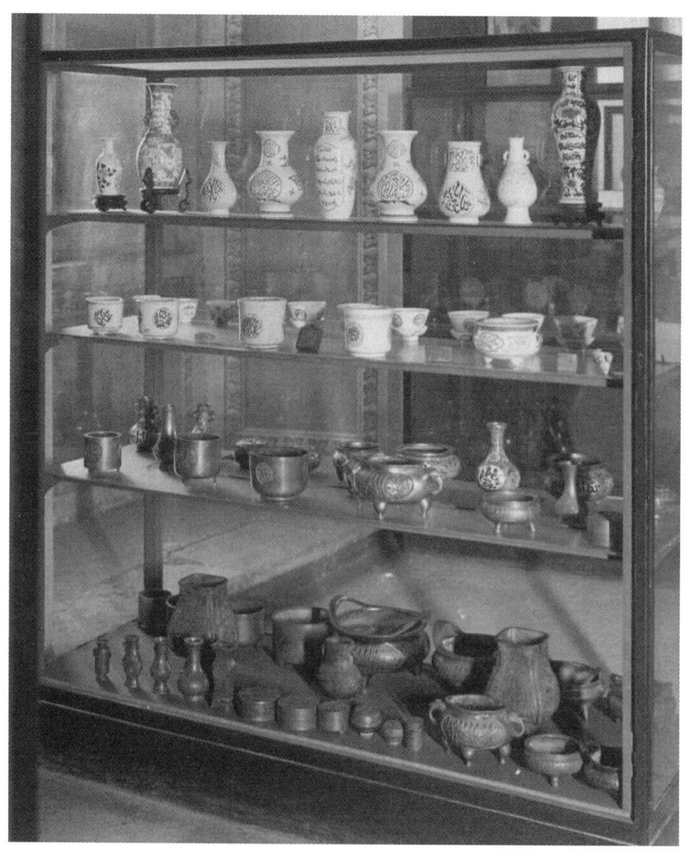

Figure 4: The Ros objects in the Lateran Ethnological Museum, 1962

of the most valuable contributions to Chinese art. Cobalt, the deep blue pigment used in the Abbasid wares, as well as probably some ware shapes and decorations, arrived in China by sea from the Persian/Arabian Gulf, hence the name 'Mohammedan blue' or *huihuiqing*. Subsequently, blue-and-white porcelain developed during the Mongol Yuan Dynasty in the 13th century, thanks to the strong political ties between the two vast Mongol empires that controlled both the eastern flank of the Islamic empire and most of Asia at the time. Interestingly, the creation of the famous blue-and-white wares from China was initially intended specifically for export to the Middle East, South-East Asia and Europe, since it did not meet the local taste. A fascinating blue-and-white item in the exhibition that also features an Islamic inscription is a Chinese incense burner dating to the 17th–18th centuries (inv. 120606, p. 107).

Other objects in the exhibition that best symbolise the intercultural fusion between Islam and indigenous cultures are selected textiles from West and Central Asia, a region with particularly active commercial networks and caravan routes intersecting in oases and resting stations, where merchants were continously exchanging goods as well as knowledge.

The intricately embroidered girl's dress (inv. 112265, p. 94) from Tal Kaif in Northern Iraq shows complicated chain-stitch embroidery with human figures, flowers, birds and water containers within floral scrolls — all age-old symbols of fertility and eternal life adopted by many cultures. The shape of the dress at the same time represents a type that appears — in many variations — all across the Middle East.

Among the most elaborate and fascinating textiles are those related to wedding ceremonies, and a wedding shawl (inv. 112406, p. 96) from Sindh in Pakistan represents very well the intricate work that goes into their creation. Embroidered on silk with traditional motifs designed to protect and bless the bride, the shawl was donated to the Vatican Museums by a prominent Italian noblewoman, Mrs Maria Brarda Barberini. Interestingly, silk is known to have been exported from China since the first century BCE, and for many centuries it was the most sought-after commodity merchants set out to exchange for spices and metals coming from the Middle East. Many items in the collections of the Vatican were collected and sent by priests and missionaries looking after Christian communities the world over. They often became deeply interested in and fascinated by the various religious and cultural groups they lived among, thus acting as intermediaries. A particularly exemplary collection in this respect is that of Paolo Bonardi, a Salesian who lived in India for many years. He donated 152 objects from India and neighbouring countries to the Vatican in 1933. The exhibition shows some outstanding Islamic objects, amulets and jewels (*ta'wiz*) from that collection, many bearing verses from the Holy Qur'an (inv. 122049; 122045; 122058; 122041, pp. 102, 103), one with Urdu inscriptions (inv. 122043, p. 104), two with Islamic prayers (inv. 122051; 122054, pp. 102, 103) and a personal seal that bears the name of its owner and a date (inv. 122047, p. 104).

The shapes are varied: circular, square, oval, hexagonal or (like that of inv. 122035, p. 101) referring to a shield for protection. The Fr Bonardi collection also includes amulets with numerical diagrams showing a grid of numbers that, when added together, give the same result both horizontally and vertically. Amulets like this were very common in India and were of particular importance in popular local Islamic culture, where the specific religious quotations and number combinations were intended to bless and protect the wearer. In many of the amulets, the style of writing adopted is particularly fine, reflecting Islamic cultures' immense respect for calligraphy due to its close link with the materialisation of the Holy Qur'an. All over the Islamic world and across Muslim cultures, calligraphy marks the most sublime art form, eternalised not only on paper but also on buildings and artefacts, such as the fine and richly decorated steel shield inlaid with black niello decoration (inv. 122028, p. 100). Its finely worked, decorative embellishment is completely dominated by an elegant Persian poetic inscription, disposed in four panels set against a background of floral decoration. Unlikely to ever have been used in battle, the shield was probably intended for ceremonial events and celebrations or simply as a decorative feature. Urdu meanwhile appears beneath the Arabic of a printed Indian Qur'an, presented on a wooden bookstand carved with a bird and flower motif and originally from Uttar Pradesh, India (inv. 122030, p. 98; 122029, p. 99). Another object (inv. 100131, p. 111) is also a Qur'an, this time from Indonesia, but on this occasion it is a printed miniature version, carefully preserved within a metal case provided with a magnifying glass to read the microscopic writing.

Moving further east, the Chinese objects in the exhibition also reveal their Islamic cultural context by means of religious quotations rendered in elegant Arabic calligraphy. They belong to the collection of 'Chinese and Mohammedans things' sent by Cav. Giuseppe Ros for the 1925 Universal Exposition and collected during his stay in Shanghai (Fig. 4).

As mentioned before, by the 13th century the trade between China and the Middle East was flourishing thanks to the safe conditions across Asia created by the so-called Pax

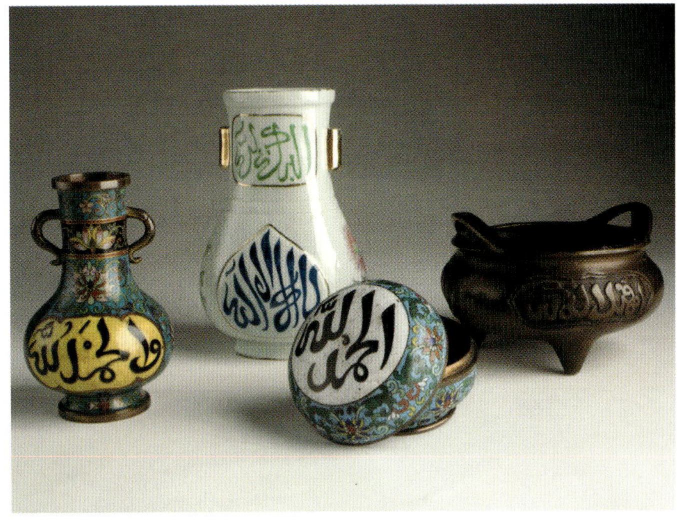

Figure 5

Mongolica, which encouraged the arrival of many Arab and Persian merchants who could enjoy the favours and protection of the Yuan rulers. Subsequently, the large Chinese–Islamic community (mainly Arab traders settled in the main cities), and the presence of Muslim eunuchs in the Forbidden City led to an extensive and valuable production of manufactured goods aimed at the Islamic market.

A particularly telling object to illustrate the peaceful cohabitation of Arab–Muslim and Chinese cultures is a jade seal showing in the middle the two Chinese characters Qing Zhen ('Muslim') surrounded by a Qur'anic quotation in Arabic (inv. 120597, p. 106). Other items displaying the same fusion are an incense burner, a pot and a circular box (Fig. 5; inv. 120613, p. 106; 120592, p. 108; 120601, p. 108; 120621). All combine traditional Chinese shapes, techniques (cloisonné) and decorative detail with Qur'anic or other Islamic inscriptions.

Interestingly, the technique of cloisonné arrived in China in the 14th century from Byzantium, where it was developed in the 10th or 11th century. The treaty *Gegu Yaolun* (*Fundamental Studies of Antiquities* 1388), by Cao Zhao, confirms this legacy. Cloisonné is called Dashi (Arabia) or Folang (Byzantium). The best production was that of the Jingtai reign (1450–1456), when Muslim artisans highly skilled in that technique arrived in China after the fall of Constantinople (1453). Even today 'Jingtai Blue' is synonymous with cloisonné.

Another item showing a peculiar and unique intercultural iconographic fusion is a porcelain vase (inv. 120613, p. 106) with four Islamic inscriptions within cartouches combined with auspicious symbols drawn from the traditional Chinese symbolic repertoire such as the bat, the pearl, the swastika and the sounding stone.

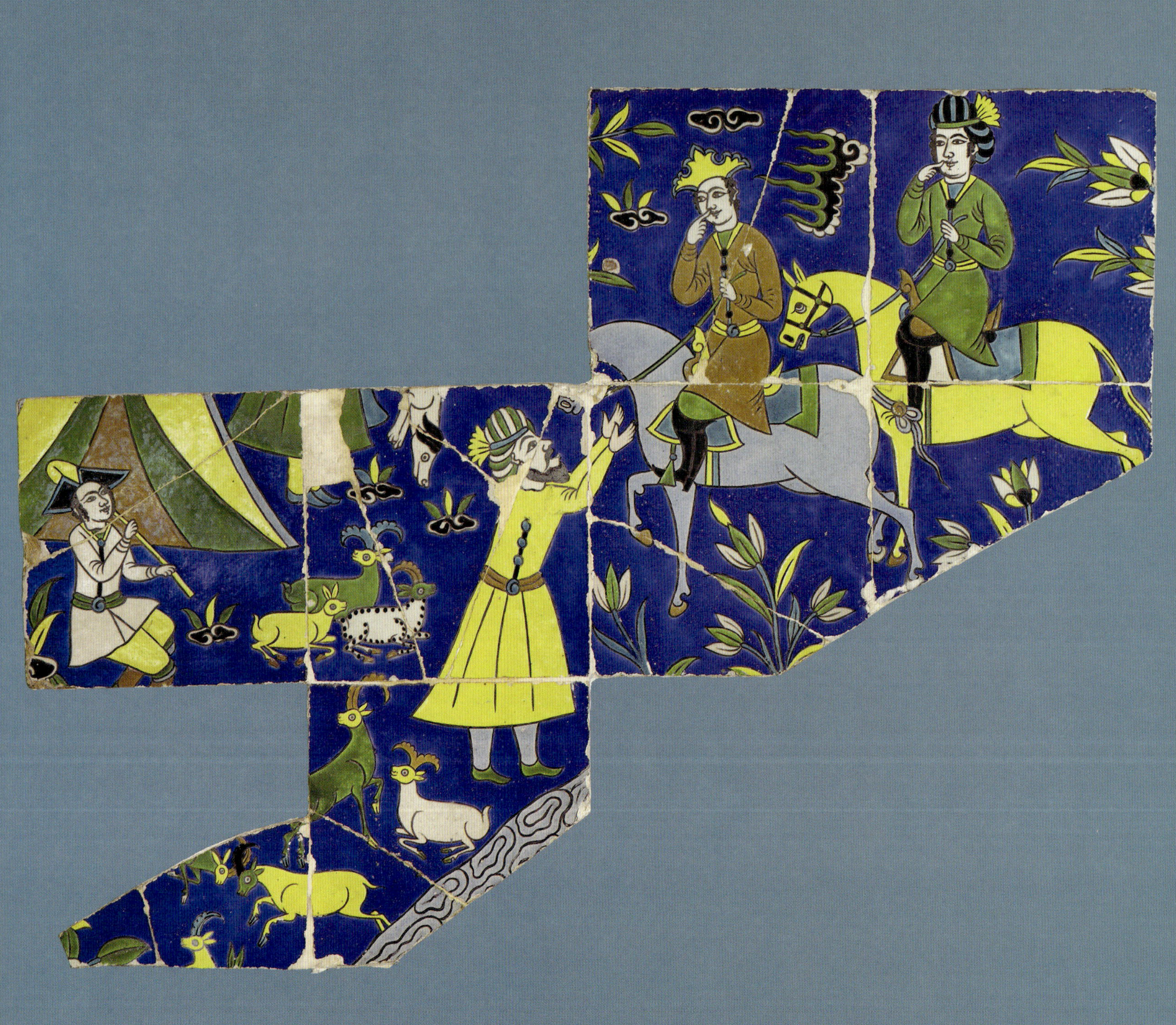

Islamic art in the Vatican *Anima Mundi* Museum

ULRIKE AL-KHAMIS

It is an entirely unexpected and exciting surprise to find among the collections of the Vatican *Anima Mundi* Museum a distinct and intriguing selection of Islamic art objects, ranging in provenance from North Africa to Iran and dating from the early Islamic period to the late 19th century CE. Most of the items are ceramics, and it is on these that this article will focus in the main. Interestingly, all the artefacts under discussion reached the museum collection at only three specific moments in its history — the result of three, specific donations — each one with its very own, fascinating historical context and story.

ISLAMIC ART FOR THE 1925 EXHIBITION

The first donation of Islamic artefacts to the Vatican collections arrived as part of a consignment of objects sent by the Vicariato Apostolico d'Egitto in Alexandria for the Universal Exposition conceived by Pope Pius XI at the Vatican in 1924–25.[1] The consignment incorporated a collection of ceramic items — mainly shards — collected in Fustat outside Cairo in Egypt, which were sent together with a number of early Islamic glass weights, flacons and fragments, coins, Fatimid bone or ivory fragments with simple scrolling, a Samarra-style Tulunid wood fragment and other disparate items.

Of great interest for the art-historical as well as scientific and analytical study of Islamic ceramics, the collection of Fustat shards comprises both unglazed and glazed items, the latter displaying a wide range of well-known styles dating from around the 10th to the 15th centuries. The unglazed items are pottery filters decorated with a simple cross design; animal figures including a bird, a rabbit and a gazelle (Fig. 2; inv. 100744); and stylised Arabic inscriptions. Conventionally, such filters — which once protected the water in utilitarian pottery jugs from becoming polluted — are attributed to Fatimid or early Ayyubid Egypt between the 10th and 12th centuries.

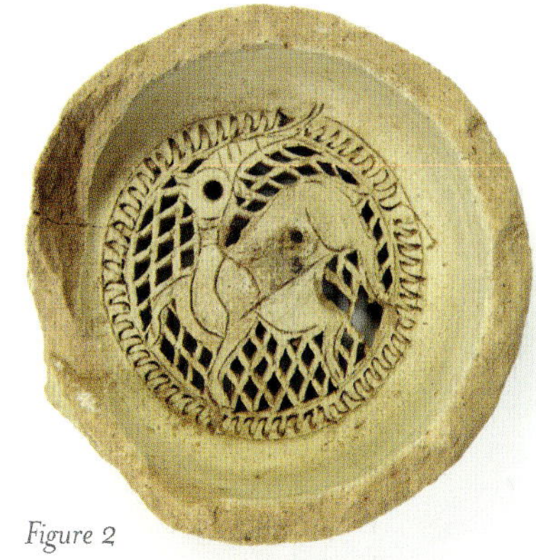

Figure 2

Figure 1: Tiled fragment from an architectural spandrel, Iran, 17th century, inv. 12564.2

Most of the glazed fragments are attributable to Syria and Egypt and range from the Fatimid to the late Mamluk periods in date, with a great variety of styles in evidence. Fatimid pieces include examples of 12th-century underglaze-painted and incised wares — the decoration of the latter applied under a rich monochrome glaze — as well as a wide range of overglaze lustre-painted fragments. Most of these are earthenware or stonepaste bases belonging to open vessels such as dishes, bowls or cups. The lustre designs — which include abstract, geometric, star and arabesque as well as animal and figural motifs — are painted on with a brush or can be reserved against a solid or incised lustre ground (Fig. 3; inv. 102702). Two slightly later ceramic types, attributed to early 13th-century Syria and/or Egypt, are represented by shards painted in black, blue and red under a clear glaze and those painted in black under a dark turquoise or blue glaze.

By the mid 13th century, major political upheavals in the Islamic world had started to impact on its main pottery centres, both in economic and artistic terms. Subsequently, new technologies, vessel shapes and styles emerged, a fact that several shards attributable to late 13th–15th-century Syria and Egypt can attest to vividly. Individual examples represent vessels painted in blue and black under a clear glaze, influenced by Iranian Sultanabad ware; slip-coated earthenwares with slip-painted and/or incised decoration — often with a central medallion executed in dark slip colours or with epigraphic elements — and stone paste vessels painted in blue under a clear glaze, clearly influenced by Chinese blue-and-white porcelain. Finally, at least two fragments represent the underglaze-blue and overglaze-lustre painted wares of Islamic Spain, made around the same period.[2]

THE LA FARINA COLLECTION

The second donation of Islamic artefacts appears to have started as a permanent loan for the Persian Hall at the Lateran Museum in June 1934 (Fig. 4), followed by further donations in the 1960s at the request of the donor's daughter. The collection in question, comprising 168 mainly ceramic pieces, had been painstakingly assembled by Salvatore La Farina from Palermo, a gentleman who confessed to having had a passion for 'ancient art' since childhood and who had dedicated most of his adult life to acquiring and studying Islamic art — mainly ceramics from Syria, Iran and Ottoman Turkey, ranging in date from the 12th to the 19th centuries. We are fortunate in that the archives of the Vatican Museums still retain a number of pertinent documents and personal letters which allow us to get a sense of La Farina's evolution as a collector and

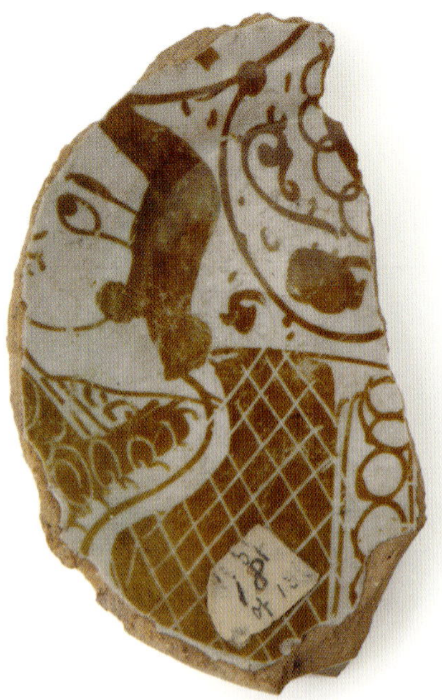

Figure 3

the serious, scholarly dedication and inquisitive concern he lavished on his objects.[3]

Interestingly, in his writings the collector states that his passion for the Orient had originally been triggered by his friendship with a highly cultured English dignitary, who had apparently lived in Sicily for many years after having served 'as the representative of the British government' at the Persian court as a young man, and who apparently was as much an eager dealer as he was a connoisseur and collector of Oriental, and particularly 'Persian', ceramics. The Englishman had considerable influence on La Farina's initial collecting efforts — indeed, his collection first took off when the former sold his pieces to La Farina, 'rather than to other collectors that had expressed their interest', as the collector recounts in a letter in 1914. Over the years, La Farina continued to acquire ceramics, at often considerable prices, keeping detailed records for each piece and apparently following relevant scholarly discussions in publications and articles with keen interest. In this, he was particularly anxious to ascertain the true worth of his collection by repeatedly consulting with internationally acclaimed scholars such as Friedrich Sarre, director of the Kaiser Friedrich Museum in Berlin.

To date we do not know the exact sequence of La Farina's acquisitions, but it seems intriguing that the collector contacted Sarre at a point in his collecting career — that is in the early 1920s — when not only Europe's fascination with the Orient and the desire of art markets to feed that interest were at their height, but also when heated debates were circulating in scholarly and dealer circles about the date and therefore

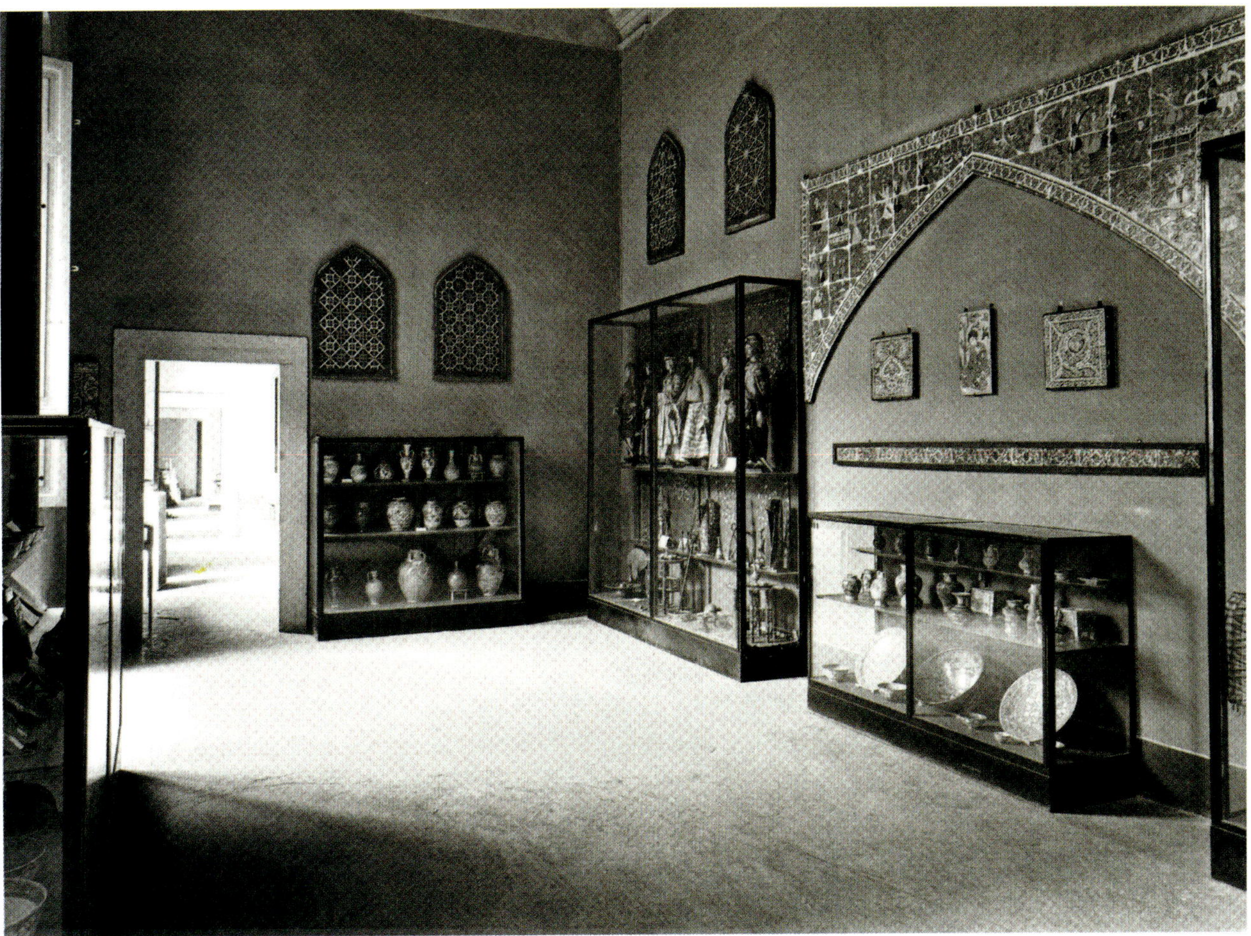

Figure 4

commercial value of certain types of Eastern ceramics, of which La Farina owned quite a few examples, in particular Syrian Raqqa ware.

Since the 1890s Raqqa ceramics, characterised by their coarse white bodies, glazes that pool above the foot and occasional lustre decoration, had appeared on the European Islamic art market, peddled by Armenian dealers as yielding from the ruins of Harun al-Rashid's palace in the city. Around 1910, the association of the ware with the famed caliph of the 'Arabian Nights' had gradually led to a buying frenzy, even though scholars had by now started to question the authenticity of such claims. Sarre, who had visited the Raqqa sites between 1908 and 1911, ascertained that the wares had no connection with Harun al-Rashid's 8th-century part of the city, but came from an area that could clearly be dated to between the 11th and early 13th centuries.[4]

La Farina entrusted a friend with an illustrated and annotated catalogue of his objects to deliver to Sarre in Berlin by hand. Some months later — undoubtedly to the collector's relief — the scholar responded reassuringly, congratulating him on the good quality of the collection and stating that he had passed the catalogue to his assistant Ernst Kuehnel to add scholarly comments and detail. Interestingly, the work of the Berlin scholars appears to not only have provided preliminary chronological dates and typological qualification, attribution and provenance, but also to have led to the suggestion that the objects should be exhibited in the Persian Hall of the Lateran Museum for the benefit of scholars and the general public. Sadly, the surviving archive material regarding the ultimate transfer is too minimal to reconstruct the subsequent proceedings at the time in detail.

Turning to La Farina's collection in more detail then, the wares that are nowadays attributed to early 13th-century Raqqa form a distinct group of squat handled jugs (Fig. 5; inv. 126953, p. 30), body-spouted ewers, albarellos, inverted pear-shaped vases and a small number of bowls of conical shape on a low foot. Their decoration is achieved either by moulding — sometimes combined with underglaze blue decoration — or underglaze painting and/or overglaze lustre, combined with either turquoise or blue glazes. One particularly interesting object among the group is a small, rectangular incense burner or stand on four low feet. It has

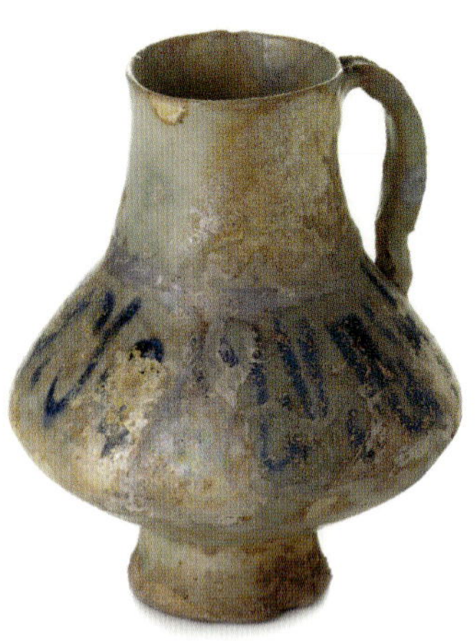

Figure 5

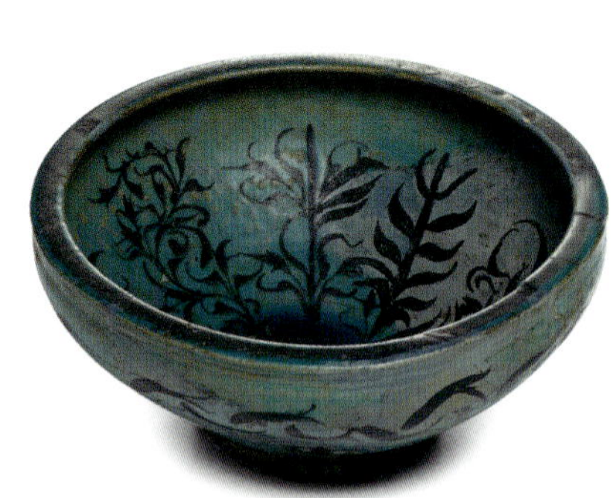

Figure 6

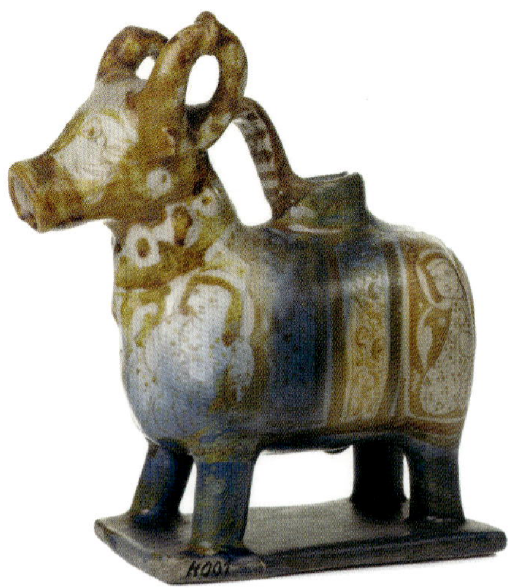

Figure 7

moulded scrolling decoration, combined with remains of a deep turquoise glaze (inv. 114361). All in all, the Raqqa objects are in a fragile condition, and some show extensive restoration.

The remaining pieces in the La Farina collection that date to this period come from Iran. The earliest pieces are attributable to the late 12th and early 13th centuries. They include a small number of fritware vessels with opaque turquoise glaze and two examples of wares with black decoration under a transparent turquoise glaze. The first piece — a squat jug or cup with epigraphic decoration carved through a black slip under the glaze — is an example of silhouette ware (inv. 126935), while the second — a wide bowl with flat inverted rim — shows underglaze painted, delicate 'water-weed' and vegetal stalks executed in black (Fig. 6; inv. 126954).

Other pieces represent the luxury lustre wares assumed to have been executed in Kashan during the same period. Bowls, dishes and jugs prevail, decorated with designs in characteristic Kashani style, including large birds, seated human figures, delicate scrolling and cursive inscriptions, arranged in geometric panels, bands or medallions. On some pieces, the ornamentation is further enhanced by detailing in underglaze blue. Among the latter is one particularly intriguing, sculptural piece in the shape of a bull or ram, apparently intended as an aquamanile (Fig. 7; inv. 102701).[5]

Twelve tiles complete the group of lustre wares. Four (damaged and restored) examples, of cross and star shape and decorated with Qur'anic inscriptions, belong to a well-known group associated with the shrine of Imamzadeh Yahya in Veramin near Teheran, dated to 1262–63 (inv. 102763; 102700; 102768).[6] Four further star tiles (one fragmented), dating to the late 13th or early 14th century, display moulded or lustre-painted floral, arabesque and figural motifs in the centre (inv. 102762; 126950; 114631; 126936; 102767). They are framed by cursive inscriptions, which in all cases but one are reserved against a blue background. Four moulded rectangular tile fragments with religious inscriptions highlighted in blue against a lustre-decorated background from the same period complete the series (inv. 102764; 102765; 125643; 102766). Originally part of architectural friezes, most have been cut or damaged, while one is a composite of two disparate fragments.

Tiles also represent the most spectacular aspect of Safavid ceramics in the La Farina collection, which furthermore include blue-and-white, lustre and monochrome wares. A richly coloured, fragmented section most probably from an architectural spandrel is executed in the *cuerda seca* technique and datable to the 17th century. It shows two riders attentively listening to the applications of a turbaned man approaching them from what appears to be a hunting camp with tents, attendants, a dog and game visible behind him (Fig. 1; inv. 125642, p. 26).

A technically and stylistically related, complete architectural spandrel with an animated outdoor scene

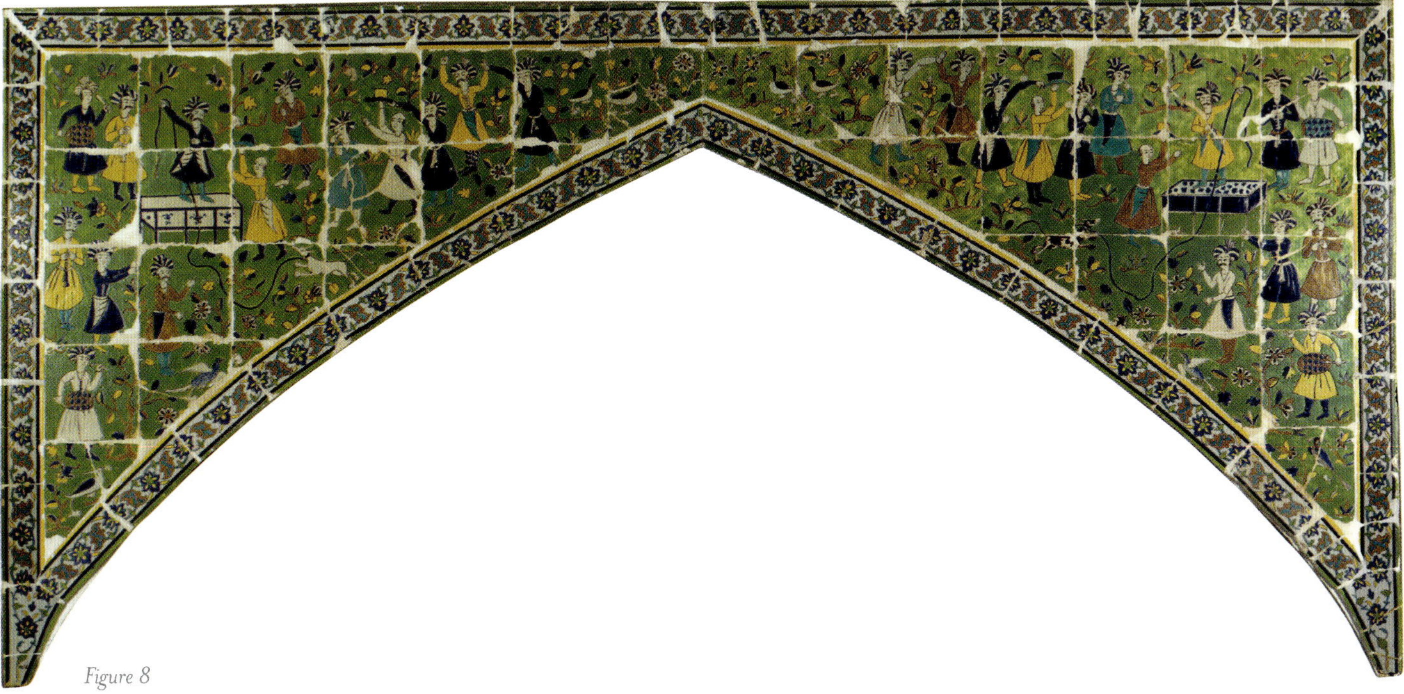

Figure 8

repeated in mirrored form on both sides (Fig. 8; inv. 125644) was sold to La Farina around 1919 as having originally belonged to a palace of Shah Abbas I (1557–1620) in Teheran, which the reigning Shah was said to have partly demolished some 80 years before the sale in order to present the tiles to a European ambassador. At the time, the dealer maintained that 'nothing equal to this ensemble could be found in any public or private museum'. However, a more sober assessment of the technical and iconographic aspects of the spandrel suggests that, more realistically, it should be dated to the late Safavid or early Qajar period, i.e. around the late 18th or early 19th century. The Iranian pieces in the collection are completed by a number of late Qajar tiles, including a well-known type depicting a mounted horserider holding a falcon (inv. 125641), and various vessels.

Ottoman ceramics in the collection are represented by a group of late 16th- to early 20th-century examples. These include a range of dishes, vases and tankards from Iznik (Fig. 9; inv. 125638; 125639), some tiles from 17th-century Syria and a diverse selection of Iznik-style and other polychrome wares from Kütahya.

The rest of the collection is made up of a small number of individual pieces from a wide range of historical contexts. They include unglazed and glazed items from the early Islamic period, a few Hispano-Moresque items and 19th-century, blue-and-white dishes from Fez in Morocco.[7]

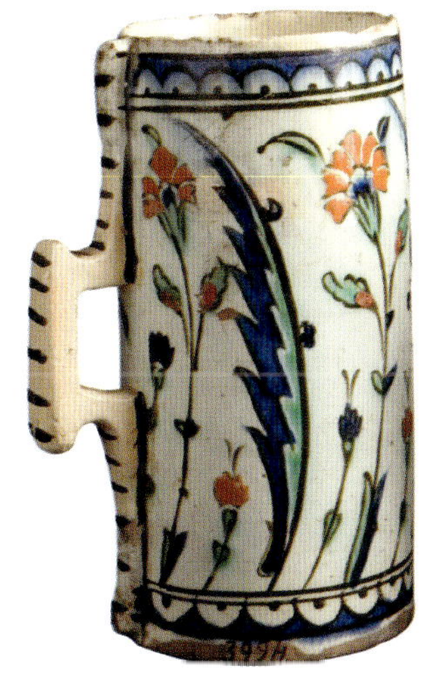

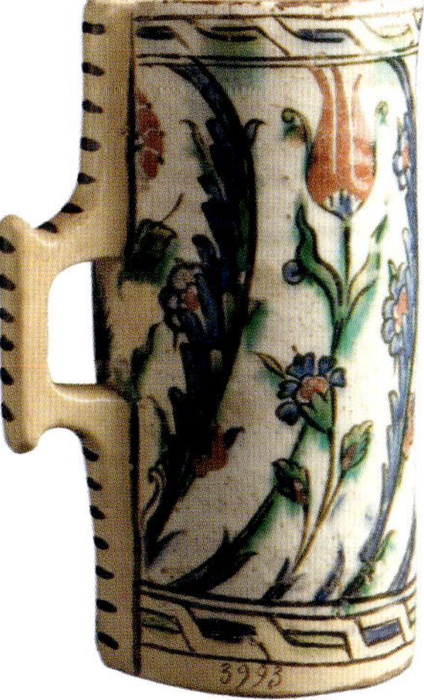

Figure 9

THE GAUTTIERI COLLECTION

The third contingent of Islamic artefacts reached the Vatican collections with the donation in the early 1960s of artefacts brought together by Count Antonio Gauttieri. The gift, which was initiated by Gauttieri's widow Countess Luisa Maria Marina Barbosi, seems to have first been discussed in 1943 but appears not to have been completed until about 1961–62. The Gauttieri collection incorporates 193 archaeological, ethnographic and art-historical pieces, including ceramics, stone inscriptions, textiles, weapons, pieces of furniture, carpets and jewels from the Middle East, India, China and Japan.

In terms of Islamic art, the collection includes yet again a small group of Syrian ceramics from early 13th-century Raqqa. In terms of shapes — jugs, vases, ewers and dishes — and decorative styles, they are very similar to the pieces already encountered in the La Farina collection, also including yet another moulded and turquoise-blue glazed incense burner or stand (inv. 114363).

More intriguing, especially as it stands entirely on its own among the diverse array of objects in the Gauttieri collection, one further Islamic artefact — although not a ceramic piece — deserves a mention here. The object in question is a Safavid-style drawing, executed in opaque watercolour and ink and finished with gold detailing (Fig. 10; inv. 112488). The painting shows a youth with flowing robes and a fur-trimmed hat enjoying a cup of wine in a garden setting, while looking back at his dog — apparently stirred by a rabbit rushing out of the bushes in front. The frame surrounding the drawing is an integral part of the object and features an array of animals and flowering plants painted in warm colours, their outlines enhanced in gold.

The documentation which accompanied this particular Gauttieri acquisition is preserved in the museum archives. It states that this painting is dated to 1600 and can be attributed to Aqa Riza (or Riza-i Abbasi; 1565-1635), one of the most important artists at the Persian court of Shah Abbas the Great and best known for his portraits of handsome young men and women in flower gardens. However, a closer inspection reveals that the stylistic execution of the drawing is too heavy and cursory to warrant an attribution to the late 16th or early 17th century. In fact, it seems more likely that the painting is a 19th-century Qajar homage to the great master — a suggestion that would sit well with the Qajar era's all-encompassing nostalgia for the political and cultural grandeur of the Safavids, which was expressed in all artistic media at the time.[8]

Notes

1 For more information on the 1925 Vatican exhibition see Katherine Aigner's article in this catalogue, p. 13.

2 For a more indepth discussion of Fustat shards see Helen Philon, *Early Islamic Ceramics: Ninth to Twelfth Centuries*, Benaki Museum, Athens, Sotheby Parke Bernet, 1980 and relevant publications listed in Susan Sinclair (ed.), *Bibliography of the Art and Archaeology of the Islamic World*, Vol. 1 Art, Brill, Leiden, 2012, pp. 458–72.

3 All the archival material relevant to the La Farina collection is housed in Contenitore 17 'Medio Oriente', Cartella 3, 'Collezione La Farina'.

4 For a detailed discussion of Raqqa ware see Marilyn Jenkins-Madina's recent study, from which the information in this section was derived: *Raqqa Revisited: Ceramics of Ayyubid Syria*, The Metropolitan Museum of Art, Yale University Press, New York, 2006.

5 A very similar piece, but without the addition of blue detailing, can be found in the Victoria and Albert Museum in London (LOAN:ADES 8).

6 Large tile panels from the same group are in the Victoria and Albert Museum and the British Museum in London, while individual pieces can be found in most public and private collections of Islamic art worldwide.

7 For a comprehensive bibliography on Islamic ceramics see Susan Sinclair (ed.), *Bibliograph*, pp. 430-516.

8 The archival material for the Gauttieri collection is housed in Contenitore 17, 'Medio Oriente', Cartella 4, 'Collezione Gauttieri'. The author is grateful to Dr Sheila Canby from the Metropolitan Museum in New York for considering this item and confirming a Qajar attribution.

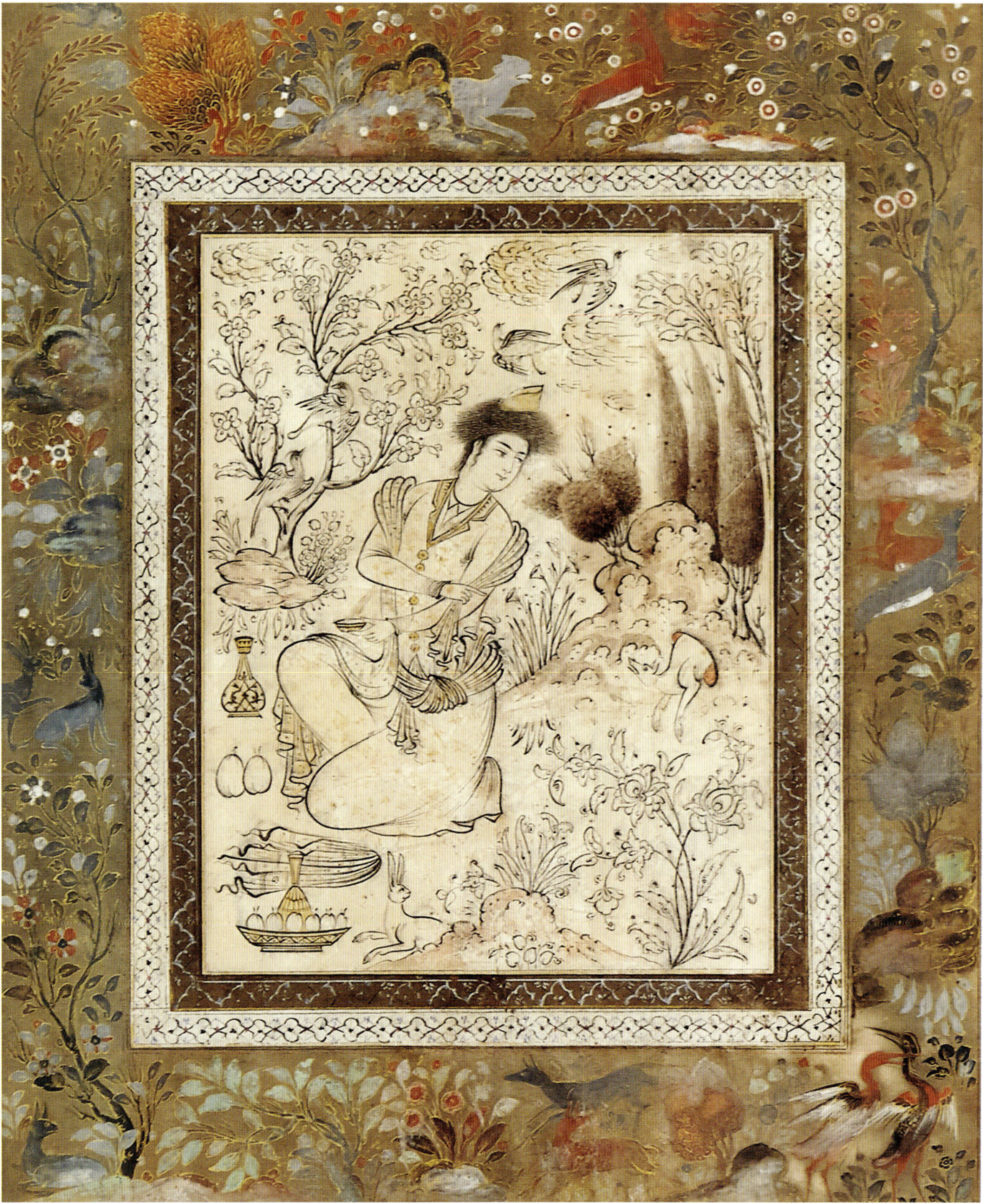

Figure 10

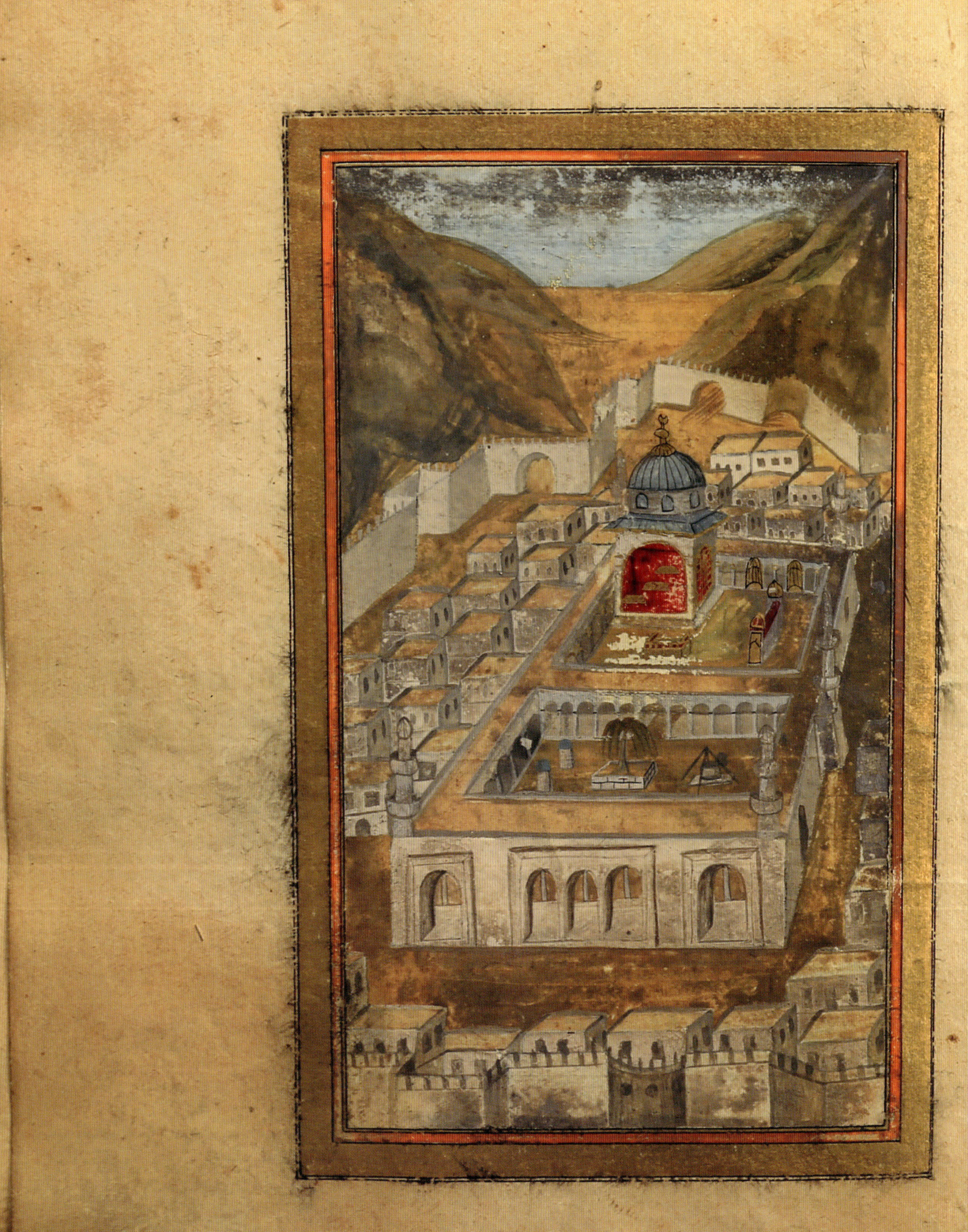

Representations of cultural heritage from the collections of Sharjah Museums Authority

HUDA ALTENEIJI

The role of Sharjah in the preservation of tradition and Islamic history is evident in the museums that His Highness Sheikh Dr Sultan bin Mohammad Al Qasimi has supported and built over the past 25 years. The Sharjah Museum of Islamic Civilization, which houses more than 5000 objects from all over the Islamic world, is one of the Emirate's 19 museums that collectively cover areas of Islamic art and culture, archaeology, heritage, science, marine life and the history of Sharjah and the region. The artefacts displayed at the Sharjah Museum of Islamic Civilization have been collected over many years from all over the Islamic world including countries influenced by Islam such as China and India. Objects also originate from Europe, obtained through extensive trade and political relationships.

The Sharjah Heritage Museum is dedicated to highlighting Sharjah's authentic heritage and the rich culture of Emirati people and Sharjah residents over the past decades. It also emphasises the value of the deep-rooted Arabic customs and traditions that are a legacy from our ancestors and a source of pride and joy to coming generations. Sharjah's most interesting marine stories and the Emirate's rich marine heritage, as collected and documented by Sharjah inhabitants (in the lives of whom the sea played a significant role) are presented through the collections of the Sharjah Maritime Museum.

For this exhibition, Sharjah Museums Authority presents 41 objects from five of its museums (the three already mentioned above, Bait Al Naboodah (The House of Al Naboodah) Museum and the Sharjah Calligraphy Museum), selected particularly to showcase the interconnected cultural and religious traditions of Sharjah and the United Arab Emirates.

By the ninth century, the Islamic world had expanded from Arabia to Spain in the west, and to South-East Asia in the east. Throughout the Sharjah Museum of Islamic Civilization, visitors can discover the story of Islam by understanding the faith and spiritual aspect of Islamic civilisation illustrated in its religious manuscripts, architectural models and in an interesting series of historical photographs of religious rituals. Furthermore, the collections reflect the timeless achievements of Islamic civilisation and its universality, including aspects of science, discoveries, culture and art.

Figure 1: Page from the D'ala'il al-Khayrat *(Guidelines to Blessings), SM2006–2181, p. 84*

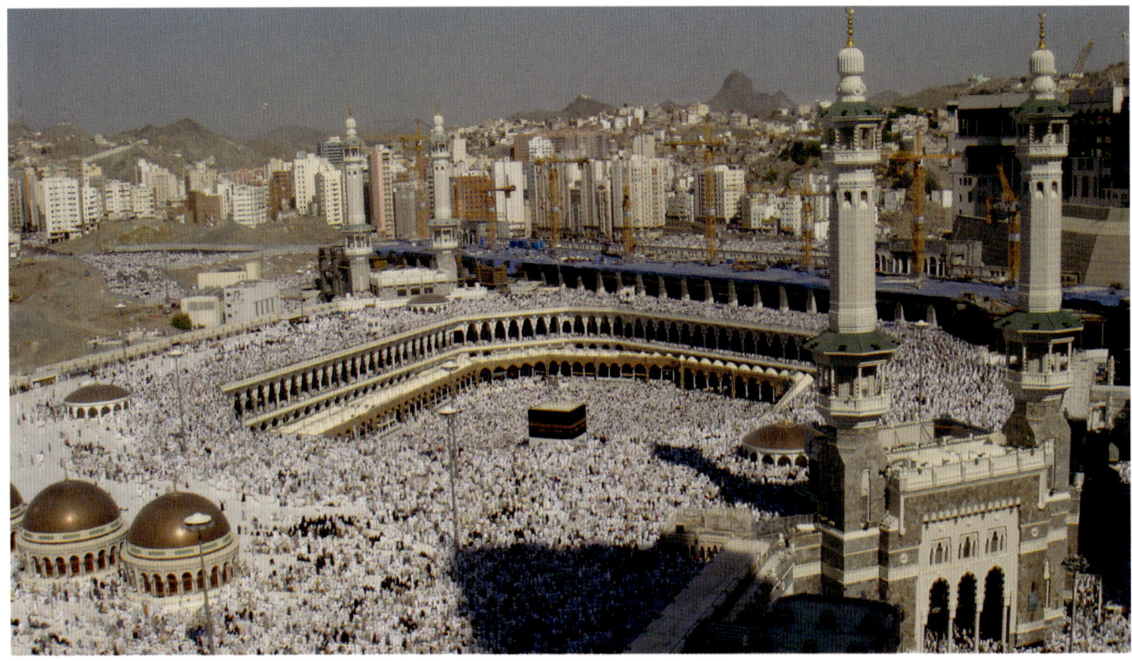

Figure 2: Grand Mosque during the Hajj, Al Jazeera Creative Commons Repository

One of the most important objects in the collection is the fragment from the Kiswah (SM1996-586, p. 80), the cloth that covers the Ka'ba. The Ka'ba, in Makkah's Grand Mosque, is the most important destination for Muslims. They direct themselves in prayer towards it five times a day and it is the site for their yearly pilgrimage (Hajj, Fig. 2). The Kiswah has been made from cloth of different colours through the years but, in recent decades, it has remained black, with additional calligraphy work sewn in silver and gold. The black silk of the Kiswah is created using a jacquard weave, where black is interwoven with black to create calligraphy of phrases such as 'Allah jala jalalah' and selected Qur'anic verses. Additional embroidered verses in gold and silver are sewn in the elegant Al Thuluth script. Each year, on the ninth day of Hajj, the Ka'ba is washed with water from the Zamzam well before the new Kiswah is draped over it. The old Kiswah is then cut into pieces and distributed, mainly as royal gifts.

Traditions – the practices and customs that are passed down from one generation to another – are an important part of everyday life in the United Arab Emirates and still play a large role in the lives of Emiratis today. Traditions are closely linked to the Islamic faith and arguably form the basis of Emirati culture, building on and giving meaning to different parts of daily life: gatherings, weddings, births and deaths, dress code and behaviour.

In the past, traditions played a huge part in people's lives and in family structure. Men and women both shared traditional roles, outwardly manifested in their clothing. Men dressed in their loose-fitting *kandoura* and, for formal events or celebrations, they would add a *bisht* (black cloak). Clothing and fabric texture varied according to the season. Men would usually carry some sort of accessory, such as a belt with dagger or a thin stick or cane.

Women would have several ways of dressing that could include *boshya* (a transparent black head and face covering), *abaya* (a loose-fitting full-length robe), *wgaya* (a head covering worn in public), and *kandoura mzariyah* (colourful embroidered fabric). The wedding costume on page 76 is an example of a traditional outfit. Women perfumed themselves with musk, sandalwood or amber, and applied kohl, a black substance made from soot, to enhance and beautify their eyes. Accessories included silver and gold earrings, rings, hand jewellery and necklaces such as *murta'isha* and *mar'eya*, two forms that were widespread in the late 1930s to the early 1960s. Accessories also included headdresses such as the *tasah* and even leg anklets.

Tradition can also be seen in the architectural designs of historical, wealthy Emirati houses as seen in Bait Al Naboodah Museum (Fig. 3). This museum was originally the house of a pearl merchant, Obaid bin Eissa Bin Ali Bin Nasser Al Shamsi, nicknamed 'Al Naboodah'. The house exterior and interiors are uniquely decorated with ornate plaster and woodwork and wooden columns. The museum provides an opportunity to experience a lifestyle of the late 19th century until the 1940s.

Pearling, an important source of income for the Gulf for thousands of years until the early 1930s, was one of the most important traditional industries in the United Arab Emirates.

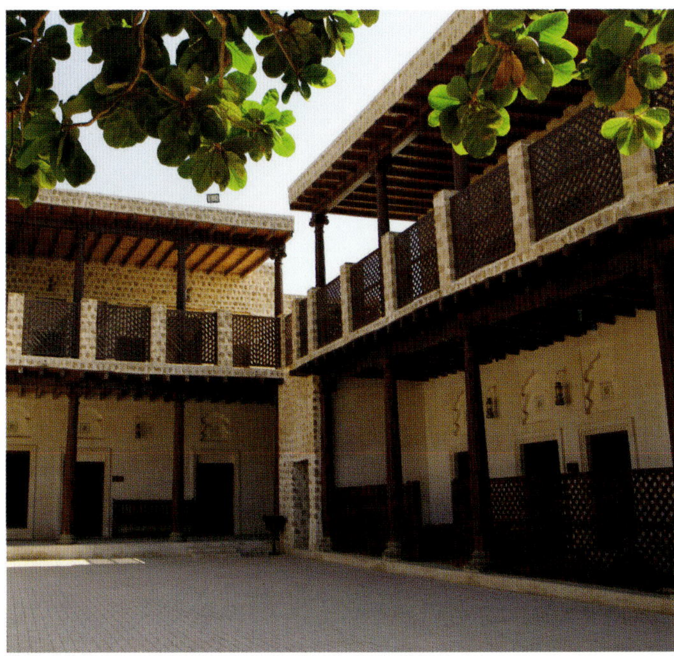

Figure 3: Bait Al Naboodah Museum, Sharjah Museums Authority

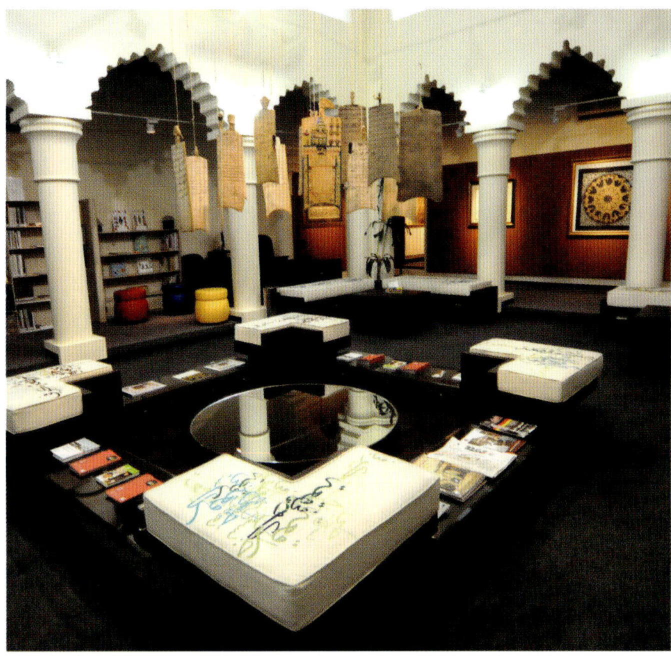

Figure 4: Sharjah Calligraphy Museum, Sharjah Museums Authority

Men would set sail in the early days of summer to harvest pearls. Following their return, a merchant known as Al Tawash (a pearl trader) would examine the pearls using his sieves and gauges and magnifying lens, equipment that he would carry in his box (SM2003-172, p. 72). The box contained many compartments to house these tools, along with a *chao* book which listed size, lustre and value for specific pearls.

The Vatican *Anima Mundi* Museum and Sharjah Museums Authority are presenting in this exhibition collections that reflect shared core themes of cultural diversity. The objects selected from both collections emphasise two common areas. First is the use of Arabic calligraphy in Islamic art. From the Chinese vases and jars sent from Shanghai by Cav. Ufficiale Giuseppe Ros (inv. 120613; 120592; 120601, pp. 106, 108) to the metal-thread embroidered textile brought probably from Cairo (inv. 112414, p. 56), we find that the art of calligraphy is found not only on religious artefacts but also on decorative art objects. Arabic calligraphy is also most prominently manifested in the manuscripts of the Qur'an written in the three most important scripts: Al Kufic, Al Naskh and Al Thuluth.[1] Many of these manuscripts were originally handwritten using a reed pen of specific thickness, nib cut, width and angle.

The second link is in the selection of traditional clothes and accessories reflecting specific aspects of life in diverse Muslim cultures. See, for example, the Palestinian woman's festive gown (inv. 112419, p. 89) and girl's jacket (inv. 112314, p. 88). The style of the jacket, with its woollen broadcloth and silk embroidery, was originally inspired by the uniform jackets of Ottoman and later British officials and officers. However, Emirati clothes were traditionally made of cotton and silk fabric, with silver or gold thread embroidery, brought from India. Another example is the dagger and scabbard made by Druze artisans (inv. 112127, p. 91).

The exhibition introduces the visitor to an Islamic presence which can be seen in many and varied forums, cultural objects and calligraphy. It provides a link to how individuals, peoples and different countries of the world interacted, beyond the aspect of political power; how religion can reflect a culture in conduct, dress code, art and even in practices for specific social occasions such as weddings. Moreover, the objects in this exhibition from both the Vatican Museums and Sharjah Museums Authority reflect the culture of Muslim communities around the world.

Note

1 The angular Al Kufic script is one of the oldest Arabic scripts. It was derived from the Nabataean writing commonly used in the North Arabian Peninsula before Islam and is named after the calligraphers from Kufa, Iraq. Al Naskh is similar to, and sometimes considered a variant of Al Thuluth. It is a legible, stately script with emphasis on a horizontal line and on the proportions between letters. It is used to make copies of the Holy Qur'an and has become the printing script. The Naskh script used by calligraphers today is basically the same as the one used during the time of the Abbasids. Al Thuluth is one of the most beautiful of the Arabic scripts and also the most difficult to write. It is considered to be the origin for many Arabic scripts and has become the standard with which the creativity of the calligrapher is measured. It is a large and elegant cursive script based on the principle that one-third of each letter slopes.

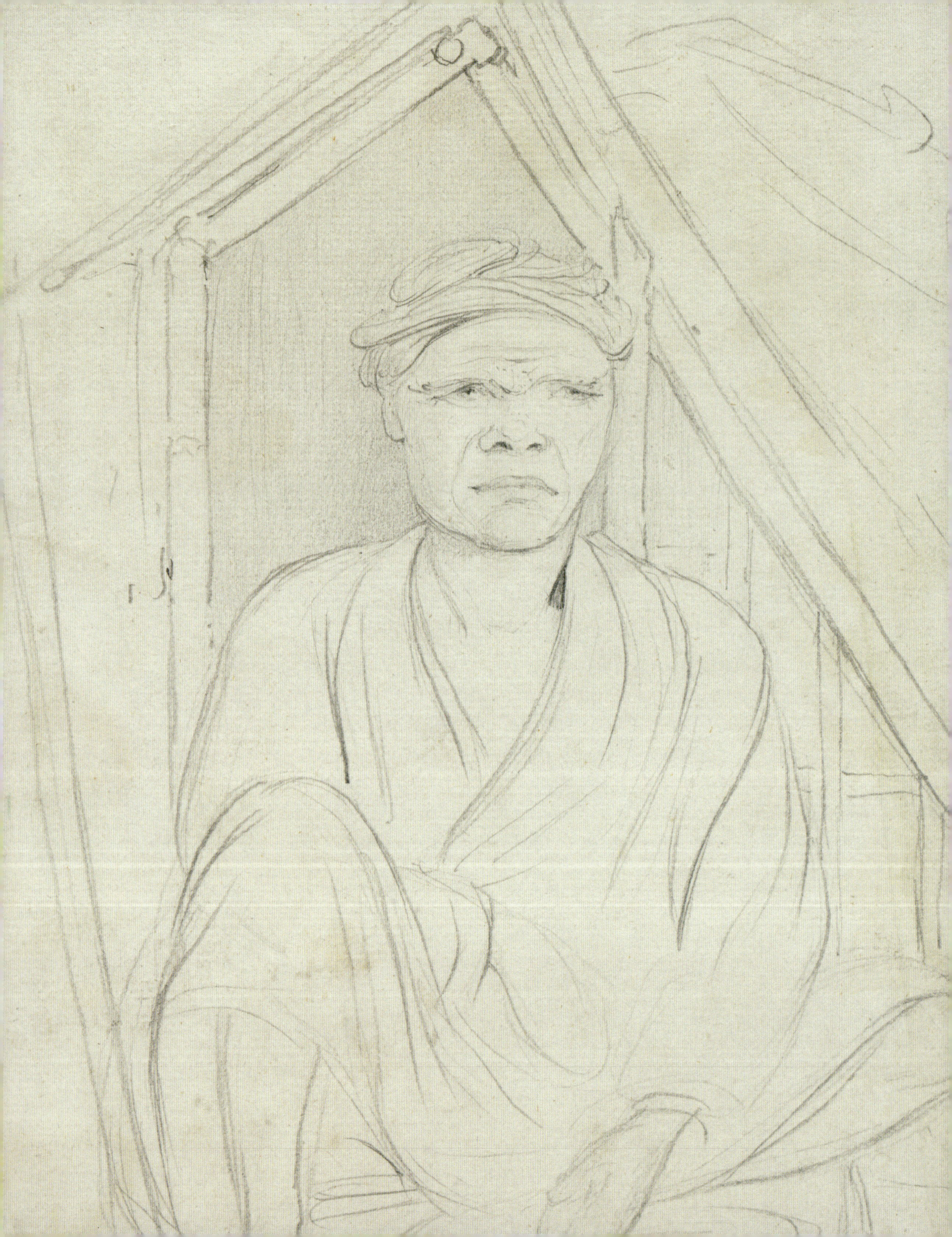

Cross-cultural encounters

The search for trepang in Australia

CAROL COOPER

It was the lure of new reserves of trepang (sea cucumber or bêche-de-mer, a culinary delicacy with medicinal properties), to supply a strong Chinese market in the 18th century, that brought the mainly Muslim Makasar traders from Sulawesi southwards.[1] It is estimated that from about 1780 to 1907, when the South Australian Government stopped issuing licences for the Makasar to harvest trepang in Australia, hundreds — perhaps thousands — of fishermen arrived each December and camped along the Arnhem Land coast, catching, boiling and preserving trepang. They met, traded and worked with local Aboriginal people. While the past 20 years have seen increased historical and archaeological interest in these non-Aboriginal visitors to the Arnhem Land and Kimberley coasts,[2] perhaps the most engaging and accurate — and earliest — written account is Matthew Flinders' description of an encounter that occurred during his circumnavigation of Australia.

CONTEMPORARY EUROPEAN OBSERVATIONS

In early December 1802, Flinders, sailing in the *Investigator*, arrived in the south-west corner of the Gulf of Carpentaria. He was surprised to find 'indications of some foreign people having visited', people seemingly as numerous as the Aboriginal population.[3] While he did not see or meet with them, he discovered tantalising traces of the sites where they had lived and worked:

> *Besides pieces of earthen ware jars and trees cut with axes, we found remnants of bamboo lattice work, palm leaves sewed with cotton thread into the form of such hats as are worn by the Chinese, and the remains of blue cotton trowsers, of the fashion called moormans.*

Flinders had stumbled upon a trepang-processing site, but what puzzled him most was 'a collection of stones piled together in a line resembling a low wall ... dividing the space

Figure 1: 'Probasso, a Malay chief', pencil drawing by William Westall, 1803, National Library of Australia, obj-138887323

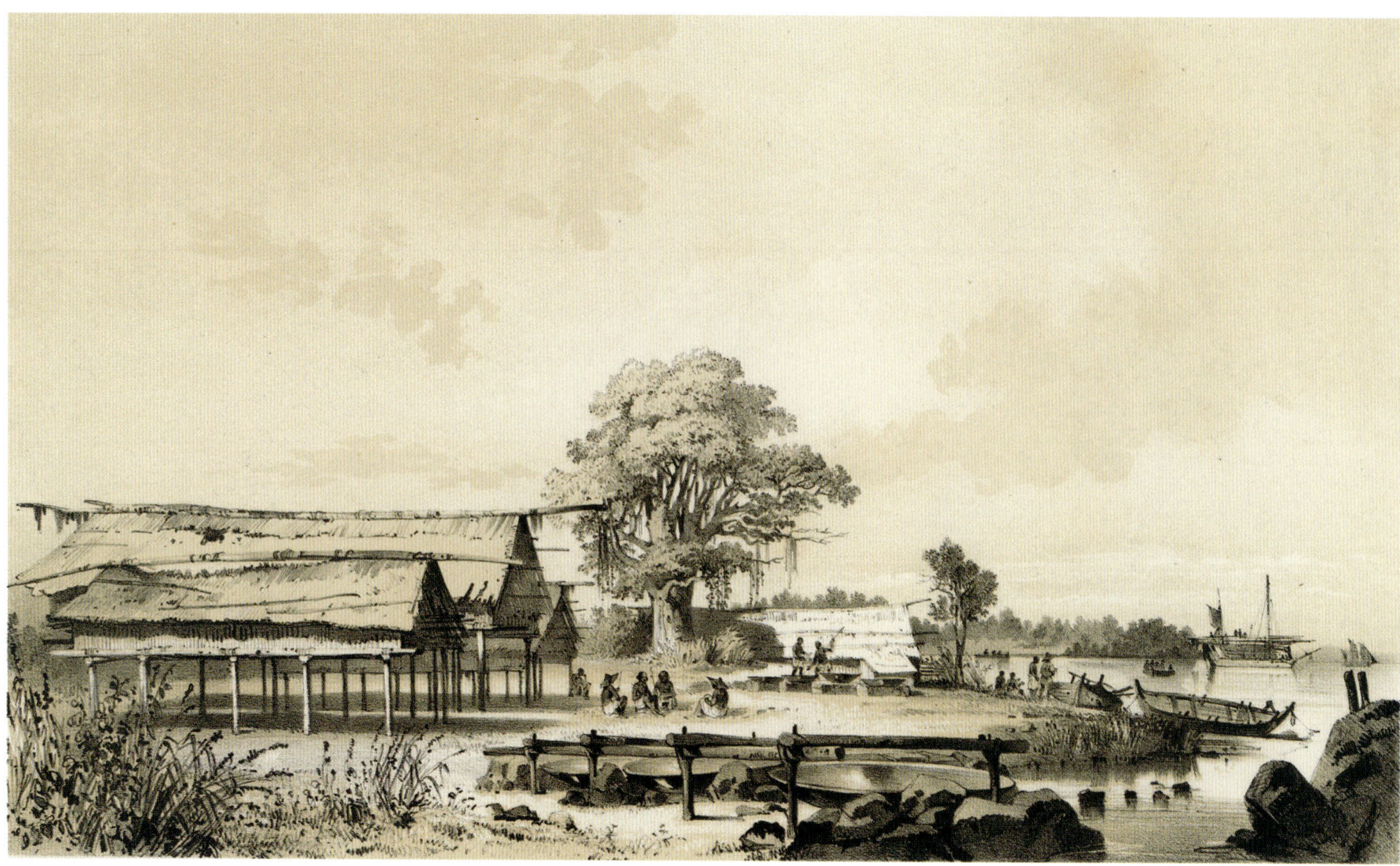

Figure 2

behind into compartments. In each of these were the remains of a charcoal fire, and all the wood near at hand, had been cut down'. He concluded, 'It was evident that these people were Asiatics', but he remained mystified about their activities. Continuing with his mapping and survey of this very complex part of the northern coastline, Flinders found further evidence of the enigmatic foreigners until, eventually, on 17 February 1803, he encountered six *prau* — part of a much larger Makasar fleet — in what he termed 'Malay Road', off the north-east corner of Arnhem Land.

Flinders' Malay cook acted as interpreter for Flinders in his communications with one of the chiefs of the fleet, Pobassoo, whose dignified portrait was captured by Flinders' landscape artist, William Westall (Fig. 1, p. 38).[4] Pobassoo is probably the first individual Asian named in published Australian history.[5] Courtesy visits were made between the Makasar vessels and the *Investigator*, and Pobassoo responded patiently to Flinders' 'numberless questions', despite his concern that he might miss the monsoonal winds necessary to commence his journey home.

Flinders' desire to 'learn everything concerning these people' revealed important details about the timing and extent of the trepanging voyages. The six *prau* were part of a much larger group of 60, with a commander-in-chief called Salloo, belonging to the Rajah of Boni.[6] Altogether, about 1000 men had left Makassar two months earlier with the north-west monsoon. Each vessel carried between 20 and 25 men, and the 'object of their expedition was a certain marine animal called trepang'. This was Pobassoo's sixth or seventh voyage to Marege' (the Makasar name for Arnhem Land) in the preceding 20 years. He explained that the earliest visiting *prau* fleet had been driven off course southwards from Indonesia, until it reached Northern Australia. Finding abundant trepang, the Makasar calculated how to use the north-west monsoons and south-east trade winds to navigate an annual visit. This chronology establishes the trepang industry in Australia as beginning in about 1780, a date that is supported by most scholars of this history.

Each man viewed the other as a stranger, in the true sense of the word. Pobassoo told Flinders that he had never before seen a European ship, or known that there was a European settlement in the country. Flinders observed that the fishermen were 'Mahometans', and was amused to see they were horrified that he kept live pigs for meat on his ship. Both Englishman and Makasar were wary in interactions with the Aboriginal population. Pobassoo confided to Flinders that the trepangers

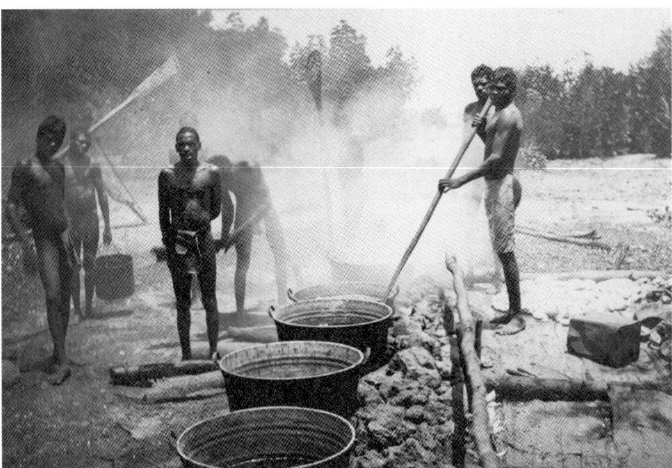

Figure 3

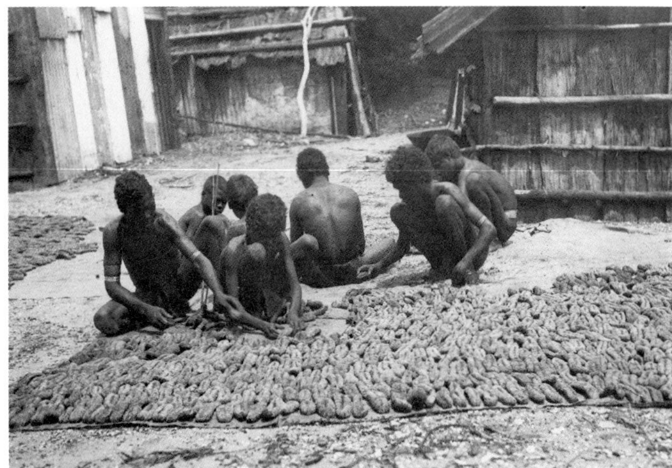

Figure 4

had often 'had skirmishes with the native inhabitants of the coast', and that he himself was once speared in the knee. While Flinders understood this warning, he also took care to keep a close and armed vigilance over the Makasar, whom he noted as wearing 'a cress or dagger, either secretly or openly'.

All early encounters on Australian shores carried grave risks, for both Aboriginal people and the visitors to their shores. The men of each group were invariably armed, and the complexity of cultural and linguistic understanding — or misunderstandings — could easily flare into violence. Only a few weeks before Flinders met with Pobassoo, a situation had occurred between crew-members of the *Investigator* and Aboriginal people living at Blue Mud Bay, when a misunderstanding led to the Master's Mate being speared. According to Flinders, and against his express orders, an Aboriginal man was shot in retribution. This death was marked by a poignant portrait by William Westall of the unnamed man, and an unfortunate observation that the man's head was removed and 'preserved in spirits' for anatomical purposes.

Flinders also recorded a number of details about the practices of the Makasar fishermen. They used small pocket compasses for navigation, and each *prau* carried one month's supply of water stored in joints of bamboo. They carried dry food such as rice, coconuts and dried fish, with a few live fowls kept for the chiefs. They supplemented this diet with live fish or turtles, which they caught themselves or obtained by trading with Aboriginal people.

Pobassoo carefully described how they obtained the trepang by diving into deep water, and that a diver could deliver eight or 10 trepang in one dive. To preserve them they were first split, then boiled in large *kawa* (cauldrons) and later stretched open with slips of bamboo, and then left to dry in the sun before being smoked and put away in bags. Flinders recorded that 1000 trepang made a *picol*, and that 100 *picols* were a suitable cargo for a *prau*.

Flinders is not the only visitor to observe and record details of the Makasar activities in Northern Australia. Three decades after Flinders sailed home, Louis Le Breton, one of two artists accompanying Dumont Durville on his second voyage of discovery, captured the scene of a trepang-processing site at Raffles Bay (Fig. 2, *Pecheurs de Tripang a la Baie Raffles*, 1846, by Louis Le Breton, National Gallery of Australia). The French landed only briefly in Northern Australia, but interacted with both Aboriginal people and Makasar fishermen. Breton depicts the lines of stone hearths and large cauldrons in which trepang was boiled, together with the bamboo and rattan smoke houses and tamarind trees. The Makasar are identified by their distinctive conical hats.

Two remarkable photographs taken by Hans Buser at an unidentified trepang processing site in Arnhem Land in about 1916 show a group of Aboriginal men, possibly working for a European trader (following the Makasar being denied fishing permits in 1907) (Fig. 3, 'Trepang processing site in Arnhem Land', about 1916, Hans Buser collection, AIATSIS, H01.BW-N5657_24A; Fig. 4, 'Aborigines drying trepang' at an Arnhem Land site, about 1916, Hans Buser collection, AIATSIS, H01.BW-N5657_29A). These images reveal a trepang-processing site just as described by Flinders, with iron cauldrons set into stone fireplaces and the boiled and slit trepang set out in the sun to dry.

The cauldron displayed in the exhibition, fragmented into two pieces (TH93/018.1; TH93/018.2, p. 116), is a rare example of a 19th-century cauldron used in Arnhem Land. It was collected from Record Point, Port Essington, in about 1909.[7] The use of iron cauldrons to boil trepang has continued in Indonesia into the present day.

REPRESENTATIONS OF THE MAKASAR IN YOLNGU ART AND CULTURE

The long association of Aboriginal people with the trepang traders in the Northern Territory left a distinct legacy for the economic, social and ceremonial life of Arnhem Land. This exhibition includes bark paintings and sculptures from the Yolngu-speaking people of north-east Arnhem Land that demonstrate this strong connection. They were all created in the 1960s, at a time when the Yolngu settlement at Yirrkala was becoming established as a centre for the production and sale of bark paintings and other Indigenous art works.

The paintings by brothers Mawalan and Mataman Marika and sculptures by Mungurraway Yunupingu are striking examples of how the story of the Makasar fishermen has been respected and absorbed into Aboriginal mythology. The two paintings demonstrate the elegant combination of representational and abstract designs characteristic of north-east Arnhem Land art.[8] Mawalan Marika (about 1908–1964), was a senior clan leader who had helped negotiate the establishment of the Methodist mission at Yirrkala in 1935. He is considered the head of one of Australia's greatest bark painting dynasties that includes his brother Mataman Marika (about 1920–1970), and his son Wandjuk Marika (1930–1987).[9] His youngest daughter, Banduk Marika (born 1954), is also a prolific and highly regarded painter, printmaker and filmmaker.[10]

In *Makasar Prau* (1967) (NMA 1985.0246.0002, p. 115) Mawalan has painted a cross-section of a typical *prau* with its tripod masts, rudders and the three cabins for the chief and crew. Inside the *prau* Mawalan has shown the valued goods that the Makasar brought with them to Australia, including a yellow goat, a red rooster, black rice sacks, three canoes and three types of steel knives or daggers. Mataman Marika's 1964 equally detailed painting *Makasar Boiling Down Trepang*, (NMA 1985.0259.0095, p. 114) conjures more *prau* and a trepang-processing site. In the lower layers of the painting the two *prau* are sailed by yellow-painted Makasar, though a black-painted Aboriginal person can be glimpsed below deck on the bottom *prau*. In the upper layer of the painting Aboriginal men are boiling the trepang in large metal cauldrons under a sheltering mangrove tree.

Munggurrawuy Yunupingu (about 1905–1979) is another of the remarkable 'old masters' of Australian bark art. His family dynasty includes his son, politician and musician Galarrwuy Yunupingu (born 1948–) and three daughters who are also artists.[11] Munggurrawuy was a prolific painter and a significant wood carver, particularly of *wuramu* mortuary figures. *Head of a Makasar* (NMA 1985.0083.0038, p. 114) and *Makasar Wuramu Figure* (NMA 1985.0083.0034, p. 115), were both made in 1946. *Wuramu* figures are derived from a ritual relating to Makasar burials that has been incorporated into Yolngu mythology and ceremony. The figures are usually depicted with a *songkok*, or Muslim cap, which can be clearly seen in *Makasar Wuramu Figure*. It was the anthropologist Ronald Berndt, who collected both of these figures in 1946, who first traced the origins of the carvings back to *wuramu* grave-post figures. Berndt considered that these in turn may have been influenced by mortuary rituals that the Yolngu are said to share with the Makasar.[12] While the Yolngu never embraced Islam as a faith, it appears that they incorporated elements of the visitors' ceremonies into their own, with multiple layers of meaning attaching to the *wuramu* figures.[13]

We know from Flinders' description that the Makasar who visited Northern Australia were predominantly Muslim. Many of the language names and the trade language that developed with Yolngu people included Arabic terms and, in some of the Yolngu song cycles, traces of classical Arabic religious music can be detected.[14] The adoption and benefits of Makasar technology in the form of iron tools and dugout canoes, including the ability to work iron itself, were major Makasar influences on Aboriginal culture.[15]

CONTINUING CONNECTIONS

These Yolngu objects speak to relationships that developed over a long period between the Makasar and Aboriginal people — the exact nature of which have been the subject of much conjecture. While they never stayed permanently in Australia, the Makasar maintained an annual cycle of economic trade that necessitated setting up camps in Northern Australia for extended periods of time. There are records of Aboriginal people travelling back to Sulawesi with the Makasar fleets. Over centuries of contact, succeeding generations of the same families made the journey from Makassar to Marege'. Pobassoo's son accompanied him on the voyage when they encountered Flinders in early 1803.[16] In about 1950, Daeng Sarro, one of the last Makasar fishermen, recounted how his own father was buried on Groote Eylandt off the east coast of Arnhem Land. In his remarkable interview with Dutch scholar AA Cense, Daeng provided many insights into the relationship between the Makasar seamen and local Aboriginal people. While in some areas they were feared and 'very aggressive' or 'unfriendly', at other places he describes them as 'peaceful' and happy to work collecting and processing trepang 'in return for food and tobacco'. He also talked about his father's relationship with some of the Aboriginal 'chiefs', saying that 'they treated each other like brothers'.[17]

The late 20th century witnessed a revival of interest in Yolngu–Makasar contact history that has led to an 'immense reinvigoration'[18] in the relationship between them. Crucial to this revival was the highly successful Hati Marege' bicentennial project, in which a *prau* captained by a direct descendant of one of the last Makasar trepang fishermen, sailed into Yirrkala on the 16 January 1988. This was exactly 200 years after the First Fleet reached Botany Bay, and more than 200 years since the first Makasar *prau* landed in Northern Australia. A long period of cultural isolation between these two groups was ended, and a multitude of other intercultural interactions began.[19]

It has been suggested that a new world heritage category of 'cultural routes' offers an opportunity to recognise and celebrate the intercultural heritage of the Makassar to Marege' trepang trade route. Sandy Blair and Nicholas Hall convincingly argue what such an acknowledgement will mean:

> *This route of intercultural connections situates Australia in the Southeast Asia region in ways that other travel routes do not, those that emphasise connections to Europe and the remoteness and distance of the colonies ... The broader story ... is of an intercultural and international route that symbolises the complex connections and seas in our region ... [and that] we will only understand it with multiple perspectives.*[20]

In the 21st century, Australian Muslims point proudly to their long and successful historical presence in Australia.[21] The history and legacy of the Makasar traders is an important part of the larger cross-cultural story of Islam in Australia.

Notes

1 Although the crews also came from other Indonesian localities, the majority originated from the port of Makassar, the point of departure and return for the trepanging fleets. This essay uses the term 'Makasar' for the people and the language; 'Macassan' is now considered erroneous. See Campbell Macknight, 'The view from Marege': Australian knowledge of Makassar and the impact of the trepang industry across two centuries', *Aboriginal History*, vol. 35, 2011, http://press-files.anu.edu.au/downloads/press/p148271/html/Text/S02%20Macknight.html?referer=&page=#footnote-13487-25-backlink, accessed 1 December 2017.

2 For an overview of this research see Campbell Macknight, 'Harvesting the memory: Open beaches in Makassar and Arnhem Land', in Peter Veth, Peter Sutton & Margo Neale (eds), *Strangers on the Shore: Early Coastal Contacts in Australia*, National Museum of Australia Press, Canberra, 2008, pp. 133–47; and Ian S McIntosh, 'Pre-Macassans at Dholtji? Exploring one of north-east Arnhem Land's great conundrums', ibid., pp. 165–80.

3 This and subsequent quotes are from Matthew Flinders, *A Voyage to Terra Australis; Undertaken for the Purpose of Completing the Discovery of that Vast Country* ... (London, 1814), quoted in Tim Flannery (ed.), *Terra Australis: Matthew Flinders' Great Adventures in the Circumnavigation of Australia*, Text Publishing, Melbourne, 2000, pp. 180, 202–7.

4 TM Perry & Donald H Simpson (eds), 1962, *Drawings by William Westall*, The Royal Commonwealth Society, 1962, p. 54.

5 DJ Mulvaney, *The Prehistory of Australia*, Pelican Books, Melbourne, 1975, p. 20.

6 Boni, or Bone, was a sultanate in the south-west peninsula of Sulawesi (formerly Celebes), now part of Indonesia. Campbell Macknight, *The Voyage to Marege'*, Melbourne University Press, Melbourne, 1976, pp. 17–18, 146.

7 Macknight, *The Voyage to Marege'*, discusses the importance of this cauldron (p. 53). He goes on to refer to 'a large Malay encampment' seen at Record Point in 1824, during the visit of Phillip Parker King (pp. 76, 158). See also Alison Mercieca, 'From Makassar to Marege' to the Museum: Trepang processing industry in Arnhem Land', National Museum of Australia Audio on demand transcript, 9 July 2008, www.nma.gov.au/audio/transcripts/NMA_Mercieca_20080709.html, accessed 3 August 2017.

8 Howard Morphy, 2013, 'Abstraction', in *Old Masters: Australia's Great Bark Painters*, National Museum of Australia Press, Canberra, 2013, pp. 25–7.

9 See *Old Masters*, pp. 218–19, for striking portraits of the two Marika brothers and pp. 160–62 for artworks.

10 'Marika, Marmburra Wananumba Banduk (1954–)', *The Australian Women's Register*, www.womenaustralia.info/biogs/AWE1169b.htm, accessed 26 September 2017. Further details of the extended Marika family of noted Indigenous artists can be found at www.nma.gov.au/exhibitions/yalangbara/the_marika_family.

11 *Old Masters*, p. 233.

12 Howard Morphy, *Aboriginal Art*, Phaidon, London, 1998, p. 245.

13 Regina Ganter, 'Histories with traction: Macassan contact in the framework of Muslim Australian history', in Marshall Clarke & Sally K May (eds), *Macassan History and Heritage*, ANU Press, Canberra, 2013, http://press-files.anu.edu.au/downloads/press/p241301/html/ch04/.xhtml?referer=294&page=6, accessed 5 August 2017.

14 ibid.

15 Sandy Blair & Nicholas Hall, 'Travelling the "Malay Road": Recognising the heritage significance of the Macassan maritime trade route', In Clarke & May (eds), *Macassan History and Heritage*, accessed 5 August 2017.

16 Flannery (ed.), *Terra Australis*, p. 206.

17 Daeng Sarro's account, 'The route of the Macassan trepang fleet', is included in Campbell Macknight, *The Farthest Coast*, Melbourne University Press, Melbourne, 1969, pp. 180–5.

18 Ganter, 'Histories with traction', accessed 5 August 2017.

19 ibid.

20 Blair & Hall, 'Travelling the "Malay Road"', accessed 5 August 2017.

21 Moustafa Fahour, *Boundless Plains: The Australian Muslim Connection*, Islamic Museum of Australia, Melbourne, 2011.

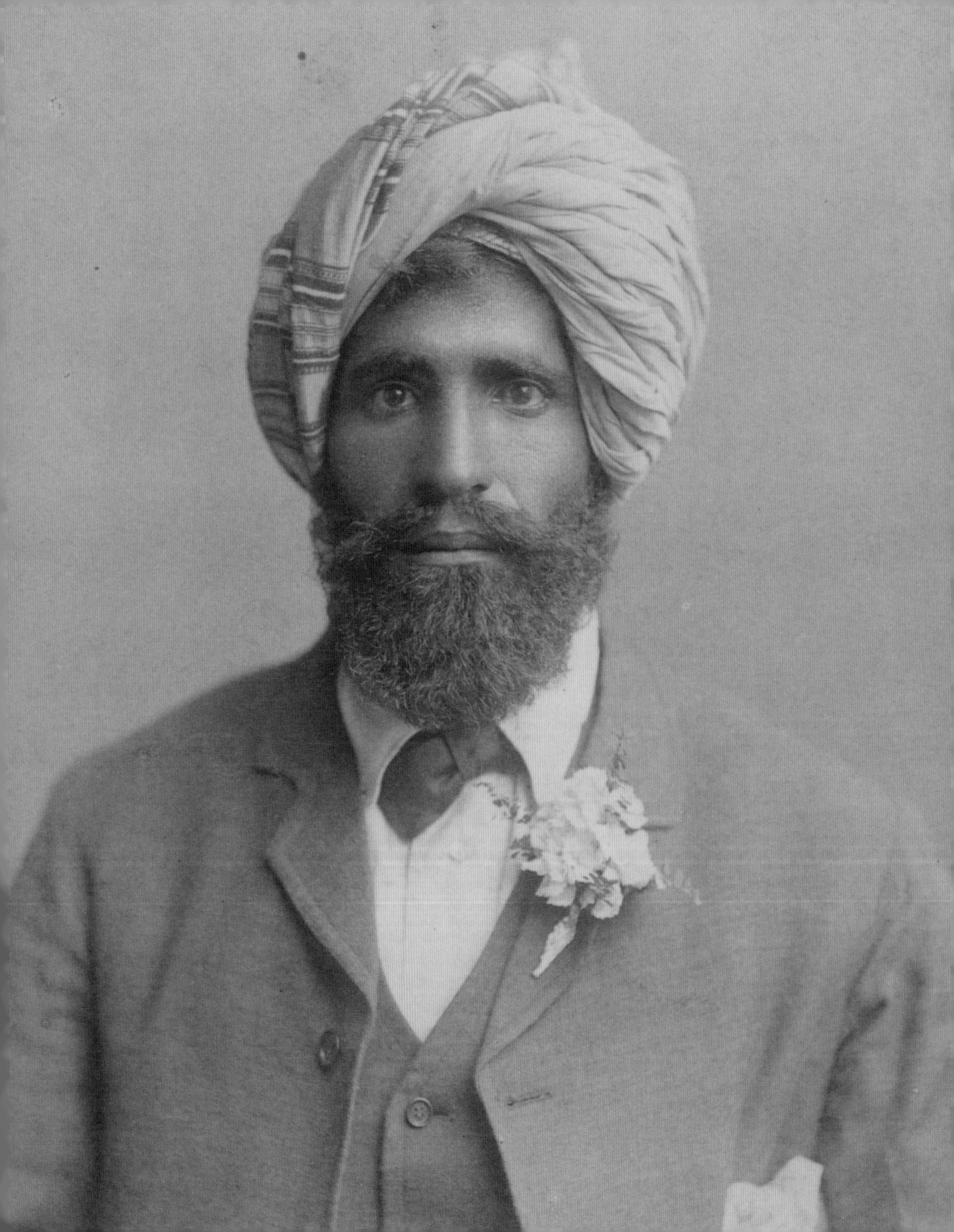

Bejah Dervish

'Australia's greatest cameleer'

CAROL COOPER

Old camel-driver, explorer, the giant Afghan
Who steered his life by compass and by Koran,
'Oh ya, believe in God; young man no care;
God save, God help; oh ya, need help out there!'
And fondled his box of brass and kissed his book
So passionately, with such a lover's look,
He whirled in deserts still, too wild for human.

Douglas Stewart, 'Afghan', 1955[1]

For 60 years, from about 1860 to 1920, an estimated 20,000 camels and more than 2000 cameleers journeyed to Australia from what was then Afghanistan and British India (now Pakistan). Uniquely suited to desert conditions because of their ability to travel long distances without regular water, the camels carried explorers, settlers, officials, domestic animals, goods, food, equipment and building materials — they were indispensable to European exploration and settlement of Australia. The men who accompanied them were respected for their navigation skills, their incredible stamina and fortitude and their love for and knowledge of their animals.

Most cameleers returned to their families and their countries after serving short contracts or indentures, but some established businesses and long-term relationships and decided to make Australia their home. It was these cameleers who formed the first Australian Muslim communities, and today their descendants proudly acknowledge their many achievements and contributions to Australian history. They brought the Muslim faith and mosques to Australia, and although they spoke many languages, all of their prayers were in Arabic.[2] Because of the transitory nature of most of these people's experience in this country, few documents or objects survive to tell the story of this remarkable episode in Australian history. The few extant physical reminders of this period in Australian history have tended to be handed down through families, while institutions have until recently shown little interest in the cameleers. When Philip Jones began assembling objects for a South Australian Museum exhibition on the cameleers in 2005, he was surprised to find that 'no Australian museum had directed its collecting efforts to material culture or documents relating to the cameleers'.[3] This is what makes the story of Muslim cameleer Bejah Dervish (Fig. 1) so important. He is typical of these first Islamic immigrants to Australia, but he is also unique in terms of his repute during his life and the details that have survived of his personal story.[4] Bejah's legacy includes not only the mementoes of his cameleering exploits and oral history of his descendants, but also vivid glimpses provided by rare documentary

Figure 1: Bejah Dervish as a young man, about 1890, SLSA B11209

sources. These include pencil drawings, photographs and diary entries — now in the National Museum of Australia's collection — created by 25-year-old English artist Noelle Sandwith, who met Bejah during a trip down the Birdsville Track in 1953.[5]

THE CALVERT EXPEDITION

Bejah Dervish was born in Baluchistan and arrived in Australia in 1890, when he was about 28 years old.[6] He arrived by ship at Fremantle and was initially employed as a camel handler, at which he excelled. In 1896, surveyor and explorer Lawrence 'Larry' Wells appointed Bejah Dervish as his head cameleer on an expedition to explore 'the remaining blanks of Australia'.[7] The expedition was seemingly well planned and funded, and a good team of men and camels was amassed.

But Wells and his team were totally 'foiled by the arid interior'.[8] The proposed 1368-kilometre route from Lake Way to Fitzroy Crossing scaled huge sand ridges. Water sources were not reliable, temperatures were extreme and, at one stage of the journey, the expedition members travelled 27 days with only the water in their canteens. Wells and Bejah both had near-death experiences, and both were saved by the other. The horrific conditions claimed the lives of two other expedition members who died of thirst, and the expedition was abandoned. The daily accounts of the expedition underscore the strength of the relationships that developed between the men and their camels, and the invaluable role of camel and cameleer to the survival of the remaining members of the team. (Fig. 2: Bejah Dervish with Larry Wells's favourite camel, Warrior, SLSA B10486/1)

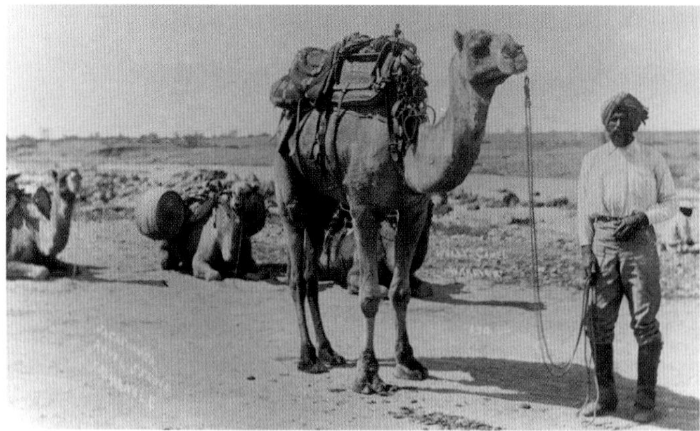

Figure 2

The first two months of their journey went relatively smoothly, although the rocky country was hard on the camels' feet — at one point the men had to clear the stones ahead of the camel caravan. On 23 July 1896, poetry was in the air when Wells named a particularly beautiful lagoon after Adam Lindsay Gordon. Not long afterwards, troubles began with poisonous grasses. Bejah was constantly monitoring the health and condition of the camels, administering potions and spending considerable time pulling up the poison plant and burning it. The team also gathered herbage so the camels could be safely tethered and fed overnight.

By 22 August 1896, team members were under considerable stress. Wells and Bejah had painful eyes, water was scarce and the country almost destitute of camel feed. A small valley provided brief respite and Wells gratefully named a hill 'after the faithful Bejah, who has proved himself a splendid fellow and an excellent camelman'. The situation soon deteriorated. Wells was almost blind, and there was neither feed nor water. On 25 August, Bejah refused breakfast: 'Camel no eat, me no eat'.[9]

As the expedition continued across the Great Sandy Desert, it was characterised by the constant battle to find water and feed for the camels, and maintain the health and sanity of the expedition members. A rare moment of relief occurred when Wells and Bejah encountered 13 camels that had been spelled to recuperate after eating poisoned grasses. Wells exclaims how good, 'even quite fat', the camels were looking, and describes Bejah being 'so delighted at seeing them that he ... ran off ... talking to and playing with them in the most excited manner. No doubt to him it was the next best thing to meeting a countryman'.[10] This is the last mention of 'delight' in Wells's report.

On 10 October, Wells reflected on the importance of finding water for his weary 'ships of the desert', declaring that it is the absence of water that is 'frequently the only danger of importance that the explorer has to encounter'. The following day the party split into two when Wells's cousin Charles and the expedition's mineralogist and photographer, George Jones, together with three camels, headed off to Joanna Spring, intending to reunite with the others in two weeks.[11]

Forced to travel at night, the main party made slow progress. Larry Wells and Bejah shared responsibility for leading the group, often undertaking extra journeys to locate feed and water, while the other men and camels rested in camp. By 17 October, the camels had refused to 'eat a morsel' for three days, and Wells began to doubt that 'any of us would be alive a week hence'.[12]

They survived, however, for another three weeks, before finally finding good feed and water on the Fitzroy River. Six camels died on this last stretch of their journey and the team had been forced to abandon their natural history and mineral collections, including cameras and other heavy equipment. Their anxiety was now for the two missing men, who had not arrived at various rendezvous points, and of whom there was no news.

Bejah Dervish continued to tend the remaining camels and support Wells in his attempts to locate the missing team members. It was not until 27 May 1897 that they finally discovered the mummified remains of the two men. From the notes made in Jones's official journal it appears they had died of thirst towards the end of November 1896. One camel had died and another two had strayed at a time when the men were two weak from dysentery to recover them. On his return to Adelaide, Wells was pilloried by the press and South Australian public over the deaths, and it was two years before he was exonerated by a parliamentary select committee.

It is possible that if Bejah Dervish or the assistant camel driver, Said Ameer, had accompanied Charles Wells and Jones, the outcome might have been different. The care and knowledge of camels was obviously an enormous advantage in successfully traversing inhospitable deserts. As George Farwell has observed in his book about life along the Birdsville Track, 'Men reared in the British tradition of horsemanship remained suspicious of these gaunt, ungainly, often savage beasts, for whom they could feel no affection'.[13] The cameleers were therefore invaluable members of expedition teams. Farwell mentions that Bejah Dervish was highly praised in Larry Wells's report of the expedition, which made special mention of 'his powers of endurance', and also that the compass that Wells had given Bejah at the start of the expedition 'was the one they had used to struggle back to safety'.[14]

GHAN TOWN

In the years following the expedition, Bejah resumed camel driving and established his headquarters in 'Ghan Town', Marree, in northern South Australia,[15] which was for many years home to a huge camel camp:

> *Here — over that way — out there — all camels and camel camp. One time my people have one hundred strings. That is many thousand camel ... and now — now all gone.*[16]

Bejah bought three sections of land in Marree, and for nearly 50 years he continued working, often escorting camel strings of 50 beasts or more. 'We went all over the outback ... We carried tea, sugar, spirits, clothing. No motors then, no planes. Only my camels'.[17]

Bejah is believed to have had two sons, both of whom followed their father into cameleering. He is recorded as having a son in the early 1890s from his relationship with Arabana and Thirrari woman, Anne Murray, whose country

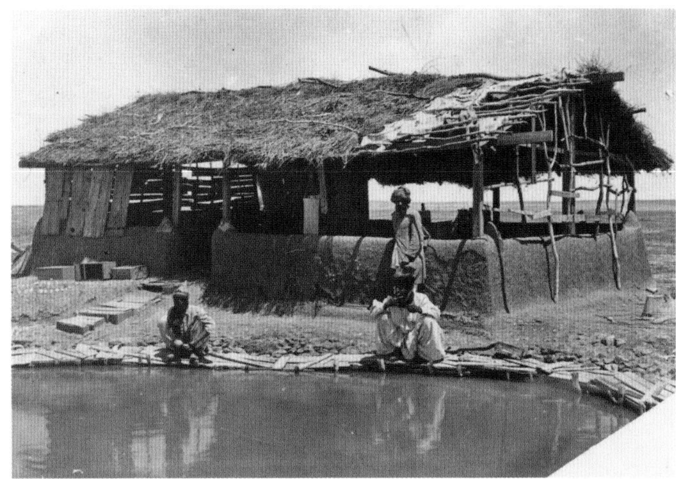

Figure 3

was on Stuart's Creek, south of Lake Eyre. Ben Murray was born at the town camp, by Frome Creek just outside Marree. By 1914 Murray was boss of his own string of 70 camels, each of whom he knew by name.[18] Linguist Luise Hercus met him in 1965 when she was conducting a study of the Arabana and Wangkangurru languages. She discovered he possessed an immense knowledge of language, tradition and history — Aboriginal, Afghan and European.[19]

In 1909 Bejah married Amelia Jane Shaw, a widow with eight children. Their son, Abdul Jubbar, or Jack Bejah, became a canny camel man himself. In 1939 Cecil Madigan asked Bejah Dervish to act as camel driver for an expedition across the Simpson Desert. Bejah, who was about 77 years old at the time, selected the camels and their saddles, but sent his son, Jack Bejah, as the driver.[20]

By the time Farwell met Bejah Dervish in the late 1940s, the former cameleer was 'over eighty, six-foot-two in height, stooping a little yet still overlooking most men'. Farwell notes his 'splendid white beard, very full, with white moustaches, and a pair of alert dark eyes'. Bejah had taken Farwell to his home to show off his prized possession, 'a brass-boxed compass ... given to him by the explorer Larry Wells' (SAM 2007A79472, p. 118).[21]

One of the most poignant passages in Farwell's narrative is his description of the Marree mosque, where he went on Bejah's invitation (Fig. 3: 'The Mosque, Marree, 1884', State Library of South Australia SLSAB15341). His initial expectations were low:

> *The mosque ... from a distance appears no more than a tin shanty. It has no minaret, no ornate exterior. Only the two tall palms, one at each end, that rise above its galvanised iron roof cause the eye to travel skyward, as spires, towers, minarets are designed to do.*

But his mood changed when Bejah took him inside the mosque and opened a lattice window:

> *The sunlight slanted upon a beautifully-worked prayer mat on the stone flagged floor. The prayer mat, woven in Bagdad, had the design of an Arabian mosque upon it ... He went over to an alcove in the eastern wall ... In the centre was a low stool, and upon it the Koran, swathed in coloured silk. Then he bent down swiftly, touched the Koran with his lips ... [and] I felt that somehow he had drawn strength from these few minutes in this sanctuary ... he was undefeated ... there was no bitterness in him. Resignation, yes — disappointment, a sense of nostalgia for the days that were past. Bejah Dervish was a courageous old man, for he had seen his world slowly crumble around him, [yet] he continued to stride through the town with measured dignity.*[22]

'LIFE IN THE OUTBACK'

By the time Noelle Sandwith met Bejah Dervish in 1953, he was the sole survivor of the Calvert expedition. Sandwith was on a mission of her own: to 'make a record of life in the Outback'. It was advice from the Australian Inland Mission that had set her on a course to travel the 500 kilometres down 'the Track', from Birdsville to Marree, to capture 'something out of the ordinary!' She wanted to preserve an enduring record of the unique characters and ways of outback life, and she was particularly keen to meet the legendary camel driver Bejah Dervish, whom she had heard about in Sydney.[23]

Sandwith's manuscript account resonates with the excitement she felt as she accompanied Marree's bush nurse to visit the aged veteran of 'Ghan Town', where the cameleers inhabited an area on the northern side of the railway line:

> *We were to call on Bejah Dervish — Bejah Dervish! — that famous name! How I had wished for an introduction to Australia's greatest cameleer! ... Away we trudged from the shanties and shacks [of Marree's European township] ... towards a distant cluster of date palms, growing behind a small wooden homestead ... We arrived at a gate in the wire-netting fence, which neatly surrounded the homely back-yard. A collection of ducks were enjoying the shade provided by the five or six date palms, planted more than fifty years before.*[24]

Sandwith describes Bejah proudly retrieving the expedition compass: Out he stumped again, dark old eyes gleaming his right palm guarding a sacred object of brass — the very same compass presented to him by his Leader on the 'Trip'![25]

Bejah described to her the devastating final days of the expedition:

> *Very dry desert country — no water. Camels good things, camels — go twenty-six, twenty-seven days without water. We have little water, nearly die of thirst. Two men die; very sad.*[26]

Sandwith was struck by the dignity with which Bejah faced the decline in the use of camels for desert transport in the early 1930s. She had been told of his great affection for one of his last camels, called 'Schilling'. 'Once he rode this gaunt and tireless brute across four hundred miles in five-and-a-half days to collect a ballot box from outlying stations'. When Schilling grew old and decrepit, Bejah freed him, 'watching his staunch companion totter away into the scrub'.[27]

Also in the National Museum of Australia's collection is a sketch Sandwith made of Bejah Dervish and another retired cameleer, Said Goolamadeen (NMA 1993.0100.0044; 1993.0100.0042, pp. 118–19).[28] Sandwith was struck by his aristocratic profile and expressive eyes that reached into 'the depths of his consciousness'. She describes how she fixed a holder onto her pencil, to sweep in 'the folds of his turban, shirt, the wide, heavy drapes in the huge pantaloons — consisting of at least six yards of material'.[29]

Sandwith also attempted an oil painting of Bejah, sending away for the canvas and paints. She describes his enthusiasm for this venture, dressing in his smartest clothes, including 'a short loose jacket like a bolero of magnificent scarlet adorned with gold braid', and an 'exquisite pair of Ottoman slippers whose flowery pointed tips curved right up in the air'. Unfortunately, this painting was damaged, and although she intended to repair and finish it, its current location is unknown.[30] Some of this clothing has been preserved by Bejah's descendants, including his silk turban and blue pantaloons, the woven inner cap for his turban, and at least one of the glittering gold, silver rings that 'flashed from both his little fingers'.[31] The precious compass was recently donated by the family to the South Australian Museum (Fig. 4: William Bejah with his grandfather's compass, photograph by P Jones).

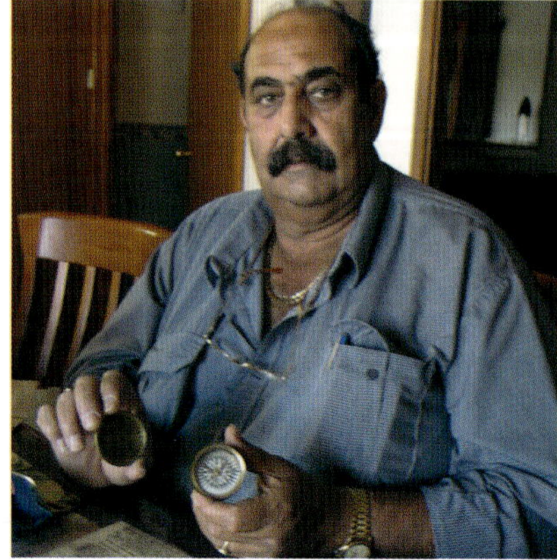

Figure 4

Sandwith's final memory of Bejah was of him farewelling her at his gate, 'the ducks all quacking and flapping at his ankles'. He told her that he would 'never go back to Baluchistan — too old, no money'.[32] He had other compelling reasons to stay. Bejah's daughter-in-law, Bebe Bejah, wrote to Sandwith in 1953 that 'Old Mr Bejah has been to Adelaide and came back looking extra fit. He will not go to India Noelle, as I don't think he will ever leave the [grand]children'.[33] Sandwith herself observed that 'he boasted four grandchildren now and nothing on earth would induce him to leave them'.[34]

Bejah never did return to his country of birth, dying at Port Augusta, South Australia, on 6 May 1957. He was 95 years old.

Another enduring record of Bejah can be found in the 1954 film *Back of Beyond*, where he is briefly shown at prayer. A devout Muslim, he prayed at the mosque at Marree at least three times a day and attributed his lasting good health to his deep faith. Today his many descendants and others of Islamic faith in Australia are proud of his strong legacy and the high esteem with which he is held in Australian history.[35]

Notes

1 Douglas Stewart, 'Afghan', in *Collected Poems, 1936–1967*, Angus & Robertson, Sydney, 1967, p. 126. First published in 1955, the poem's subject is Muslim cameleer Bejah Dervish.

2 George Farwell, *Land of Mirage: The Story of Men, Cattle and Camels on the Birdsville Track*, Rigby Ltd, Adelaide, 1971 (1950), p. 24; Philip Jones & Anna Kenny, *Australia's Muslim Cameleers*, Wakefield Press, Adelaide, 2007, pp. 27, 82; Moustafa Fahour, *Boundless Plains: The Australian Muslim Connection*, Islamic Museum of Australia, Melbourne, 2011.

3 Philip Jones, 'Australia's Muslim cameleer heritage', *reCollections: A Journal of Museums and Collections*, vol. 2, no. 2, September 2007, http://recollections.nma.gov.au/issues/vol_2_no2/notes_and_comments/australias_muslim_cameleer_heritage, accessed 21 November 2017. See also Philip Jones & Anna Kenny, 'Reflecting on Australia's Muslim cameleer heritage', in *Australia's Muslim Cameleers*, pp. 9–15, where Jones discusses the rarity of genuine cameleer objects in Australian museum collections and the significance, in the case of Bejah Dervish, of the role of his grandchildren in preserving his relics.

4 Valmai A Henkel published the first biography of Bejah, 'Bejah Dervish (1862–1957)', *Australian Dictionary of Biography*, National Centre of Biography, Australian National University, http://adb.anu.edu.au/biography/bejah-dervish-5187/text8721 (1979), accessed online 6 April 2017; she updated this slightly in her more recent short biography, 'Bejah Dervish', on the *Adelaidia* website, http://adelaidia.sa.gov.au/people/bejah-dervish (2013), accessed 6 April 2017. Bejah is also unusual in the number and quality of firsthand accounts that were written about him, especially those provided by Larry Wells, George Farwell and Noelle Sandwith used in this essay, as well as the number of excellent photographs taken of him which are available in public collections, notably the State Library of South Australia.

5 In 1993 Noelle Sandwith donated to the National Museum of Australia 105 pencil sketches together with photographs and negatives, drawing equipment, letters and a manuscript, 'Outback adventure: Sketching across Australia', National Museum of Australia Research Library, AU NMA-60-1. This drew on the detailed diaries she kept on her expedition, and excerpts from this account, together with biographical information and a selection of sketches and stories, was edited by Sophie Jensen & Johanna Parker and published as *In Search of the Birdsville Track: An Artist in the Outback*, National Museum of Australia Press, Canberra, 2005. Sandwith's quotes in this essay are all taken from the original manuscript.

6 Henkel, 'Bejah Dervish'.

7 The Calvert Exploring Expedition was financed by London-based mining engineer and author Albert Calvert to explore largely unknown areas of Western Australia. It was managed from Adelaide by the Royal Geographical Society of Australasia (South Australian Branch). The expedition consisted of Larry Wells (leader); Charles Wells (his cousin, and second in command); George Jones (mineralogist and photographer); George Keartland (naturalist); and James Trainor. Bejah Dervish and Said Ameer were engaged as camel drivers. See Christopher Steele, 'Wells. Lawrence Allen (1860–1938)', *Australian Dictionary of Biography*, National Centre for Biography, Australian National University, http://adb.anu.edu.au/biography/wells-lawrence-allen-9043/text15931 (1990), accessed online 4 October 2017; LA Wells, *Journal of the Calvert Scientific Exploring Expedition*, 1896–7, Government Printer, Perth, 1902.

8 Steele, 'Wells. Lawrence Allen (1860–1938)'.

9 Wells, *Journal*, pp. 17–18.

10 ibid., p. 23.

11 ibid., p. 30.

12 ibid., p. 32.

13 Farwell, *Land of Mirage*, p. 24.

14 ibid., p. 27: the compass was a treasured heirloom of Bejah's descendants until it was donated to the South Australian Museum following the *Australian Muslim Cameleers* exhibition in 2007. See Jones & Kenny, *Australia's Muslim Cameleers*, p. 59, for a photograph and description of the compass which is inscribed 'Calvert Exploring Expedition/ Bejah/ 25 May 1896'.

15 Marree was called Hergott Springs until 1883. From the time of Marree's establishment, Europeans, Muslims and Aborigines all lived in distinct areas, with the Muslims living in an area known as 'Ghan Town'. Jones & Kenny, *Australia's Muslim Cameleers*, pp. 122–3, includes early photographs of Marree's two mosques and a plan of Hergott Springs in the early 1880s, showing the cameleers' residences.

16 Farwell, *Land of Mirage*, p. 26; Henkel, 'Bejah Dervish'.

17 Noelle Sandwith, 'Outback adventure', p. 187.

18 Ben Murray attributed calling out words learned from his father, and his father's name, to saving his life when he was spared after being shot by Turkish soldiers in Palestine during the First World War. See Phoebe Spurrier, 2015, 'Ben Murray: Aboriginal WW1 Gallipoli veteran', http://anzaccentenary.sa.gov.au/wp-content/uploads/2015/03/Ben-Murray-by-Phoebe-Spurrier.pdf, accessed 15 April 2017; Luise A Hercus, 'Afghan stories from the north-east of South Australia', *Aboriginal History*, vol. 5, no. 1, 1981, 39–68 ; Peter Austin, Luise Hercus & Philip Jones, 'Ben Murray (Parlku-nguyu-thangkayiwarna)', *Aboriginal History*, vol. 12, no. 2, 1988, p. 162.

19 Hercus, 'Afghan stories'; Austin, Hercus & Jones, 'Ben Murray (Parlku-nguyu-thangkayiwarna)'.

20 Henkel, 'Bejah Dervish'. For an account of the Madigan Simpson Desert Expedition, see Jones & Kenny, *Australia's Muslim Cameleers*, pp. 62–3, especially photographs of Jack Bejah loading one of the expedition camels (p. 62) and Bejah Dervish standing next to his daughter-in-law, Bebe Noor Bejah, at the completion of the expedition at Marree (p. 63).

21 Farwell, *Land of Mirage*, p. 26.

22 ibid., pp. 27–8. Bejah Dervish's prayer mat has also survived in the care of his descendants and featured in the South Australian Museum's 2007 exhibition: see Jones & Kenny, *Australia's Muslim Cameleers*, p. 124.

23 Sandwith, 'Outback adventure', p. 180.

24 ibid., p. 180.

25 ibid., p. 186.

26 ibid.

27 ibid., p. 187.

28 Said Goolamadeen, born about 1870, left his birthplace of Quetta-Pishin in 1901, contracted to drive camels for the agricultural firm of Elder Smith. He first settled at Broken Hill in New South Wales, then lived in Marree where he helped take care of the Marree mosque, and where he died, the last cameleer in the town, in the 1960s. There is a small photo of him in Jones & Kenny, *Australia's Muslim Cameleers*, p. 185, and a portrait sketch by Noelle Sandwith in the National Museum of Australia collection, 1993.0100.0042.

29 Sandwith, 'Outback adventure', p. 182.

30 ibid., pp. 190–2.

31 ibid., p. 183; Jones & Kenny, *Australia's Muslim Cameleers*, pp. 194, 195.

32 Sandwith, p. 193.

33 Letter from Bebe Bejah to Noelle Sandwith, 18 May 1953, National Museum of Australia Research Library, AU NMA-60-1, p. 47N.

34 Sandwith, 'Outback adventure', p. 193.

35 Shell Film Unit Australia, *The Back of Beyond*, 1954, https://aso.gov.au/titles/documentaries/back-of-beyond/, accessed 21 July 2017. More recently, Kuranda Seyit, of Whirling Dervish Media, researched and filmed the documentary *By Compass and Quran: History of Australia's Muslim Cameleers*, which was broadcast on ABC TV in 2015. It includes the excerpt from *Back of Beyond* (1954), and many short interviews that Seyit has conducted with descendants of Bejah Dervish, such as William 'Butch' Bejah, Marie Williams and others. See http://www.roninfilms.com.au/person/13755/kuranda-seyit.html, accessed 5 October 2017.

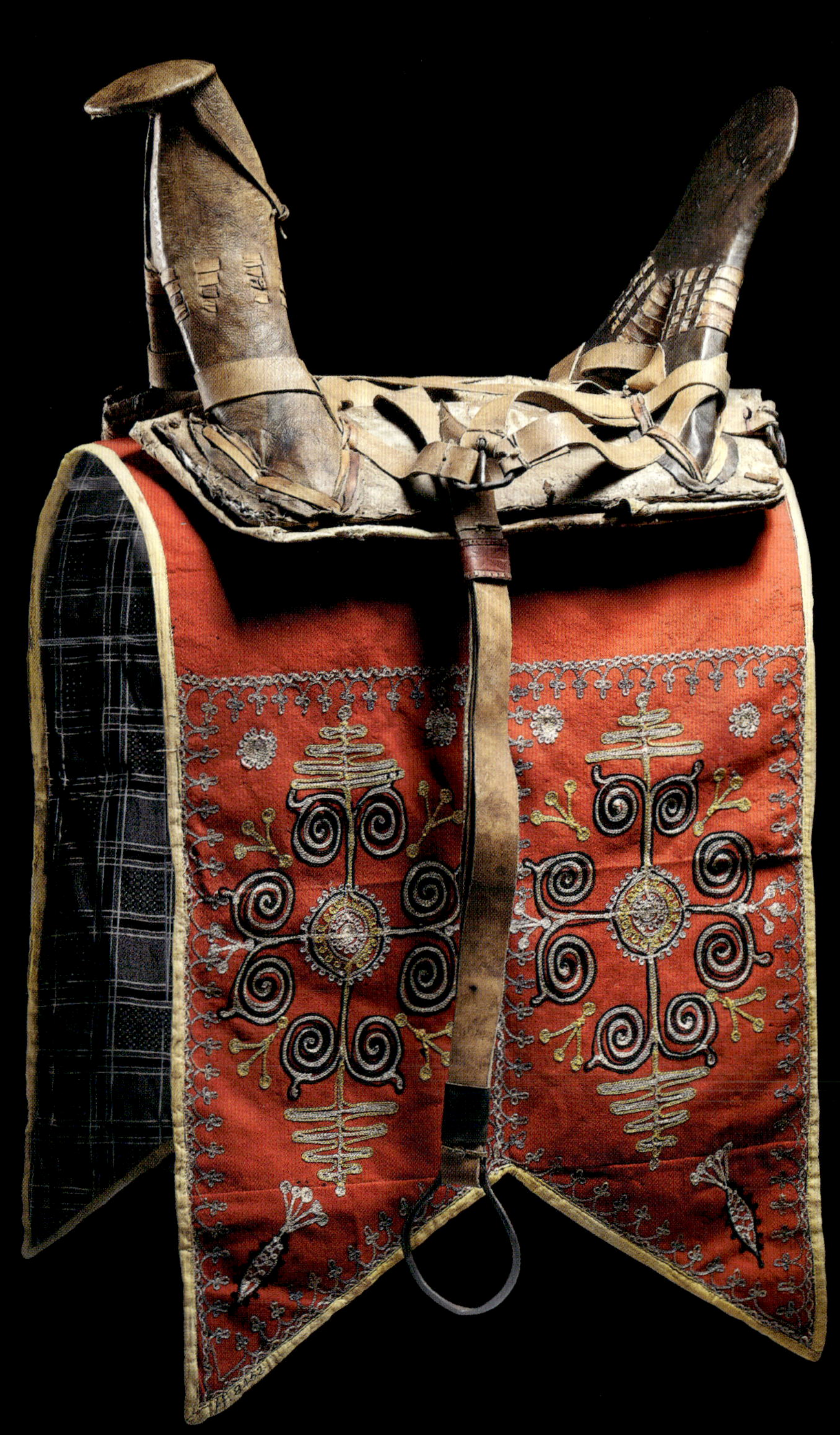

About the exhibition

This exhibition is the result of an unprecedented collaboration between the Vatican *Anima Mundi* Museum, the Sharjah Museums Authority and the National Museum of Australia. It follows the successful exhibition of the same name held at the Sharjah Museum of Islamic Civilization in 2014.

Objects have been selected from the Vatican's extensive collections to highlight and celebrate the diverse cultures of traditional Muslim societies from Africa to China by telling stories of ordinary people's lives, beliefs and cultural traditions. Complementing these are objects from the collections of the Sharjah Museums Authority, which extend the representation of the Middle East, particularly the Emirate of Sharjah, Saudi Arabia and Ottoman Turkey. The National Museum of Australia has contributed two important historical stories, with associated objects, which highlight the earliest journeys of Muslim people to Australia, and the establishment of its first Islamic communities.

As the exhibition title — inspired by a verse from the Holy Qur'an — suggests, visitors are invited to learn more about each other's lives and at the same time reach out across religions and cultures in a spirit of mutual respect and open dialogue. The exhibition, like this catalogue, takes the visitor on a journey of discovery, starting in Africa before heading eastwards into Asia, including the Middle East, India, China and South-East Asia, before eventually arriving in Australia.

Saddle and saddlecloth with harness straps, inv. 112384.2, *p. 57*

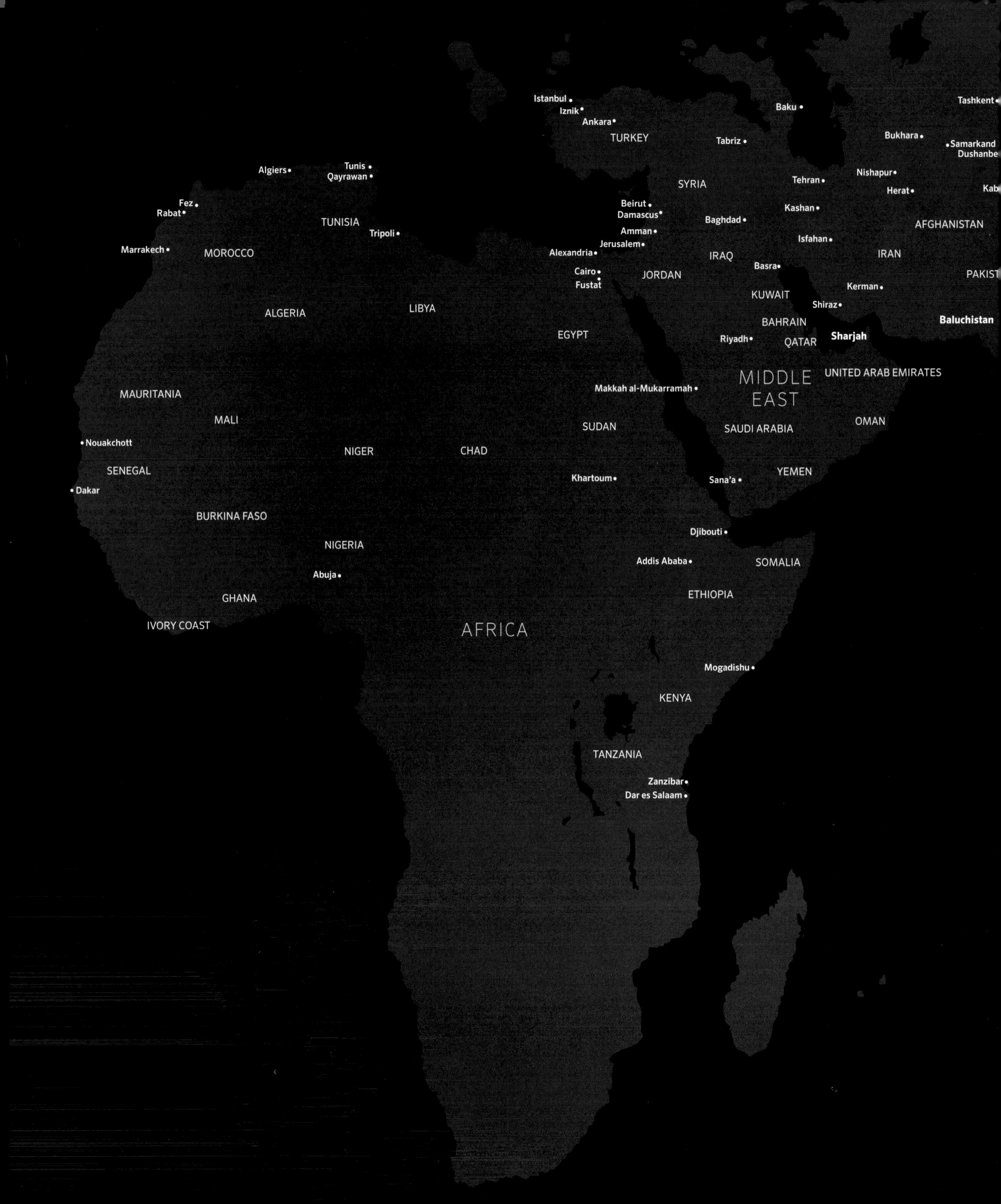

Istanbul
Iznik
Ankara
TURKEY
Baku
Tabriz
Tashkent
Bukhara
Samarkand
Dushanbe
Algiers
Tunis
Qayrawan
Fez
Rabat
TUNISIA
Tripoli
Marrakech
MOROCCO
SYRIA
Tehran
Nishapur
Herat
Kab
Beirut
Damascus
Amman
Jerusalem
Alexandria
Baghdad
Kashan
Isfahan
AFGHANISTAN
IRAQ
IRAN
Cairo
Fustat
JORDAN
Basra
Kerman
PAKIST
KUWAIT
Shiraz
ALGERIA
LIBYA
BAHRAIN
Baluchistan
EGYPT
Riyadh
QATAR
Sharjah
MIDDLE EAST
UNITED ARAB EMIRATES
MAURITANIA
Makkah al-Mukarramah
MALI
SUDAN
SAUDI ARABIA
OMAN
Nouakchott
NIGER
CHAD
SENEGAL
Khartoum
Sana'a
YEMEN
Dakar
BURKINA FASO
Djibouti
NIGERIA
Addis Ababa
SOMALIA
Abuja
ETHIOPIA
GHANA
IVORY COAST
AFRICA
Mogadishu
KENYA
TANZANIA
Zanzibar
Dar es Salaam

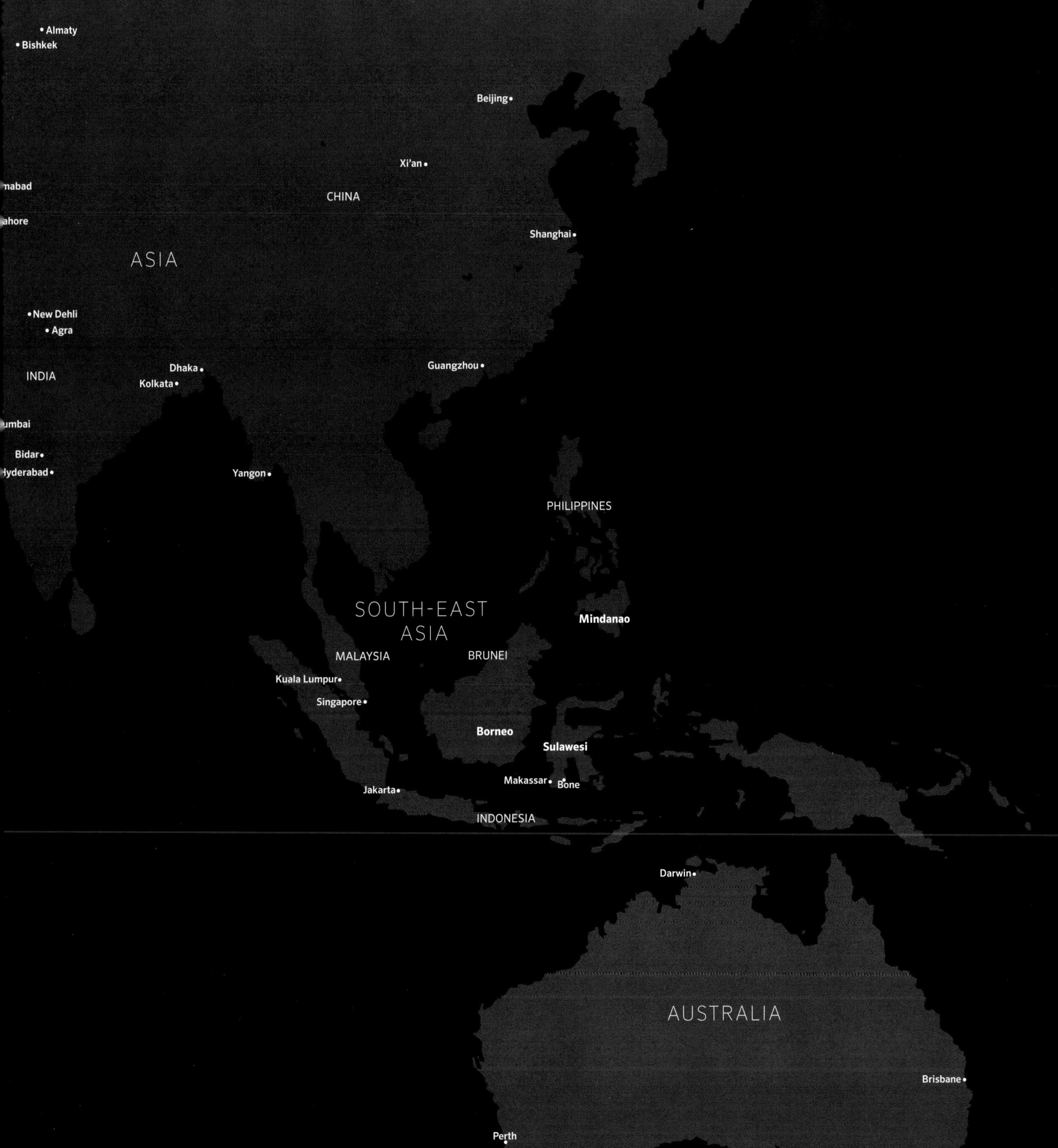
Almaty
Bishkek
Beijing
Xi'an
mabad
CHINA
ahore
Shanghai
ASIA
New Dehli
Agra
Dhaka
Guangzhou
INDIA
Kolkata
umbai
Bidar
lyderabad
Yangon
PHILIPPINES
SOUTH-EAST ASIA
Mindanao
MALAYSIA
BRUNEI
Kuala Lumpur
Singapore
Borneo
Sulawesi
Makassar
Bone
Jakarta
INDONESIA
Darwin
AUSTRALIA
Brisbane
Perth
Sydney
Adelaide
Canberra
Melbourne
Hobart

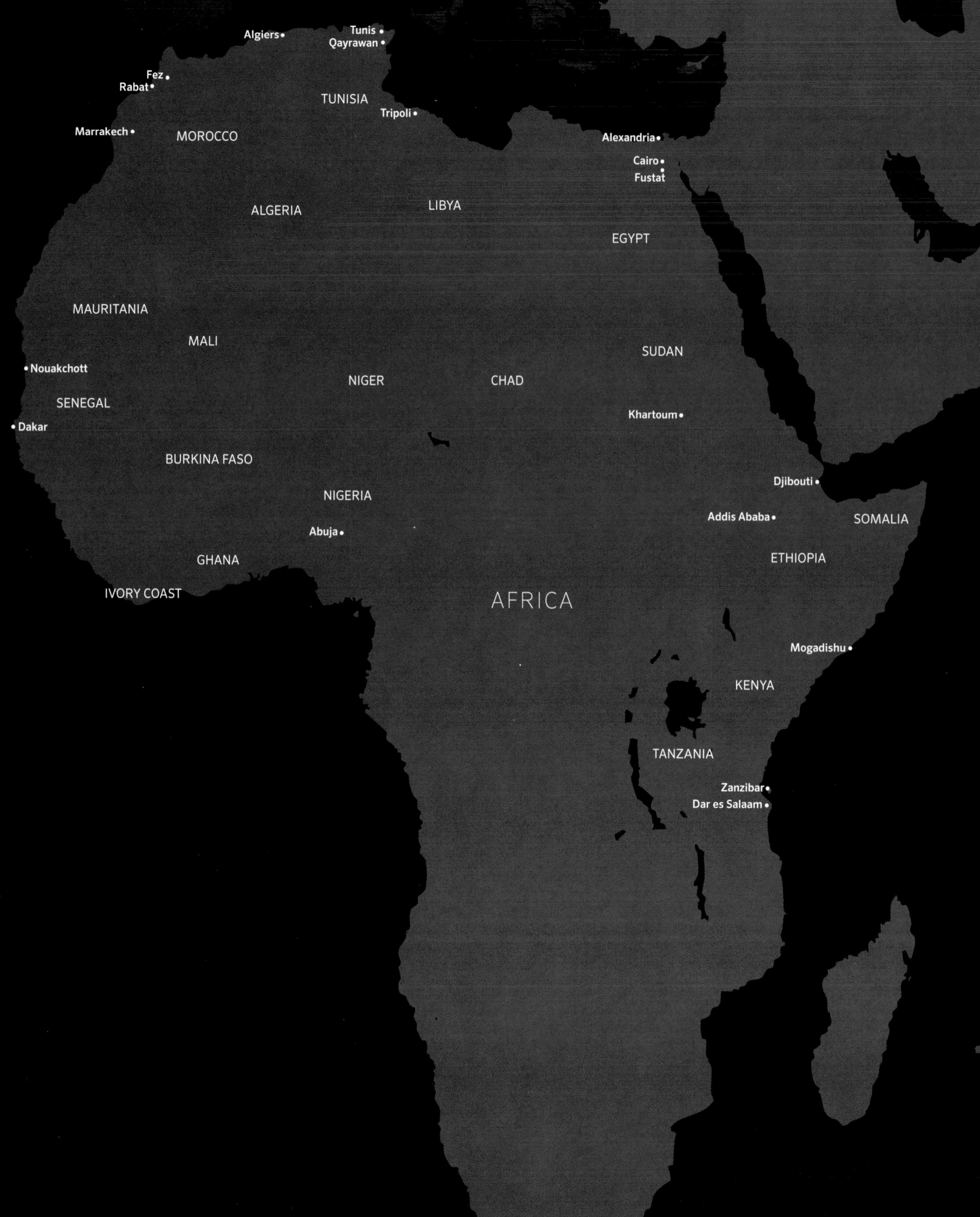
Algiers
Tunis
Qayrawan
Fez
Rabat
TUNISIA
Tripoli
Marrakech
MOROCCO
Alexandria
Cairo
Fustat
ALGERIA
LIBYA
EGYPT
MAURITANIA
MALI
SUDAN
Nouakchott
NIGER
CHAD
SENEGAL
Khartoum
Dakar
BURKINA FASO
Djibouti
NIGERIA
Addis Ababa
SOMALIA
Abuja
ETHIOPIA
GHANA
IVORY COAST
AFRICA
Mogadishu
KENYA
TANZANIA
Zanzibar
Dar es Salaam

Islam in Africa

Since its arrival in the seventh century, Islam has played a key role in Africa's history, with Muslims establishing sophisticated trading networks, powerful states and far-reaching educational initiatives. Meanwhile, Arab–Islamic and African traditions merged to form local cultures of great diversity.

Across North Africa, Islamic culture intermingled with that of the Berber people, already infused with age-old Egyptian and Coptic, Phoenician, Greek, Hellenistic, Roman and Early Christian influences.

Muslim Arab and Berber merchants meanwhile took Islam south to West and Central Africa across trans-Saharan trade routes. Over time, influential, multi-ethnic Muslim states emerged, incorporating diverse cultures and belief systems, while Sufi brotherhoods began to spread. By the 19th century, powerful kingdoms and Sufi orders drove the accelerating dissemination and anti-colonial reassertion of Islamic values across the region.

In East Africa, Muslims arriving from southern Arabia and the Gulf came to intermarry with the local population and built powerful, multicultural trading hubs and city-states, creating a unique culture and identity, characterised by the fusion of Gulf, Indian Ocean and indigenous traditions.

Metal-thread embroidered textile

Istanbul, Damascus or Cairo, early 20th century
cotton cloth, cotton- and metal-thread embroidery
2000 x 2800 mm
Vatican *Anima Mundi* Museum, inv. 112414

Metal-thread embroidery first became popular by around the 17th century in the Middle East. First used in imperial Istanbul workshops to make luxurious textiles for the Ottoman court, the technique was soon adopted in other, commercial textile-producing centres such as Damascus and Cairo. The wide variety of embroideries produced often combined Islamic designs with the emblem (*tughra*) of the ruling sultan in the centre, as here that of the last effective Ottoman ruler, Mehmed VI (1918–22).

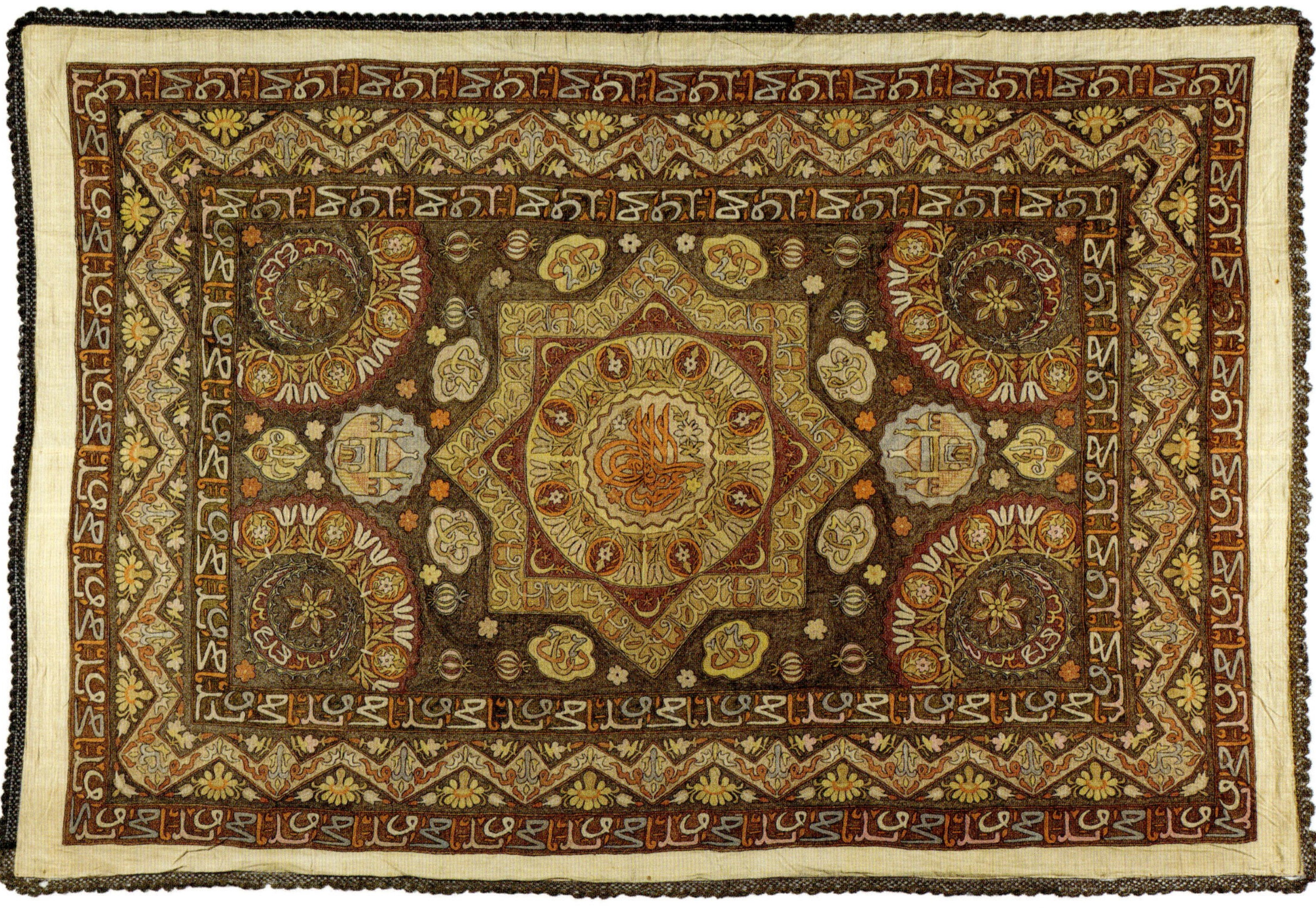

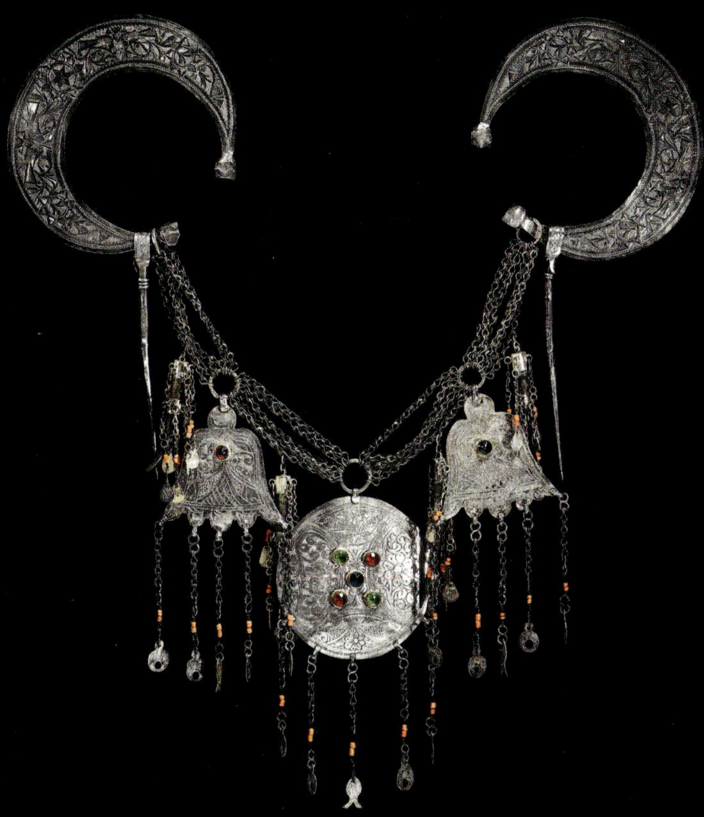

Necklace

collected in Libya, Cyrenaica region, late 19th - early 20th century
silver, coral, horn, glass beads
530 x 425 x 20 mm
Vatican *Anima Mundi* Museum, inv. 112705

This object was a bequest in 1936 from Commander Alessandro Salvadori, a high-ranking Italian colonial official, who had worked in the Cyrenaica region of Libya and in what was then Italian Somaliland. The stylised hand motifs, the central medallion with its colourful stones and the tiny crescent and fish motifs were meant to avert the evil eye, and protect and bring good luck to the wearer. The silver itself was believed to be beneficial as the preferred metal of the Prophet (pbuh). The necklace was probably fixed to the wearer's dress with the large pins attached to the crescent shapes.

Saddle and saddlecloth with harness straps

North Africa, possibly Tunisia, late 19th century
wood, leather, felted wool, wool embroidery
1120 x 850 x 400 mm
Vatican *Anima Mundi* Museum, inv. 112384.2

Domesticated some 5000 years ago, the horse has always been central to Muslim-Arab civilisation — as a beast of burden, for mounted warfare, hunting and sports such as archery, polo or falconry. It was on the back of the horse that Islam was carried far and wide and that much of Islamic history was acted out. Ruling and military elites everywhere prided themselves in the art of horsemanship (*furusiyya*) and lavished the greatest care and expense on their animals as symbols of their prowess, status and power.

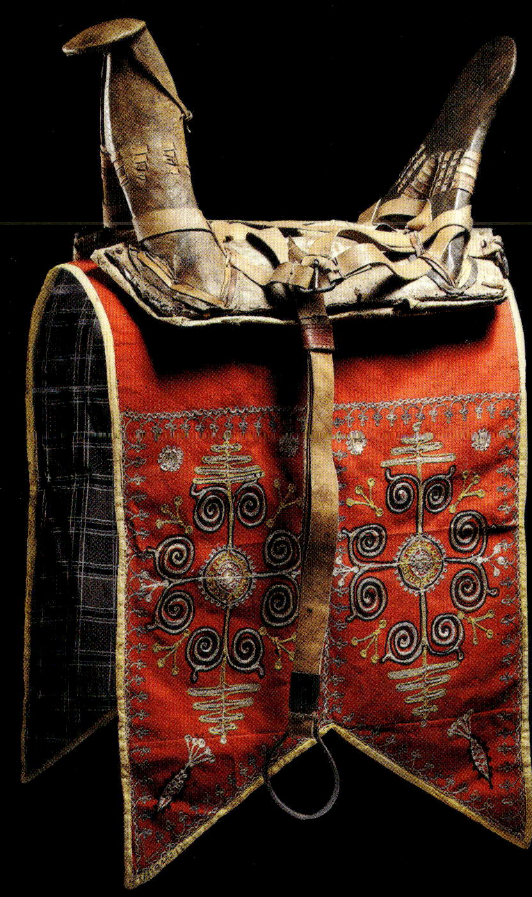

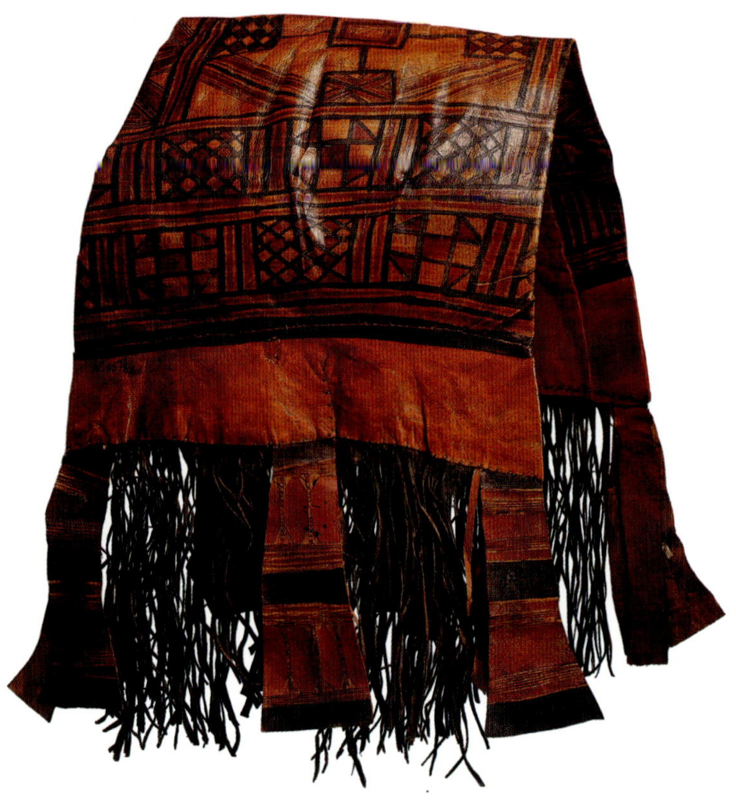

Saddle cloth

Algeria, late 19th century
leather, natural pigments
1250 x 600 x 35 mm
Vatican *Anima Mundi* Museum, inv. 112240

The rigid geometric decoration on this piece shows close similarities to the Kabyle pottery of Algeria, but it was probably made by the Tuareg Berbers, famous for their leatherwork. The Tuareg are largely nomads and pastoralists, who move and live across the Saharan areas of North and West Africa, particularly Libya, Algeria, Mali, Niger and Burkina Faso. The most famous Tuareg centres for leatherwork have traditionally been Agadez and Tahoua in Niger. Most items were made by women. The abstract decoration reflects tribal and talismanic symbolism.

Sword and scabbard

Algeria, late 19th – early 20th century
metal, carved and engraved wood, plant fibre
550 x 90 x 40 mm
Vatican *Anima Mundi* Museum, inv. 112103.2

Swords of this type have been associated with the largely Muslim Kabyle (from Arabic 'Qaba'il', meaning 'tribes') people of Northern Algeria. Centred traditionally on the Atlas mountain regions, the Kabyle are Berbers with a distinct cultural heritage and art. They form the second largest Berber-speaking group in Africa. The abstract ornamentation on this sword is typical of Kabyle art. Highly decorative, it combines tribal and protective symbols.

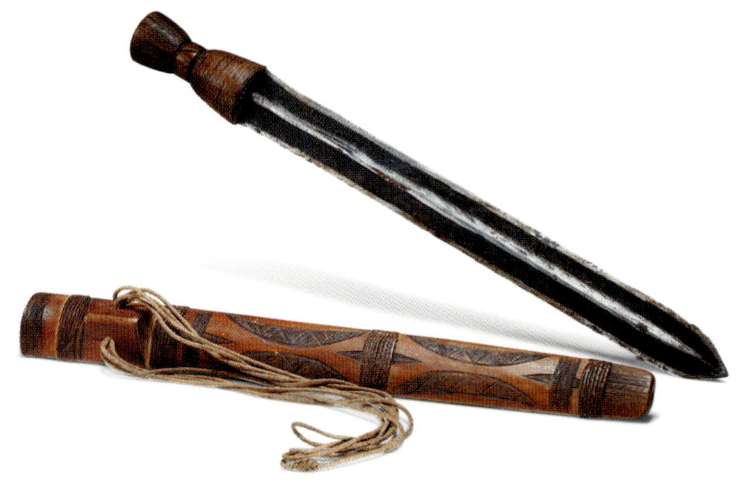

Qaraqab (castanets)

Morocco, late 19th - early 20th century
iron, leather, plant fibre
300 x 115 x 32 mm
Vatican *Anima Mundi* Museum, inv. 112087

Acquired in 1925, these castanets are still used today in one of the most important musical genres of Morocco: Gnawa music. The Gnawa are Muslims of Subsaharan origin, whose music combines traditional African elements and rhythms with Islamic spirituality and celebration. Traditionally, Gnawa music is performed in the evening, when the whole community comes together for prayer and spiritual renewal. A typical Gnawa ensemble comprises musicians playing bowed and plucked lutes, drums and the distinctive castanets seen here.

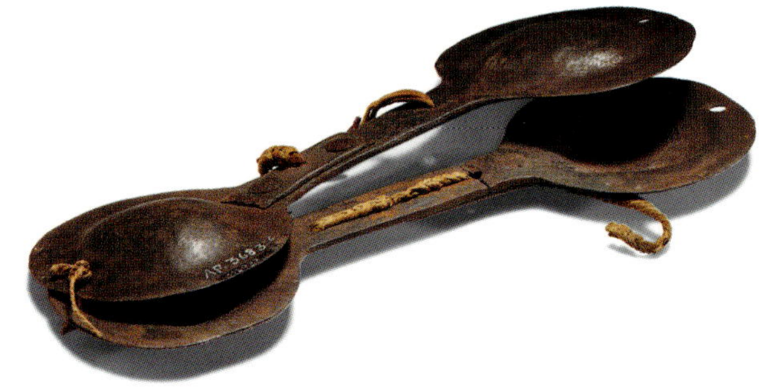

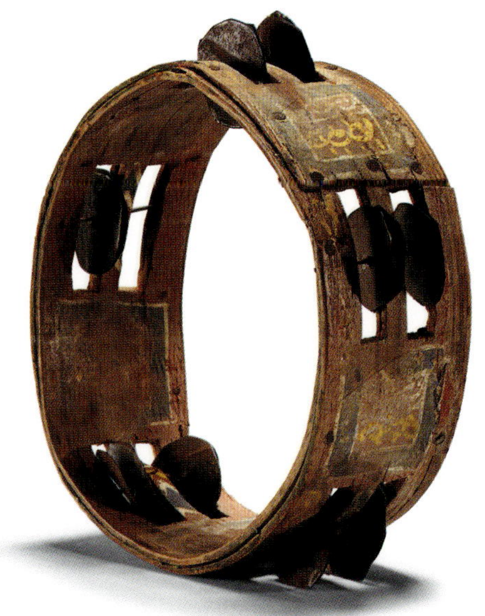

Ornamented tambourine

Morocco, late 19th - early 20th century
metal, wood, pigments
80 mm x 240 mm (diameter)
Vatican *Anima Mundi* Museum, inv. 112085

This tambourine was collected in Tangier during the early 1920s. It originally had a membrane and was probably used by an ensemble performing religious and spiritual music.

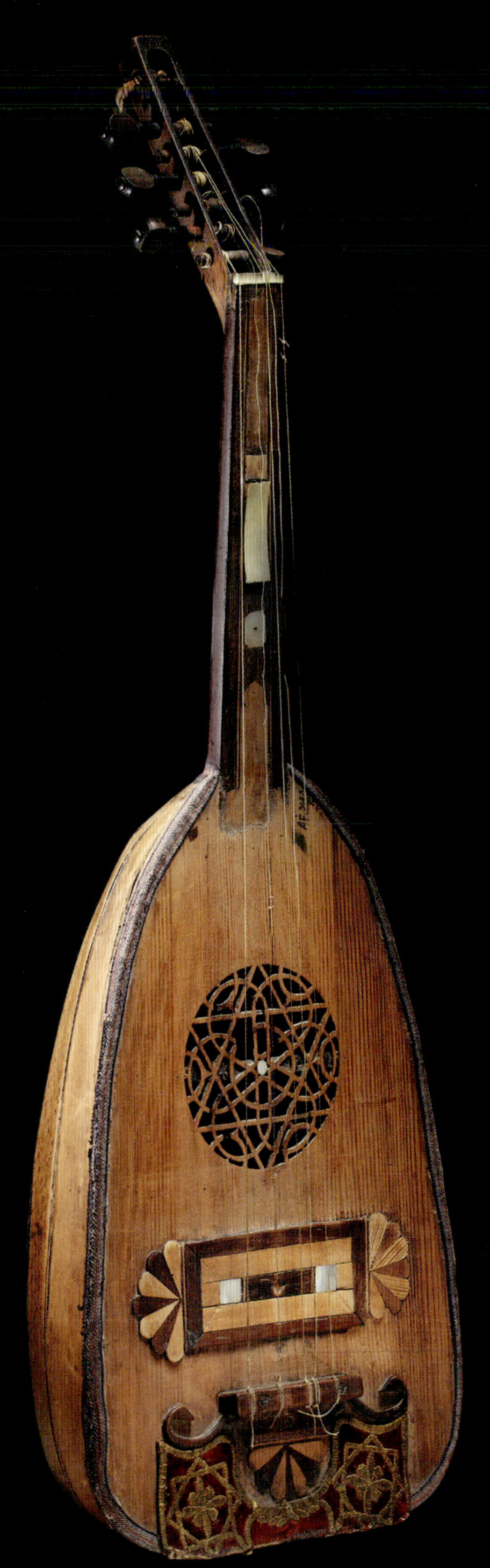

Kuitra (lute)

Morocco, late 19th – early 20th century
wood, mother-of-pearl, cloth, gut
950 x 315 x 190 mm
Vatican *Anima Mundi* Museum, inv. 112083

The short-necked lute is one of the classical instruments of the Islamic world. Played with a long thin plectrum (*risha*), lutes have been used in the region for over 5000 years. Most popular in Arab lands are the large Middle Eastern *'ud* and the North African *'ud ramal* or *kuitra*. This lute is smaller and more elongated than the eastern version, with a less steeply bent neck, and four rather than six strings. Through Southern Spain and Sicily, the Arab lute was introduced to Europe in the Middle Ages and had a profound impact on its music and instruments.

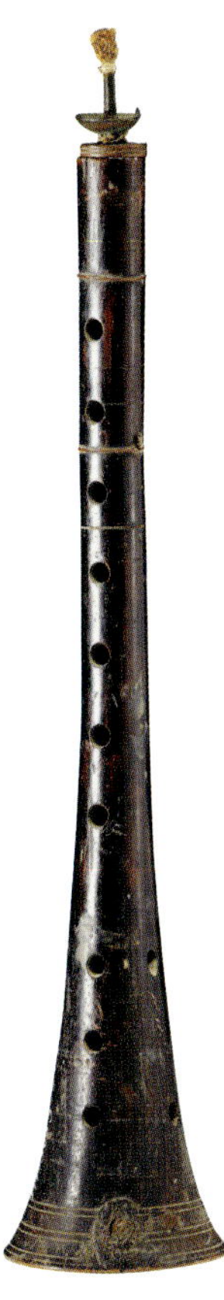

Ghaita (oboe)

Morocco, late 19th – early 20th century
wood, metal
425 x 77 mm
Vatican *Anima Mundi* Museum, inv. 112096

This *ghaita* is very similar to the Arab *mizmar* played all over the Middle East. It has a spectacular, penetrating sound that can be heard from far away. As a result, it has always been popular in music played at weddings and celebrations. It also plays an important part in the traditional religious music of the southern Rif mountains of Morocco. The centre of this region is the town of Joujouka, which sprang up around the sanctuary of Sidi Ahmed Sheikh, who arrived in Morocco in the early ninth century in his quest to spread the word of Islam.

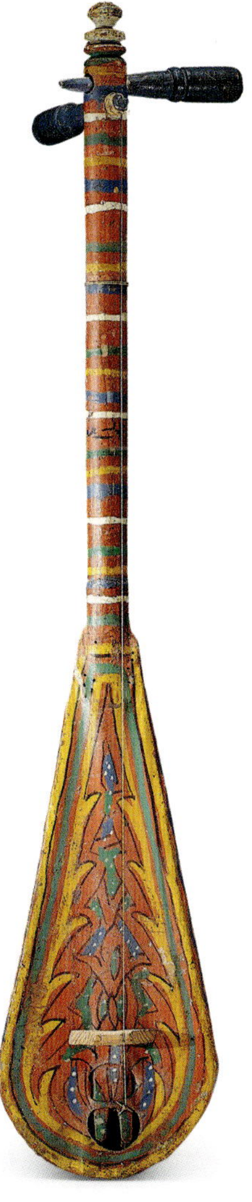

Gimbri or *lotar* (lute)

Morocco, late 19th – early 20th century
wood, skin, gut, pigments
505 x 105 x 45 mm
Vatican *Anima Mundi* Museum, inv. 112093

This instrument was used by the Berbers of the Middle and High Atlas regions of North Africa. The Berbers (or Imazighen) are the Indigenous inhabitants of North Africa and parts of West Africa, with an age-old family of languages and a distinct culture. After the Arab invasions of the seventh century, they gradually converted to Islam and played an important role in the Islamic history of Spain and the Maghreb. Their musical traditions combine Islamic themes with Imazighen songs, stories and poetry. One of their most important traditional musical genres is '*rwais*', performed by a small group of musicians playing the *lotar*, the *rebab* (see inv. 112355, p. 89), drums and a bell.

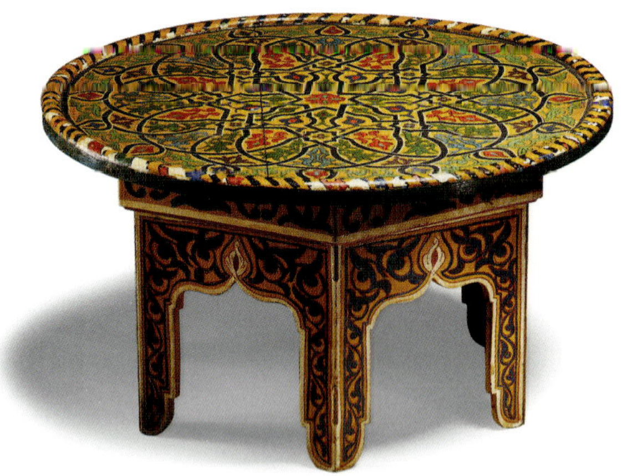

Table with geometric and arabesque decoration

Morocco, late 19th - early 20th century
arar wood, metal, pigments, varnish
390 x 600 mm (diameter)
Vatican *Anima Mundi* Museum, inv. 112566

This colourful table, collected in 1925, tells two important stories about traditional Moroccan and Islamic culture. As a piece of furniture, its design and dimensions reflect the traditional custom of sitting, eating and relaxing on the floor or on low divans. As domestic spaces had no designated function, the table is designed to be collapsible and portable, to be used wherever it is needed. The decoration meanwhile reflects the non-figural preferences of Arab-Islamic art. Geometric decoration remains prominent in the Islamic architecture and decorative arts of North Africa.

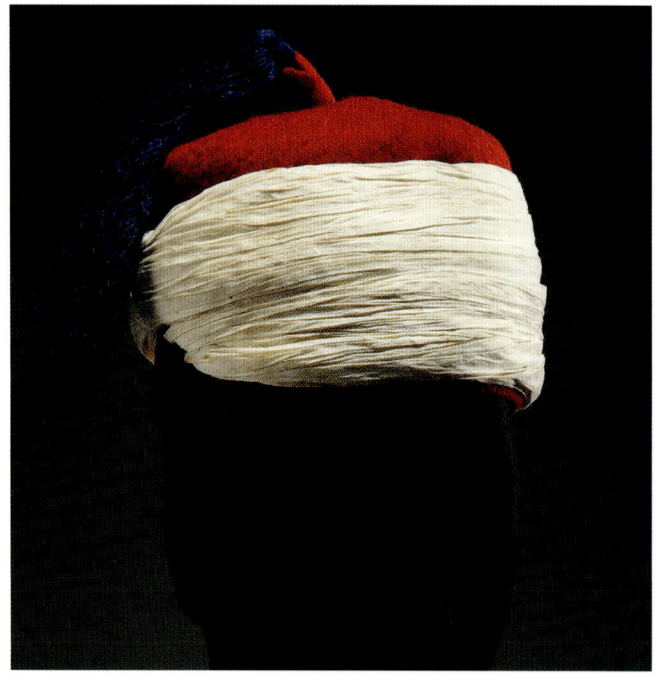

Fez or *tarboosh*

Morocco, late 19th - early 20th century
felted wool, silk, cotton
170 x 200 mm (diameter)
Vatican *Anima Mundi* Museum, inv. 112034

The fez, a distinctive type of felt hat characterised by its deep red colour, became popular throughout the southern Mediterranean and North Africa during the 19th century. It came in many shapes and was worn by government officials, members of the urban elite and religious personalities, who generally combined it with a white turban cloth. According to museum records, this particular example was originally worn by a Moroccan Sufi.

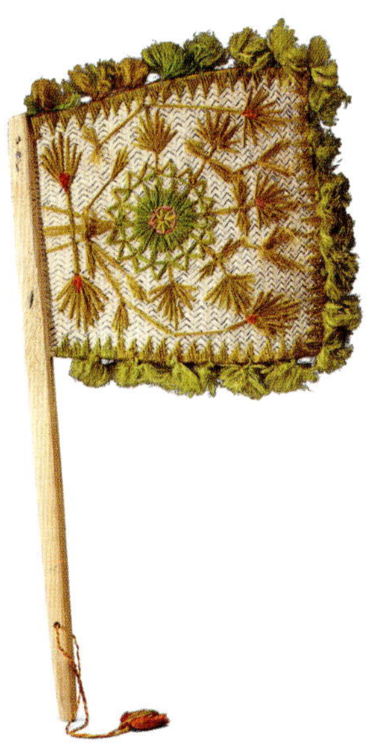

Embroidered fan

Morocco, late 19th - early 20th century
plant fibre, silk, wood
380 x 215 x 25 mm
Vatican *Anima Mundi* Museum, inv. 112101

Fans are popular across the Middle East and wide areas of North and East Africa. They were often made with basketry work or, as in this case, woven from plant fibre such as palm fronds to form a fabric. The decoration was often woven into the fan, but here it has been embroidered onto the surface. Plant fibre fans had many purposes — cooling the air, keeping away insects or fanning a small fire. Judging by its elaborate ornamentation, this fan may have been used for special occasions.

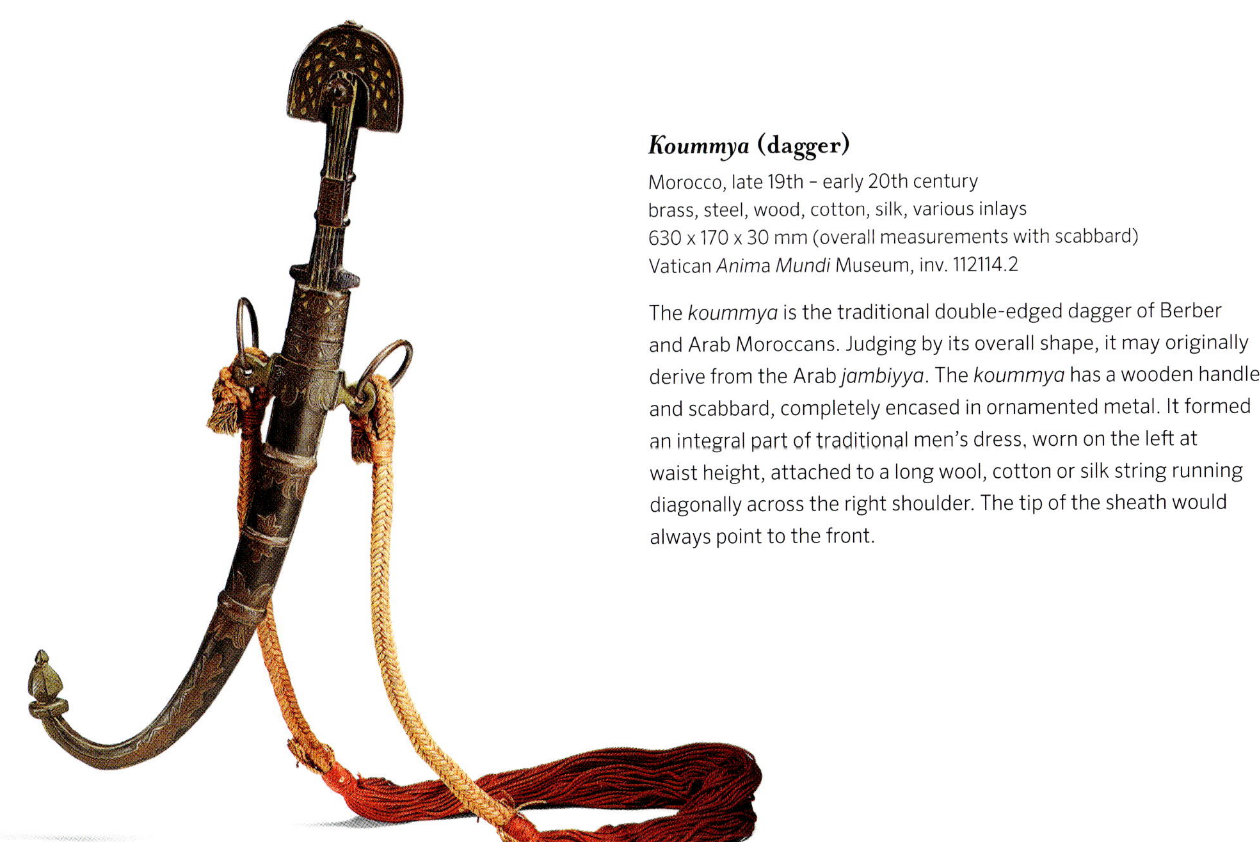

Koummya (dagger)

Morocco, late 19th - early 20th century
brass, steel, wood, cotton, silk, various inlays
630 x 170 x 30 mm (overall measurements with scabbard)
Vatican *Anima Mundi* Museum, inv. 112114.2

The *koummya* is the traditional double-edged dagger of Berber and Arab Moroccans. Judging by its overall shape, it may originally derive from the Arab *jambiyya*. The *koummya* has a wooden handle and scabbard, completely encased in ornamented metal. It formed an integral part of traditional men's dress, worn on the left at waist height, attached to a long wool, cotton or silk string running diagonally across the right shoulder. The tip of the sheath would always point to the front.

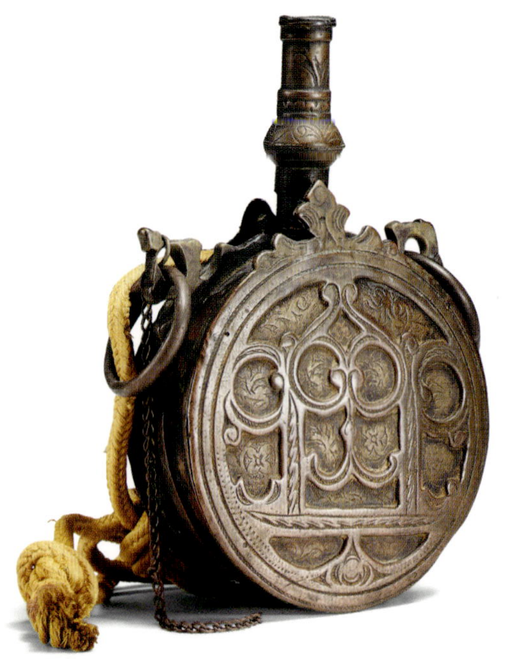

Powder flask

Morocco, late 19th - early 20th century
engraved and embossed brass, cotton
180 x 120 x 40 mm
Vatican *Anima Mundi* Museum, inv. 112123

This object represents one of the most popular types of powder flasks traditionally used in Morocco. It has a flat circular body, a narrow profiled neck and rich abstract decoration derived from both Islamic and local tribal traditions.

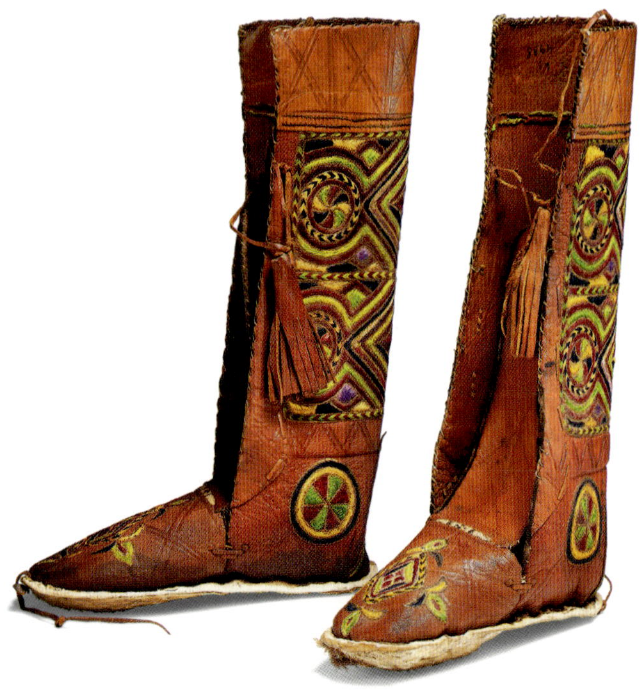

Embroidered boots

attributed to Senegal, late 19th - early 20th century
leather embroidered with coloured cotton threads
370 x 250 x 95 mm
Vatican *Anima Mundi* Museum, inv. 111984

Although it is documented that these boots originate in Senegal, their colourful style relates them to the embroidered leatherwork done by Berber people all over North, Central and West Africa. Women dedicated much time to making and embroidering these boots, which were worn on special occasions and during wedding celebrations.

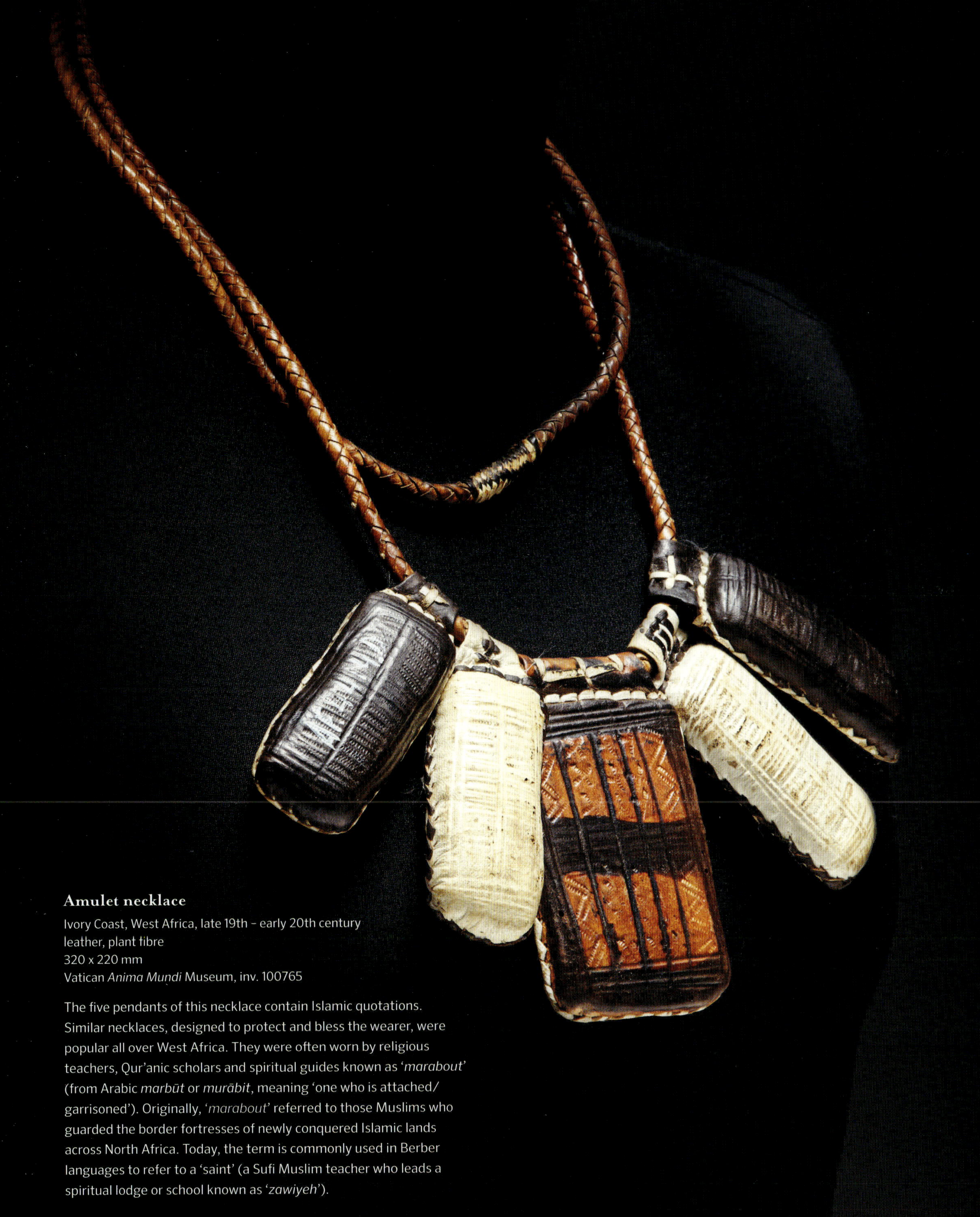

Amulet necklace

Ivory Coast, West Africa, late 19th – early 20th century
leather, plant fibre
320 x 220 mm
Vatican *Anima Mundi* Museum, inv. 100765

The five pendants of this necklace contain Islamic quotations. Similar necklaces, designed to protect and bless the wearer, were popular all over West Africa. They were often worn by religious teachers, Qur'anic scholars and spiritual guides known as '*marabout*' (from Arabic *marbūt* or *murābit*, meaning 'one who is attached/ garrisoned'). Originally, '*marabout*' referred to those Muslims who guarded the border fortresses of newly conquered Islamic lands across North Africa. Today, the term is commonly used in Berber languages to refer to a 'saint' (a Sufi Muslim teacher who leads a spiritual lodge or school known as '*zawiyeh*').

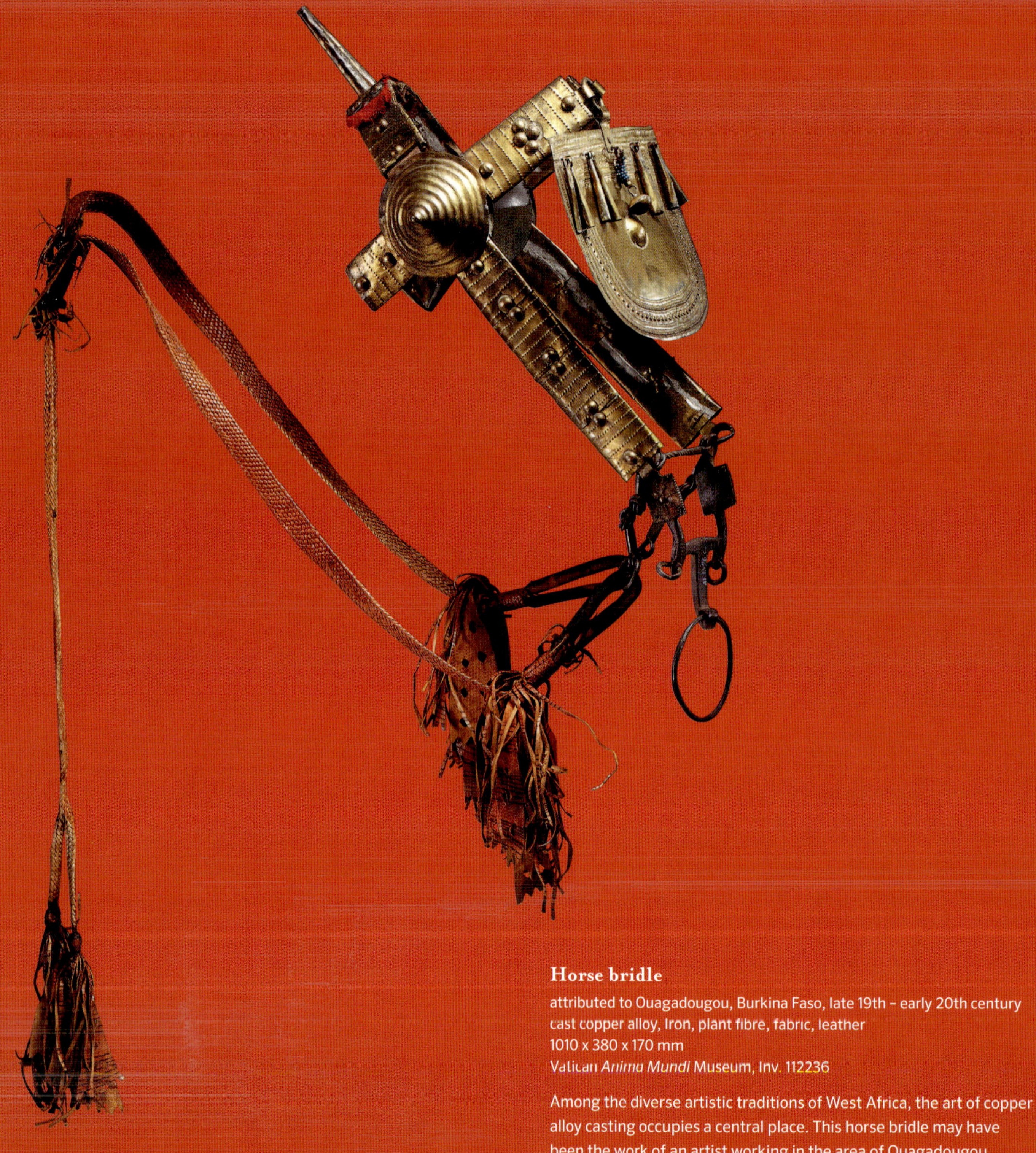

Horse bridle

attributed to Ouagadougou, Burkina Faso, late 19th – early 20th century
cast copper alloy, iron, plant fibre, fabric, leather
1010 x 380 x 170 mm
Vatican *Anima Mundi* Museum, Inv. 112236

Among the diverse artistic traditions of West Africa, the art of copper alloy casting occupies a central place. This horse bridle may have been the work of an artist working in the area of Ouagadougou, the capital of Burkina Faso and an important political, cultural and economic centre since the 15th century.

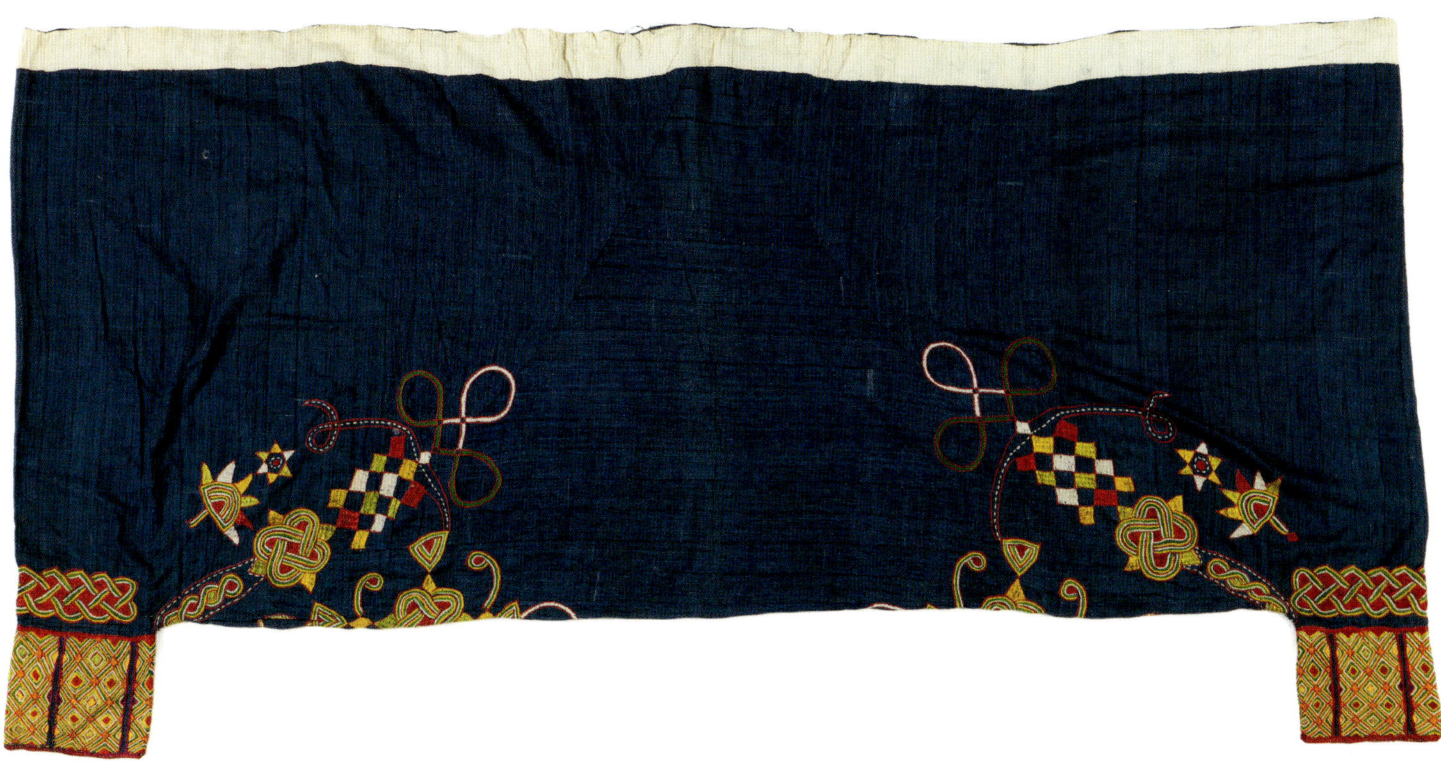

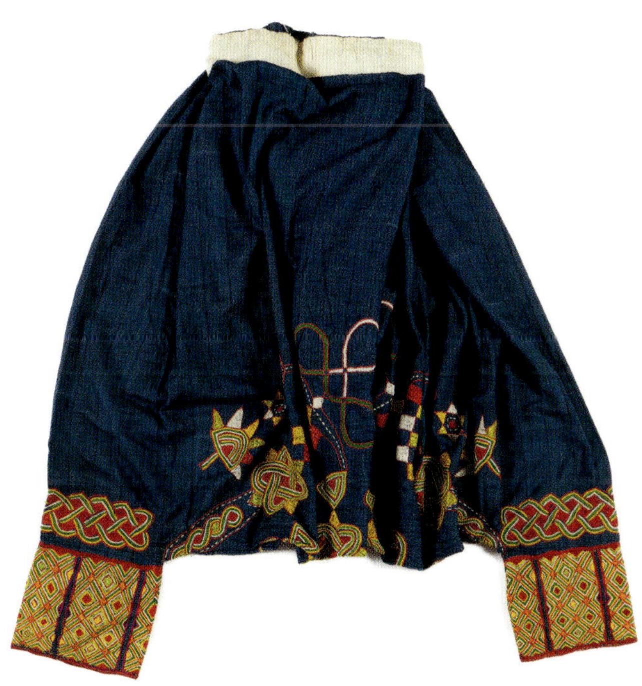

Wando mai kamun k'afa
(embroidered trousers with anklebands)

Nigeria, Hausa people, late 19th - early 20th century
indigo-dyed cotton, embroidered with silk
1000 x 1940 mm
Vatican *Anima* Mundi Museum, inv. 112183

After the arrival of Islam in Subsaharan Africa, many local people adopted Muslim codes of modesty and dress. These voluminous trousers were once combined with a full, wide-sleeved robe. Its colourful embroidery is the work of professional Muslim embroiderers and particularly associated with the Hausa people of Nigeria, the largest ethnic group in West Africa. In 19th-century Kano — the Hausa's economic and cultural centre — even the emir's sons prided themselves in embroidering *wando* trousers, which were often used for riding.

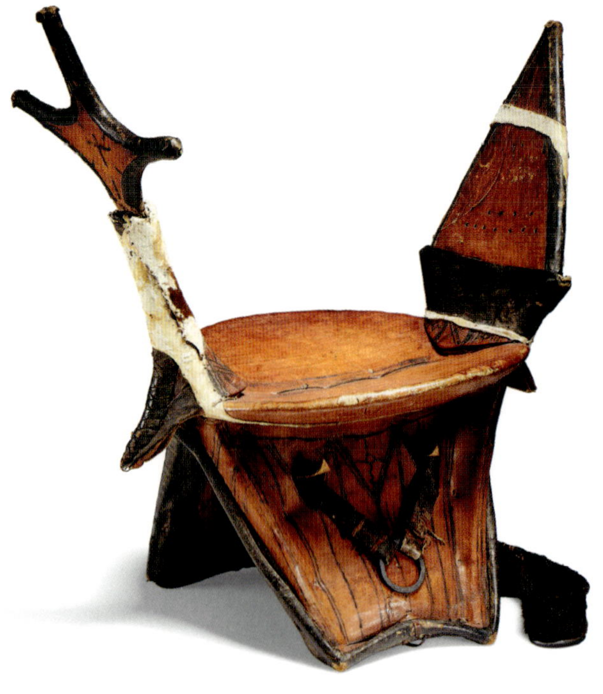

Camel saddle

Niger, Tuareg people, late 19th - early 20th century
wood, cut metal, leather, natural pigments
1030 x 700 x 380 mm
Vatican *Anima Mundi* Museum, inv. 100774

One of the most distinctive and eye-catching objects of Tuareg culture, this type of camel saddle has traditionally been made in Agadez, Niger. It is placed on a layer of several saddle cloths at the front of the camel's neck, supported by its strong shoulders. Riders sit on it, with their legs extended, cross-legged, along the camel's neck. This position allows them to keep their balance and direct the camel during long treks across the Sahara Desert.

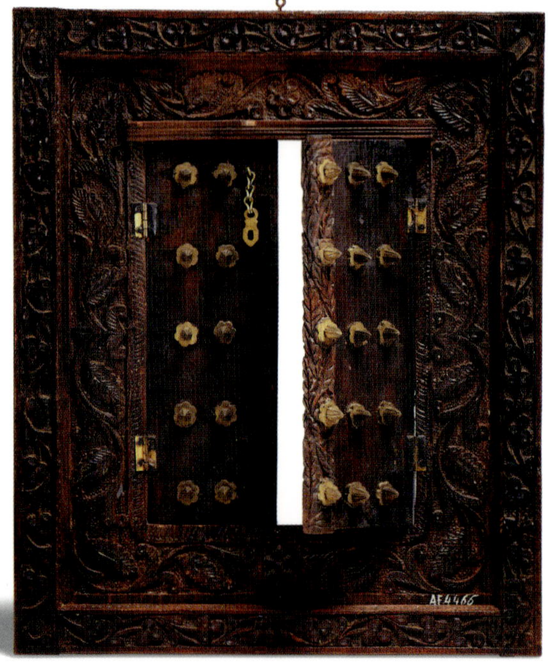

Decorative carving inspired by traditional Zanzibari doors

Zanzibar, Tanzania, late 19th - early 20th century
hardwood, brass
350 x 295 x 25 mm
Vatican *Anima Mundi* Museum, inv. 100775

Zanzibar has been an important centre of Islamic culture since the 10th century. Many traders from the Arabian Peninsula, Arabian Gulf, Iran and India settled and intermarried with the local East African population, leading to the emergence of a distinct culture and language, known as Swahili (from Arabic '*sawahil*', 'of the coast'). This carving recalls Zanzibar's famous doors, which traditionally combined Omani Arab and Indian influences. In Zanzibari society, such doors symbolised the status, wealth and honour of their owners.

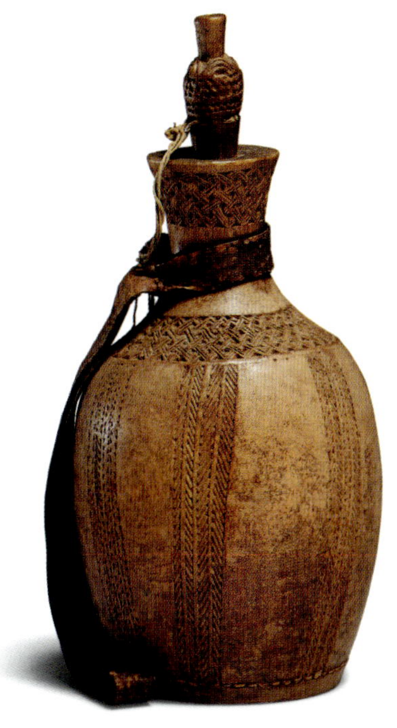

Ablution flask

Harar, Eastern Ethiopia, late 19th - early 20th century
gourd, wood, leather, plant fibre
280 x 130 mm
Vatican *Anima Mundi* Museum, inv. 100753

Carefully engraved with abstract designs, this simple flask was used for ablutions. In Ethiopia, the Islamic presence is strongest in its eastern and south-eastern regions. It was here that some of the first Muslims fleeing persecution in their Arabian homeland found shelter. The city of Harar, from which this flask originates, has been an important religious, cultural and commercial centre for centuries. Here, trade routes from all over Africa, the Arabian Peninsula and across the sea converged.

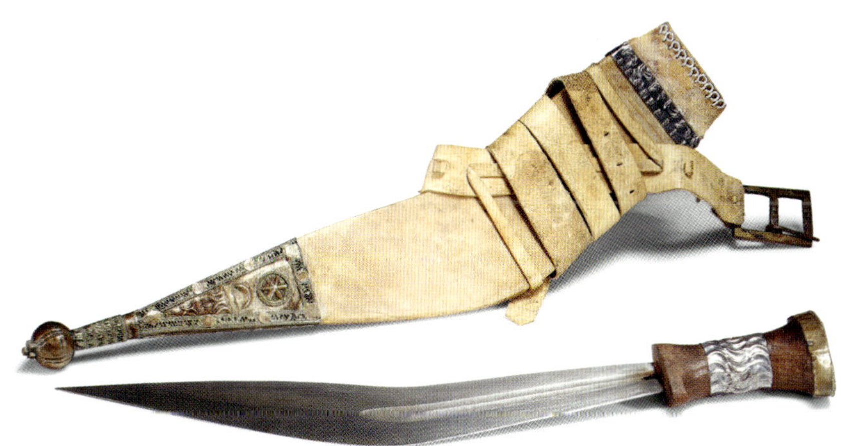

Qilé or *jile* (dagger and scabbard)

Afar region of Ethiopia, late 19th - early 20th century
metal, wood, leather, silver
475 x 70 mm (dagger); 550 x 100 mm (scabbard)
Vatican *Anima Mundi* Museum, inv. 100752.2

The distinctive, sharply bent dagger style seen here is associated with the Muslim Afar people, living in north-eastern Ethiopia and parts of Eritrea and Djibouti. It is worn horizontally on the right side or across the front, fixed to a belt worn below the hip. Traditionally pastoralists with a distinct language and culture, the Afar have often played an important role in the history of East Africa and even established their own sultanates.

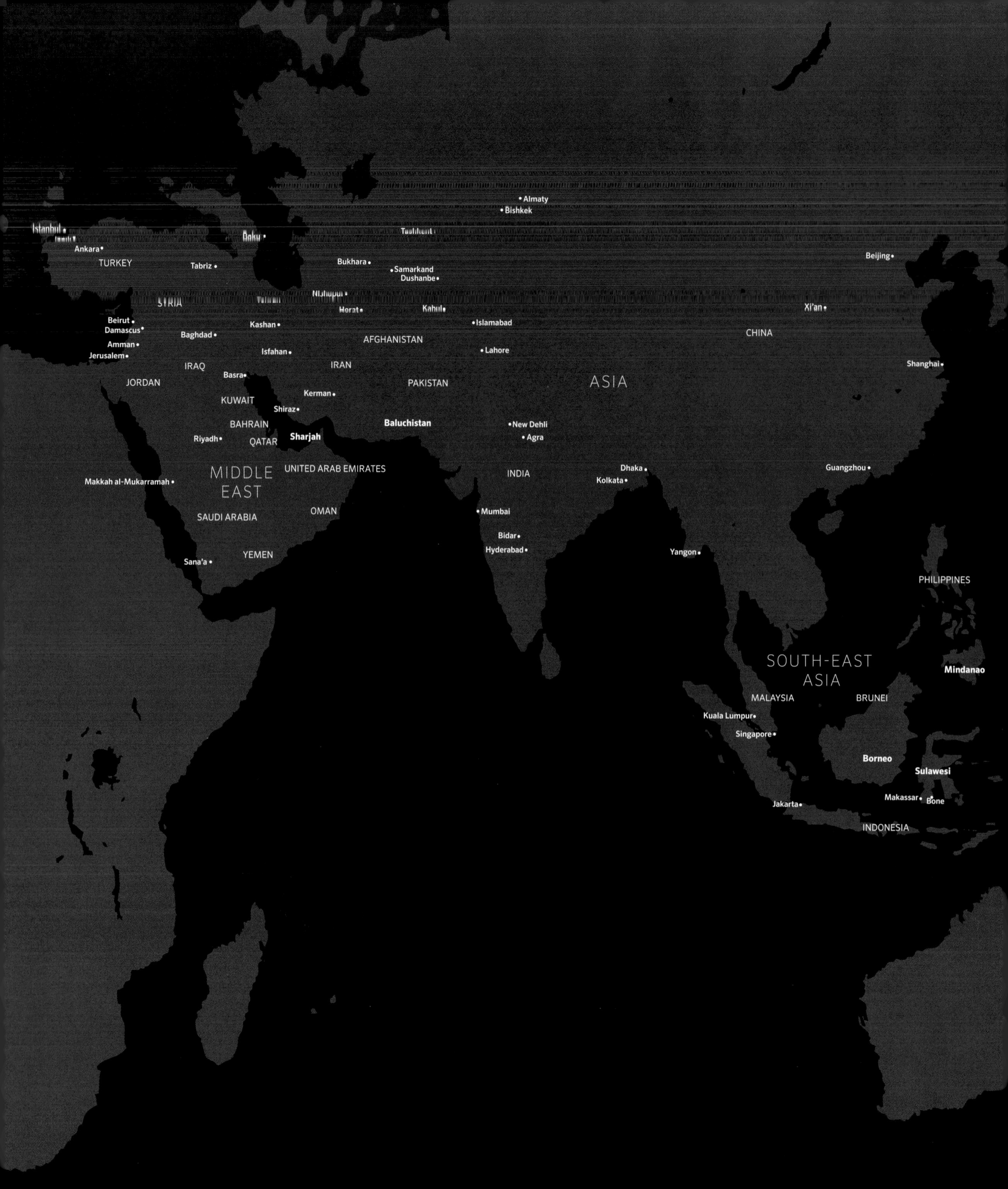

Almaty
Bishkek
Istanbul
Baku
Tashkent
Ankara
TURKEY
Tabriz
Bukhara
Samarkand
Dushanbe
Beijing
SYRIA
Tehran
Nishapur
Herat
Kabul
Xi'an
Beirut
Damascus
Kashan
Islamabad
Baghdad
AFGHANISTAN
CHINA
Amman
Jerusalem
Isfahan
Lahore
IRAQ
IRAN
Shanghai
JORDAN
Basra
PAKISTAN
ASIA
Kerman
KUWAIT
Shiraz
BAHRAIN
Baluchistan
New Dehli
Riyadh
QATAR
Sharjah
Agra
MIDDLE EAST
UNITED ARAB EMIRATES
INDIA
Dhaka
Kolkata
Guangzhou
Makkah al-Mukarramah
SAUDI ARABIA
OMAN
Mumbai
Bidar
Hyderabad
Sana'a
YEMEN
Yangon
PHILIPPINES
SOUTH-EAST ASIA
Mindanao
MALAYSIA
BRUNEI
Kuala Lumpur
Singapore
Borneo
Sulawesi
Makassar
Bone
Jakarta
INDONESIA

Islam in the Middle East and Asia

The continent that stretches from the Suez Canal to the Pacific is home to the largest Muslim population in the world. From the seventh century — the first century of the Hijri (Islamic) calendar — Islam quickly expanded from the Arabian Peninsula across Palestine and Syria into Iraq, Iran and other parts of the region. After the first conquests, it was often merchants who carried the new faith along the extensive trade routes that linked the Middle East and China by land and sea.

Over the centuries, influential and powerful Muslim dynasties emerged, often ruling with the support of indigenous social hierarchies over multicultural, multilingual and multi-faith societies. Thriving Muslim trading communities were established, particularly along India's and South-East Asia's sea coasts; their rulers, scholars and merchants maintaining close links with the Arabian Peninsula while at the same time absorbing many influences from the dynamic and sophisticated cultures of the region. Arab and Muslim traders soon dominated the South-East Asian trade networks and set up colonies all across the region, including China.

Here, Muslim communities emerged mainly in the port cities and near the end point of the Silk Road in the north-west — with the explicit permission of the Chinese emperors. Subsequently, many Muslims became valued soldiers, bureaucrats and intellectuals in Chinese society. From the 19th century, Islamic reform movements in many parts of Asia led to further Islamisation of indigenous societies, particular in the face of Imperialist colonialism.

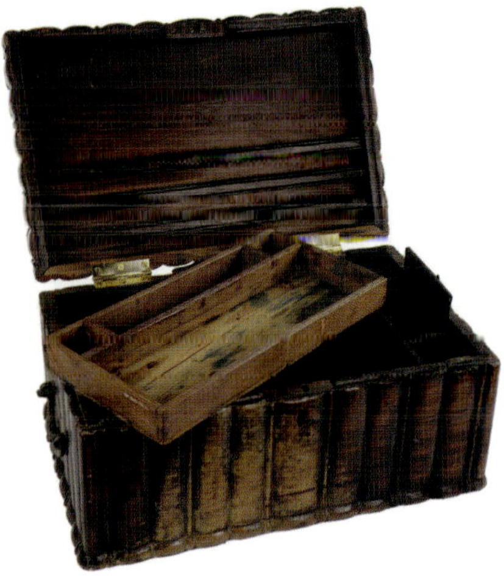

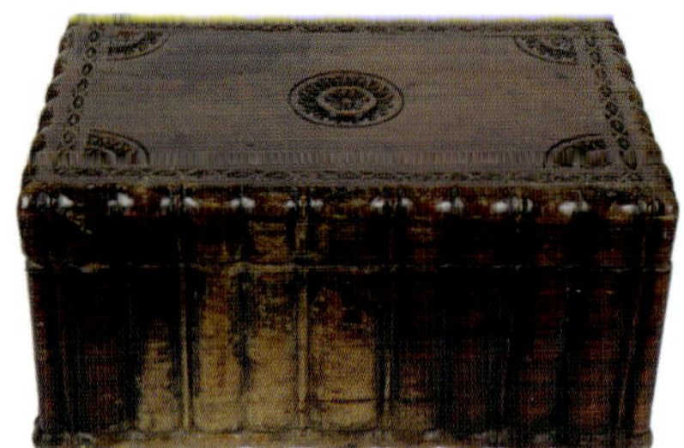

Bishtakhta (pearl merchant's chest)

Sharjah, late 19th - early 20th century
hardwood, copper alloy (probably made in India)
475 x 225 x 295 mm (closed)
Bait Al Naboodah Museum, Sharjah Museums Authority, SM2003-172

Before the discovery of oil, pearling was a crucial industry in Sharjah and throughout the Gulf region. Between early June and late September every year, over a thousand pearling boats were engaged in harvesting the rich offshore pearl banks for merchants (known as Al Tawash) who specialised in the sale of pearls.

A chest like this one was an indispensable piece of equipment for the pearl merchant, containing not only all his equipment, but also his valuable bags of pearls. Often elaborately decorated, these chests varied in size and were designed to hold pearling scales with their agate weights, scoops, graded sieves, small discrete boxes for cash (often hidden in secret compartments), bags of pearls and the *chao* book, used to calculate the value of specific pearls on the basis of their weight. By the turn of the 20th century, pearl merchants in the Gulf oversaw the export of pearls worth well over US$1 million.

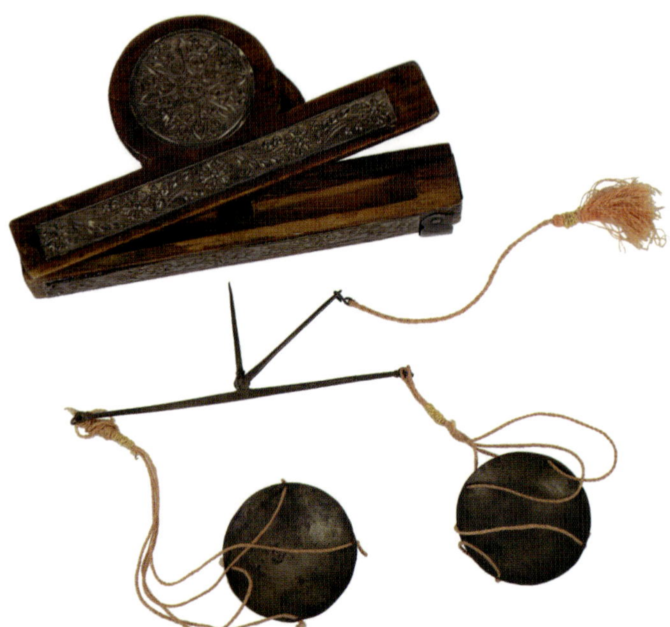

Mizan (pearl merchant's scales)

Sharjah, late 19th - early 20th century
wood, copper alloy, silver, fibre
156 x 71 x 28 mm
Sharjah Maritime Museum, Sharjah Museums Authority, SM1999-77

Pearling scales were an essential tool for any pearl merchant. All aspects of a pearl's appearance — shape, hue, perfection, size and weight — determined its value and saleability.

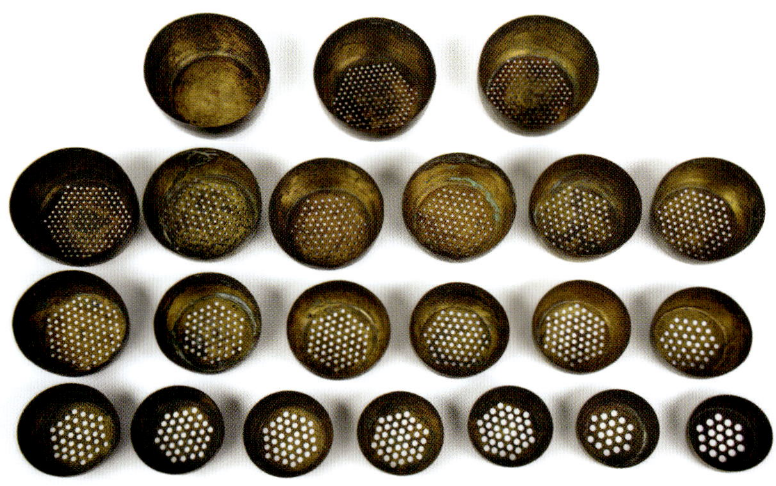

Pearl merchant's grading equipment

Sharjah, late 19th – early 20th century
copper alloy
container 41 x 88 mm (diameter); sieves range from 49 x 86 mm (diameter) to 21 x 54 mm (diameter)
Bait Al Naboodah Museum, Sharjah Museums Authority, SM2003-167

This set of brass sieves with holes of different sizes was used to grade pearls. The larger, heavier and more luminous a pearl was, the higher price it was able to fetch among the traders in the marketplace.

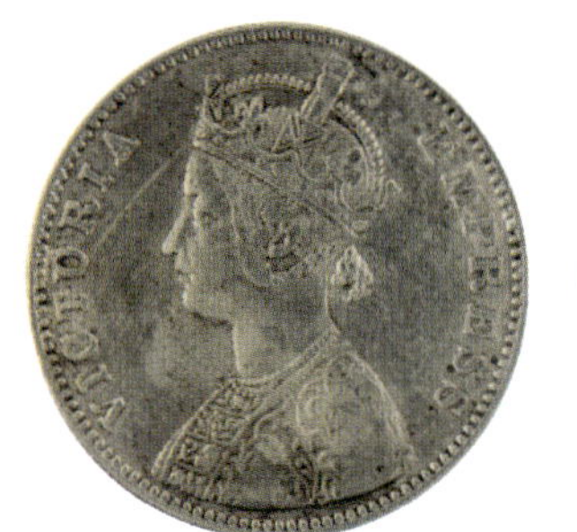

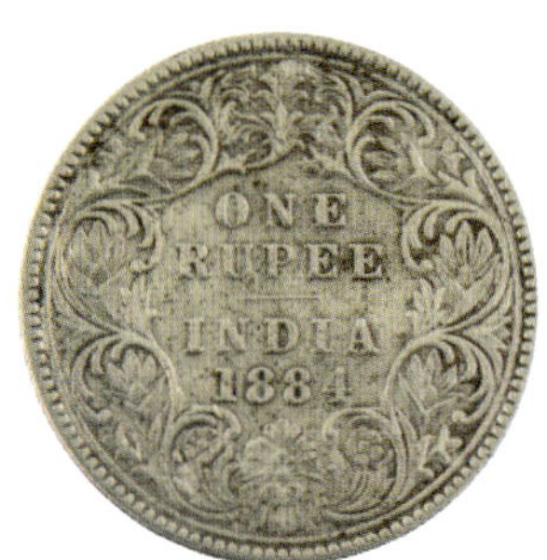

Indian rupee of Empress Victoria (Um al Bint)

India, 1884
silver
28 mm (diameter)
Sharjah Heritage Museum, Sharjah Museums Authority, SM2004-825

Imperial British Indian rupees were first used in the Gulf region in the second half of the 19th century. The currency began circulating in about 1857 as a result of the pearl trade and the gold exchange between local and Indian merchants. It continued in use throughout the Gulf region until 1947 when India regained its independence. After 1947 the Gulf rupee replaced the Imperial British rupee.

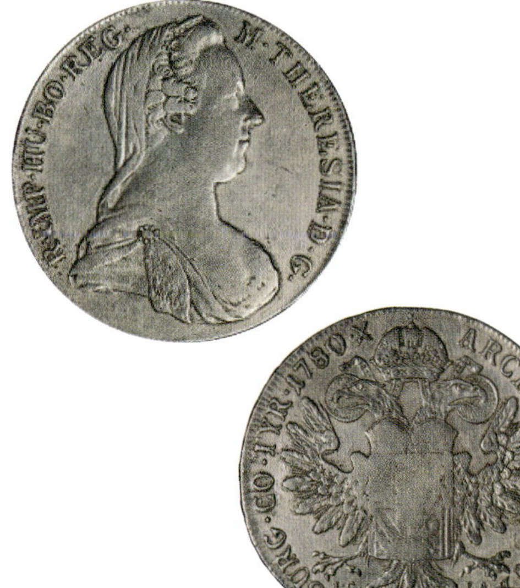

Maria Theresa *thaler* (dollar)

Austria, 1780
silver
41 mm (diameter)
Sharjah Heritage Museum, Sharjah Museums Authority, SM2004-834

European currencies increasingly infiltrated the Gulf region in the 19th century, to the detriment of traditional local currencies. Originally minted in 1741 in Austria, the Maria Theresa *thaler* became extremely important for trade throughout the Middle East. It was eventually declared an official trade coinage in 1857, one year before it ceased as currency in Austria itself. In the Arabian Peninsula and the Gulf region, the Maria Theresa *thaler* remained popular until 1920, and was highly regarded for its high silver content. A quantity of *thalers* was minted just for the Gulf in 1920.

Sha'sha (palm frond raft) model

19th – 20th century
palm frond, plastics, cotton
1430 x 240 x 315 mm
Sharjah Maritime Museum, Sharjah Museums Authority, SM1999-345

The *sha'sha* is a raft traditionally used for fishing and short-distance travel along the east coast of the United Arab Emirates and in Oman. Made entirely from local palm leaf midribs, it could hold between two and five men, depending on its size. It formed an integral part of the lifestyle and coastal economy along the United Arab Emirates's eastern coastline for hundreds of years.

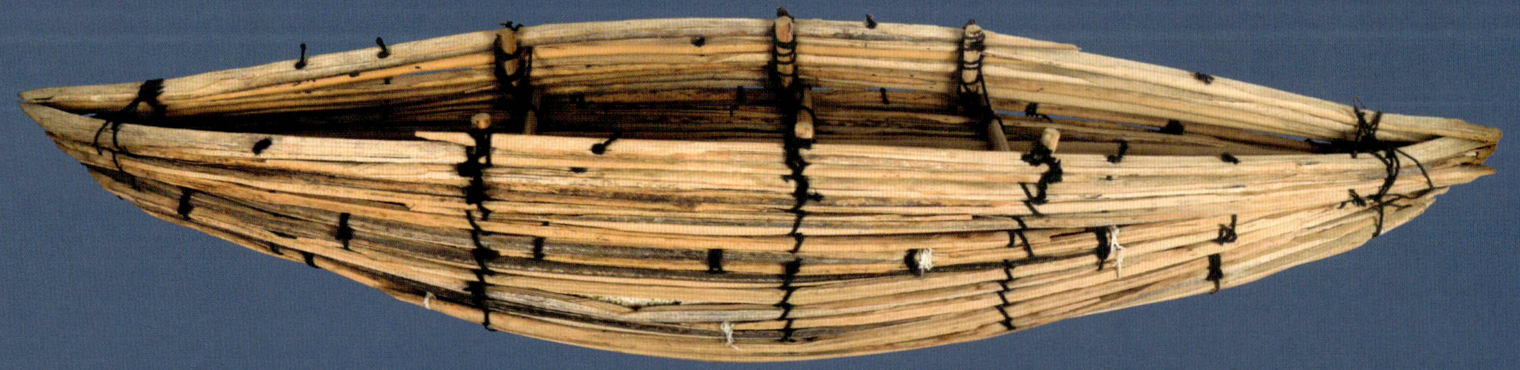

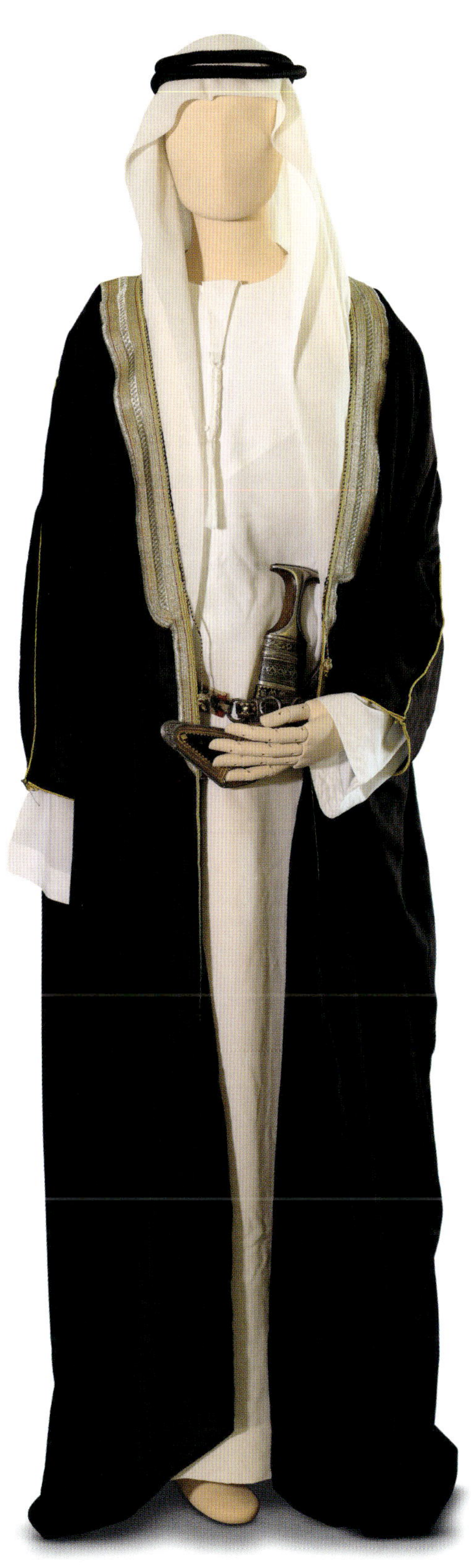

Emirati Arab man's traditional ceremonial outfit

Sharjah, 20th century
cotton, wool, gold thread (clothing); iron, silver, gold, leather, wood, textile, horn (dagger)
1860 x 570 x 500 mm (dressed mannequin); 300 x 190 mm (dagger)
Sharjah Heritage Museum, Sharjah Museums Authority, SM2017-38, SM2017-35, SM2017-37, SM2017-34, SM2017-39, SM2017-36; SM1996-3848 (dagger)

The man's ceremonial attire comprises the following:
kandoura (long, loose-fitting garment)
wizar (undergarment)
bisht (robe)
ghutra (head cover)
agal (cord used to keep the *ghutra* in place)
gahfya (cotton cap worn under the *ghutra*)
khanjar (traditional dagger, see below)

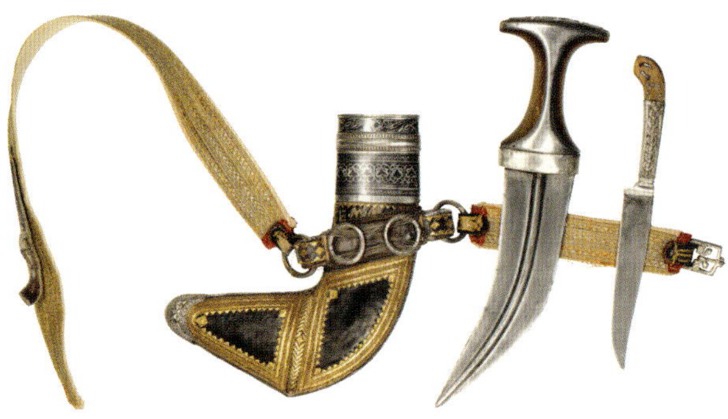

Al khanjar (traditional dagger with knife)

Sharjah, late 19th century – early 20th century
steel, silver, gold, leather, wood, fabric, horn
290 x 160 mm; 800 mm (belt length)
Sharjah Heritage Museum, Sharjah Museums Authority, SM1996-3848

Now only worn on special occasions, daggers like this were once worn daily for personal protection and for hunting; they were also symbols of social standing, courage and manhood. A *khanjar* was given to a boy at about the age of 10 to mark his entry into manhood.

The blades of this curved dagger and the knife are steel and the handles are made from horn, decorated with silver and niello (engraving powder). The scabbard is constructed of wood, covered with leather, and decorated with gold and silver wires. The fabric belt is decorated with silver thread and has a leather strap and a silver buckle. The degree of decoration often signified the owner's social status and wealth.

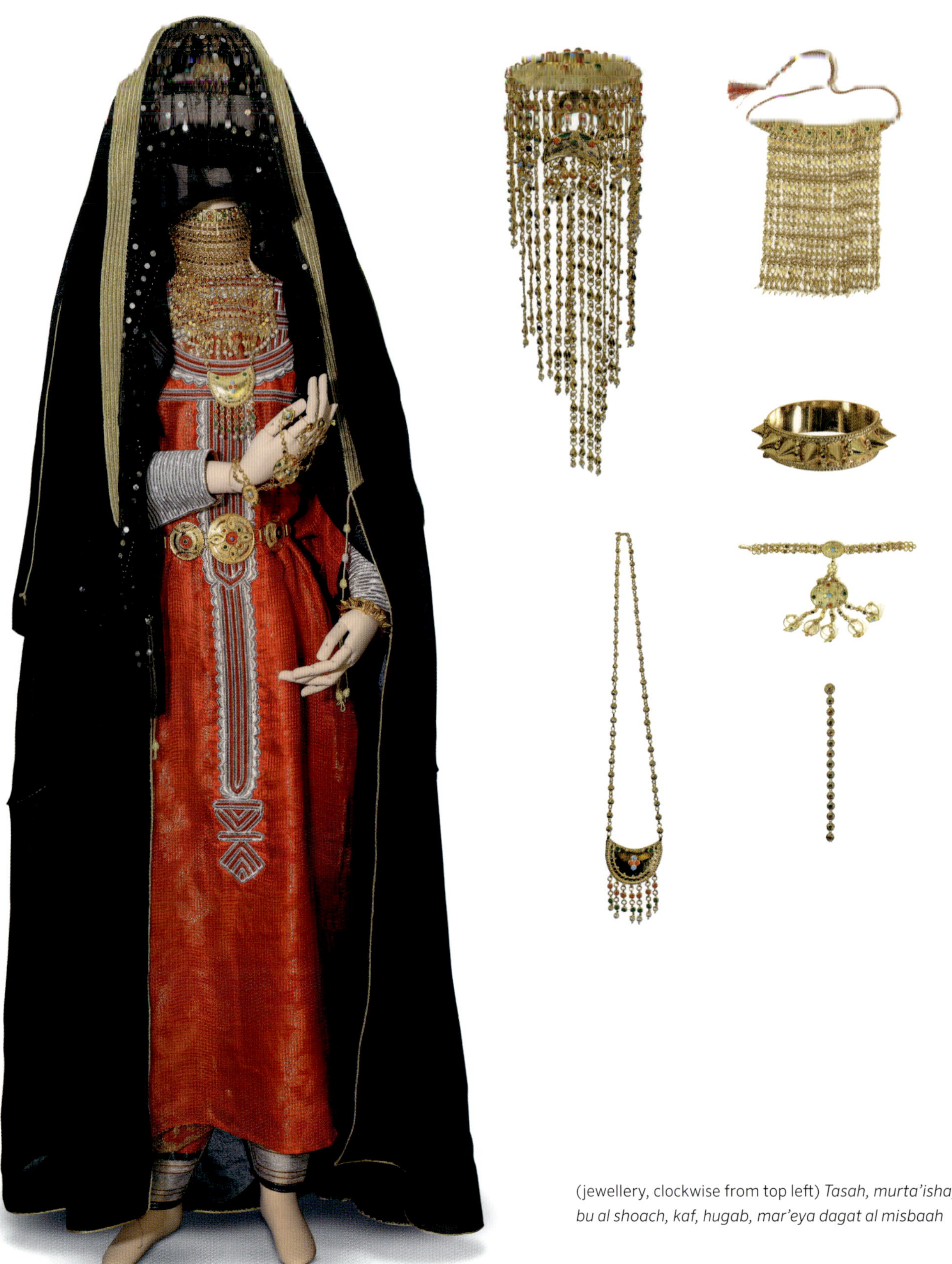

(jewellery, clockwise from top left) *Tasah, murta'isha, heel bu al shoach, kaf, hugab, mar'eya dagat al misbaah*

Traditional wedding costume

Sharjah, 20th century
silk, gold thread, silver thread, cotton, wool, pearls
1750 x 540 x 500 mm (dressed mannequin)
Sharjah Heritage Museum, Sharjah Museums Authority, SM2017-54, SM2017-50, SM2017-59, SM2017-55, SM2017-61, SM2017-60, SM2017-66, SM2017-67, SM2017-68, SM2017-69, SM2017-65, SM2017-71

Within the United Arab Emirates, marriage rituals vary from one region to another. They often take place outdoors at the bride's family home. A traditional band performs as the two families serve traditional foods to guests and neighbours, who wear their best clothing and jewellery.

In the past, people's wealth was often measured by the jewellery they owned. Instead of keeping money in banks, people invested in silver, gold, pearls and precious stones. Women were given jewellery as wedding gifts, which they were entitled to keep in the event of a divorce. Men sometimes wore silver jewellery (watches and rings); Sharia' (Islamic law) forbids men from wearing gold.

Textiles made from cotton, wool and silk were used to create traditional clothing. Decorative and expensive fabrics were generally reserved for special occasions.

The costume here would be worn by a bride for a traditional Emirati wedding. It comprises:

- *murta'isha* (wide necklace)
- *mar'eya dagat al misbaah* (long beaded necklace that resembles a rosary)
- *kaf* (bracelet connected to rings by decorative chains)
- *heel bu al shoach* (wide bracelet decorated with a row of prominent cones)
- *tasah* (decorative head jewellery)
- *hugab* (belt worn to decorate a women's waist)
- *thoab bu qafas* with *telli* (red over-dress with silver embroidery on the sleeves)
- *kandoura mzariyah* with *telli* (red dress with silver embroidery)
- *serwal* (undergarment)
- *wegaya mnaqdeh* (headscarf decorated with silver)
- *burqa* (face cover, worn for modesty)
- *abah suwaye'yah* (black *abaya*, or overgarment, made from wool and decorated with gold thread)

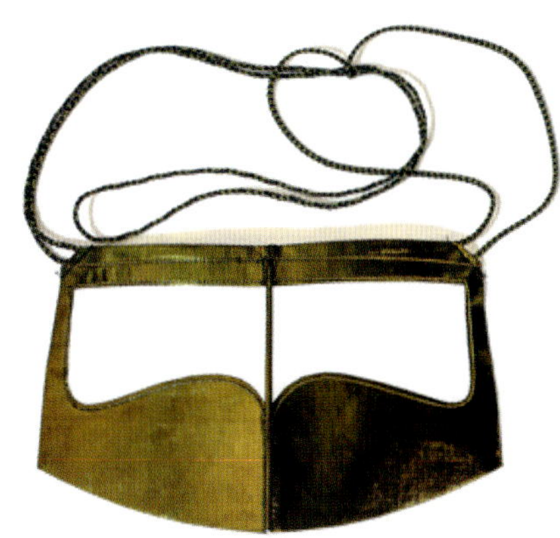

Burqa (face mask)

Sharjah, 20th century
dyed and burnished cotton, wood, thread
123 x 210 mm
Sharjah Heritage Museum, Sharjah Museums Authority, SM2017-65

Across the United Arab Emirates and the Gulf region, the term *burqa* denotes a traditional face mask, worn to both protect and adorn a woman's face. In the past it was adopted by a young woman on her engagement. This one is made from a special type of Indian cotton or linen cloth, dyed with indigo, cut and burnished until golden. Red, yellow and green fabrics are also used. With regular wear, the dye of the underside would come to stain the woman's face. This stain, known as the 'sunset' effect, was considered a sign of beauty. Under the fabric, a *saef* (thin stick) rests against the nose and supports the fabric. *Betanat al burqa* is used as a lining to absorb sweat and protect the face from the dye. The *burqa* is secured in place with *shabaq* (red wool or cotton thread) tied around the head.

Burqa designs vary from emirate to emirate. The design most common in Dubai and Abu Dhabi is known as the 'Zabeel cut'. It features a narrow top and broad, curved bottom. *Burqa* from Al Ain feature both a narrow top and bottom. In Sharjah, the *burqa* resembles the Zabeel cut, but is shaped so the top of the mask is inclined forwards.

Today, the traditional *burqa* is only worn by older women in the more traditional parts of the United Arab Emirates, or on special occasions.

Medkhan (incense burner)

Sharjah, 20th century
ceramic, painted decoration
170 x 165 mm (diameter)
Bait Al Naboodah House Museum, Sharjah Museums Authority, SM1995-55

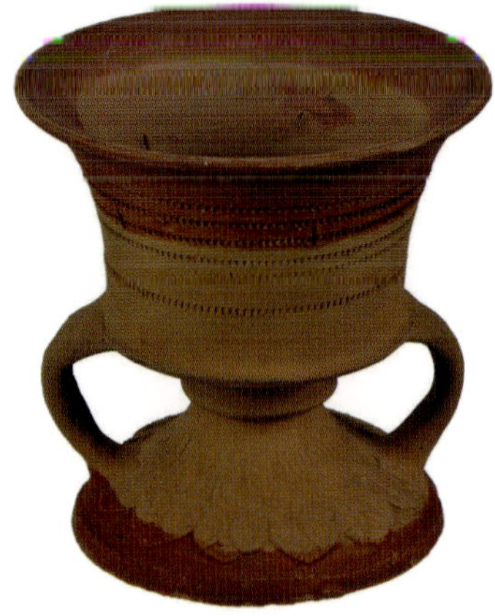

Incense is traditionally used — and particularly on special occasions — to perfume one's clothing, hair and body, and fill the home and its furnishings with a scent that is both pleasant and health-inducing and that welcomes and honours guests. Two popular types of incense in the United Arab Emirates and the Gulf region are Bukhoor, a mixture of aromatic woods, spices and oils; and the rare and expensive Oud, made from shavings of agarwood infected by a mould known as *Phialophora parasitica*. The infected wood produces a dense and fragrant protective resin, which releases a unique scent when heated. Both types of incense are burnt in a special container like the one shown here, slowly releasing their perfume over a glimmering piece of charcoal.

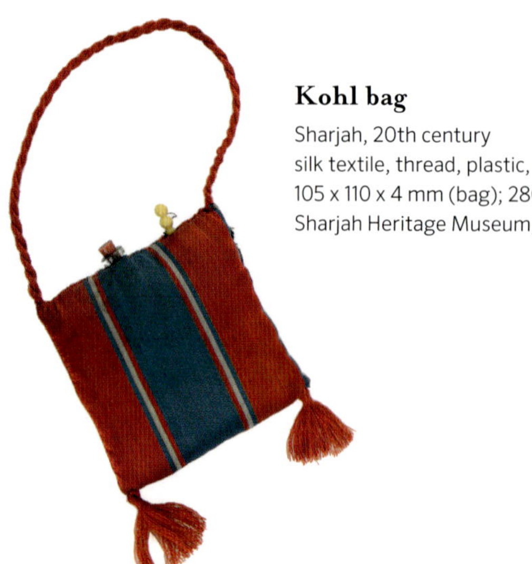

Kohl bag

Sharjah, 20th century
silk textile, thread, plastic, glass, rubber, kohl
105 x 110 x 4 mm (bag); 280 mm (length with strap and tassels)
Sharjah Heritage Museum, Sharjah Museums Authority, SM2004-559

Assaya (cane)

Sharjah, 20th century
bamboo cane, steel
980 x 9 mm (diameter)
Sharjah Heritage Museum, Sharjah Museums Authority, SM2017-62

Among the Arabs of the peninsula and the Gulf region, canes like this one were used for walking, herding and — on occasion — self-defence. They continue to play an important part in tribal dances, particularly in the uniquely Emirati *ayyala*, in which men line up in two facing rows, shoulder to shoulder, in a show of tribal unity and support. The men sway forward and backward to the rhythm of drums, waving their sticks in front of them. Each row sings in turn, addressing a jovial challenge to the group opposite.

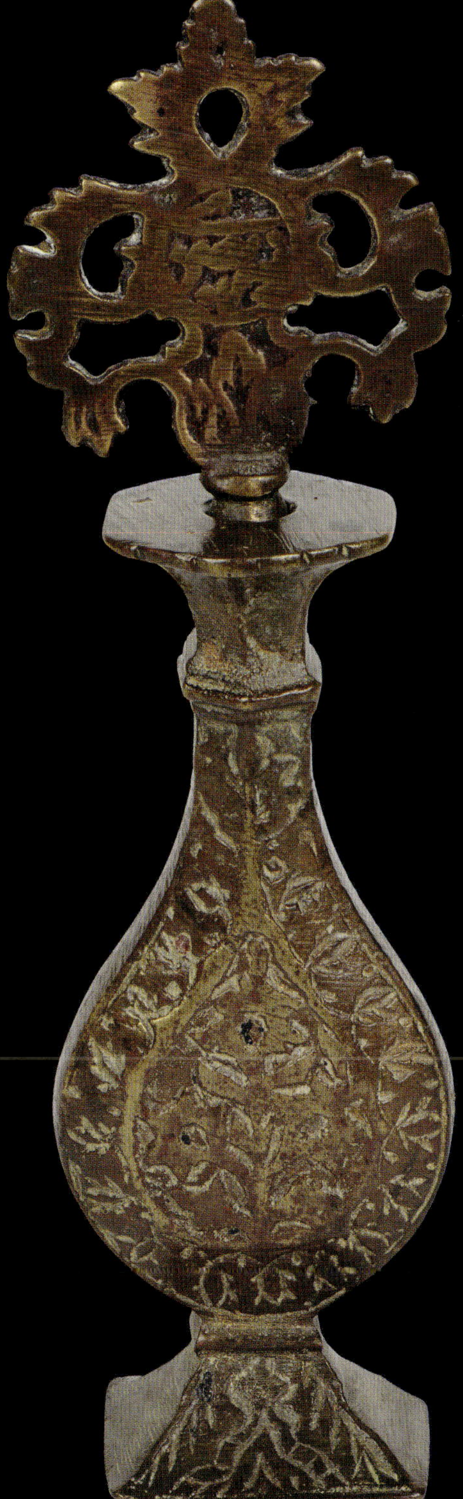

***Mekhala* (kohl bottle)**

used in Sharjah during the late 19th and 20th centuries
copper alloy
114 x 35 x 24 mm
Sharjah Heritage Museum, Sharjah Museums Authority, SM2004-560

Kohl is a black material made from soot or antimony, used to beautify the eyes. First used in Ancient Egypt and Iraq some 5000 years ago, kohl became popular throughout the Arab-Islamic world, and was believed to protect the eye from the effects of the sun, airborne eye diseases and the effects of the 'evil eye'. This kohl container has a screw-in, floral applicator.

In the Emirates *mekhala* (kohl bottles) were made from silver, glass or copper. *Athmad* (antimony kohl) was kept in small pieces of paper and cork-topped bottles and applied using *merwad* (applicator sticks) made from silver, shell, mother-of-pearl, ivory and copper. *Athmad* kohl is derived from antimony ore imported from Iran and Makkah, soaked in Zamzam (well water from Makkah) or rainwater for a month, then dried, crushed and sieved into a fine powder. *Sarrai* (soot) is the carbon left on the bottom of cooking pots heated over a fire. It can also be collected from inside traditional fuel-burning lanterns. *Sarrai* is used by children and adults.

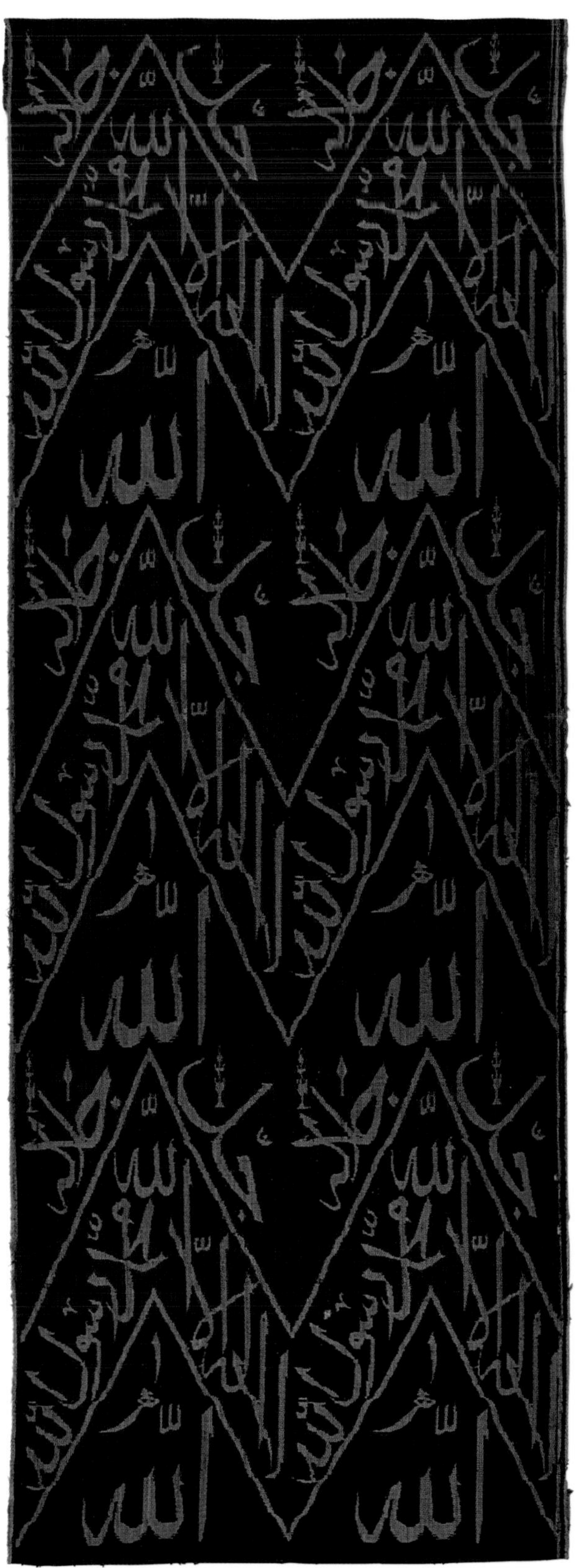

Kiswah fragment

Ottoman Turkey, 17th–18th century
silk
2310 x 790 mm
Sharjah Museum of Islamic Civilization,
Sharjah Museums Authority, SM1996-586

This fragment is believed to come from the Kiswah, the ceremonial cloth, changed annually during the Hajj, that is draped over the exterior of the Ka'ba building at the heart of Islam's most sacred mosque in Makkah. Dating back to pre-Islamic times, the Ka'ba plays a crucial part in Islamic history and — most importantly — lies at the very heart of Islamic ritual. Muslims are held by God to direct their five daily prayers towards it. During the Hajj pilgrimage, which Muslims should undertake during a particular month in the Islamic year once in their lives if they are financially and physically able, believers walk around the Ka'ba seven times anticlockwise. This action symbolises the unity and communal spirituality of all Muslims in the worship of the One God.

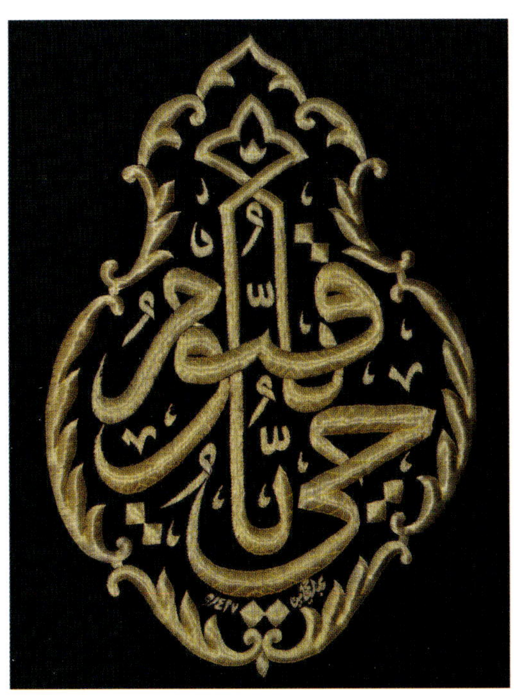

Qandil (embroidered separator from a Kiswah)

Umm Al Jood, Saudi Arabia, 2005
gilt silver wire, silk, cotton
757 x 555 mm
Sharjah Museum of Islamic Civilization, Sharjah Museums Authority, SM2013-4

The Kiswah is made from black silk lined with cotton and embroidered with gilded silver and silver threads. Although it has been made in various countries over the centuries, including Egypt, Saudi Arabia and Iraq, since 1977 it has been made in a purpose-built factory in Umm Al Jood, Saudi Arabia.

The Kiswah has three main parts: the jacquard fabric with the Arabic words, 'There is no God but God and Muhammad is the messenger', repeatedly woven through the fabric; the *sittara* (curtain) that hangs over the door; and the *hizam* (belt) that is a continuous run of embroidered calligraphy around the sides of the Kiswah. Other components of the Kiswah are *qandil*, embroidered separators positioned below the belt, between sections of embroidered calligraphy and *samadia*, square pieces placed on the corners of the Kiswah. *Qandil*, which means 'lamp', are so-called because their shape resembles a traditional lamp. The designs of the *qandil*, *samadia* and other sections with silver and gold embroidery vary each year. On the *qandil* here, the phrase '*Ya Hai Ya Qayoum*' ('Oh Ever Living, Oh Who Sustains and Protects All That Exists') is embroidered in gilt silver wire in Al Thuluth script.

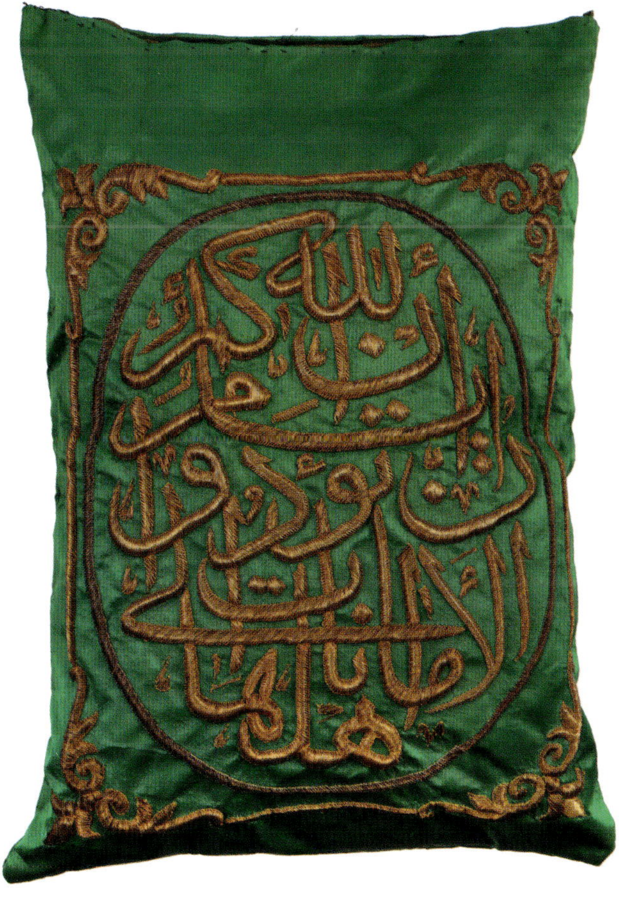

Metal-thread embroidered silk bag for the key of the Ka'bah

Umm al-Joud, Saudi Arabia, 1987
silk, gilt and silver thread
460 x 330 mm
Sharjah Museum of Islamic Civilization, Sharjah Museums Authority, SM1998-8

Since the advent of Islam, the guardianship of the Ka'ba in Makkah has been in the hands of one family, the Banu Shayba. They are the direct descendants of Uthman bin Talha, the man chosen by the Prophet (pbuh) Himself to guard the Ka'ba keys 'until the Day of Judgement'. For centuries, a special bag has been prepared to receive the magnificent key for the door of the Ka'ba. Together with the Kiswah to cloak the Ka'ba, it is presented to the most senior representative of the Banu Shayba on the onset of the Hajj season.

The inscription on this bag is taken from Chapter 4 of the Holy Qur'an (Al-Nisa'), Verse 58: 'Verily! Allah commands that you should render back the trusts to those to whom they are due ...' The inscription on the back states that 'the Guardian of the Holy Places, Fahd bin 'Abdulaziz Al Saud [King of Saudi Arabia, (1982–2005)] ordered this bag to be made in 1407 H/1987 CE'. King Fahd adopted this title instead of 'His Majesty' in 1986 to emphasise his religious authority over his secular one.

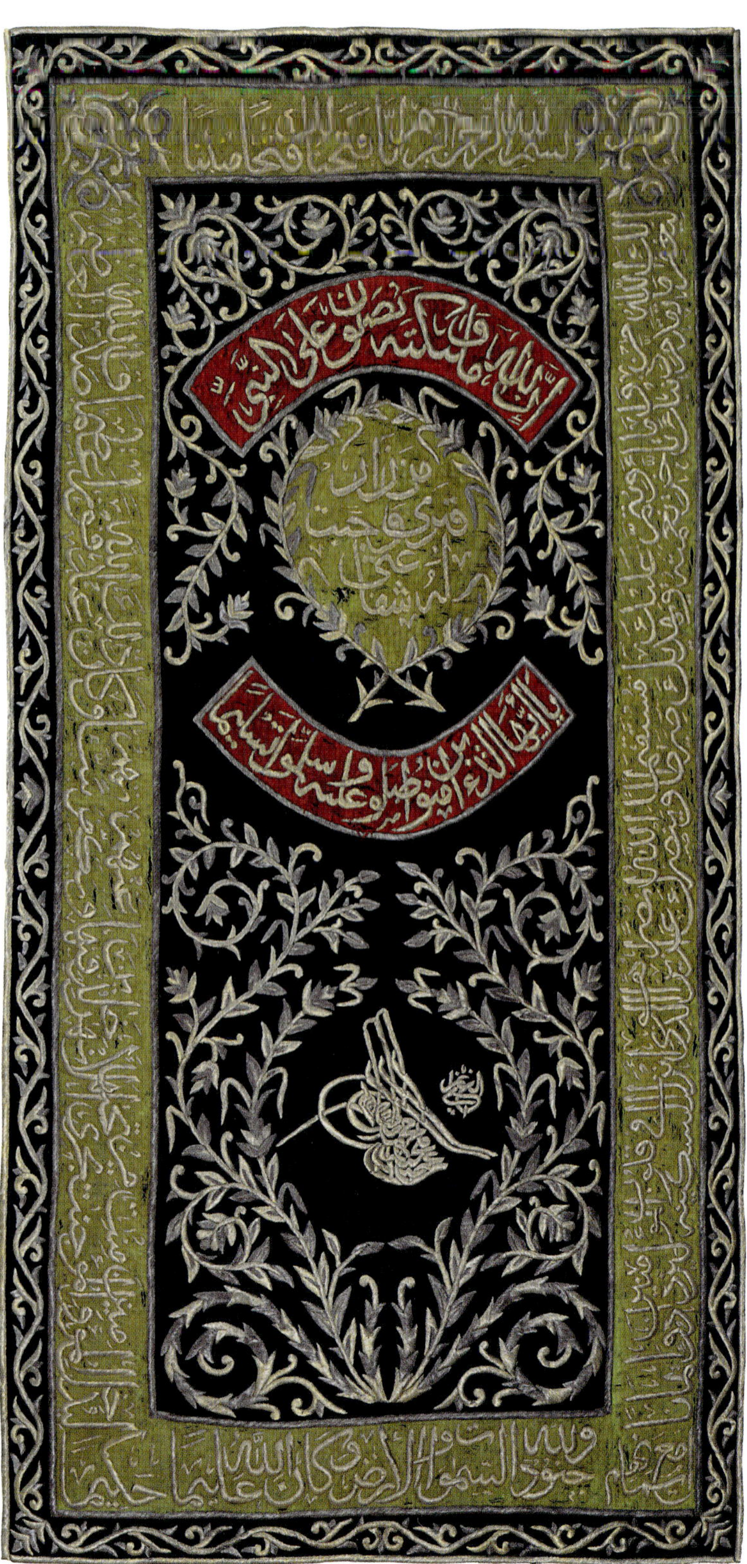

Sitara (hanging) for the Mosque of the Prophet Muhammad (pbuh) in Madinah

Egypt, mid-19th century
silk, gilt and silver thread
2600 x 1380 mm
Sharjah Museum of Islamic Civilization, Sharjah Museums Authority, SM2011-1262

During the Hajj, Muslims also endeavour to visit the Mosque of the Prophet in Madinah. The interior walls of the shrine built over his grave were traditionally covered with elaborate hangings to honour this hallowed location. During the Ottoman period, it was customary for the sultan to send hangings for the shrine on the occasion of his ascension to the throne or if the hangings had become worn. The old hangings were returned to the seat of the caliphate in Istanbul where they were used to cover the tombs of sultans or were distributed among nobles and dignitaries. Today, the Holy Places of Islam are cared for and maintained by the Kingdom of Saudi Arabia. The inscriptions on Islamic textiles always refer to their function and location. In this example, the prominent green border contains the first five verses of Chapter 48 (Al-Fath) from the Holy Qur'an:

> *In the Name of Allah, the Most Gracious, the Most Merciful. Verily, we have given you a manifest victory. That Allah may forgive you your sins of the past and the future, and complete His Favour on you, and guide you on the Straight Path. And that Allah may help you with strong help. He it is who set down As-Sakinah (calmness and tranquillity) into the hearts of the believers, that they may grow more in Faith along with their Faith. And to Allah belong the hosts of the heavens and the earth, and Allah is Ever All-Knower, All-Wise. That He may admit the believing men and the believing women to Gardens under which rivers flow to abide therein forever, and He may expiate from them their sins; and that is with Allah a supreme success ... (Almighty God has spoken the truth).*

The curved red panels show the first two sentences of Verse 56 from Chapter 33 (Al-Ahzab):

> *Allah sends his Salat (merciful blessings) on the Prophet (pbuh), and also His angels. O you who believe! Send your Salat on him, and greet him with the Islamic way of greeting.*

The panels enclose a large green medallion with an excerpt from a Hadith (report of the Prophet): '[For] whosoever may visit my grave, my intercession will become an obligation'.

Sitara (hanging) for the Mosque of the Prophet Muhammad (pbuh) in Madinah

Egypt, mid-19th century
silk, gilt and silver thread
2620 x 1430 mm
Sharjah Museum of Islamic Civilization, Sharjah Museums Authority, SM2011-1263

Hangings like this one may have been intended for the *mihrab* (prayer niche) of the Prophet's Mosque, as earlier examples of this type often include the inscription 'this is the *mihrab* of the Prophet (pbuh)'. The *mihrab* denotes a niche in the wall of a mosque. It indicates the direction of the Ka'ba in Makkah, towards which Muslims everywhere in the world must align their prayer. The religious inscriptions on this hanging include the Shahada (Profession of Faith), Ya Fattah (invocations to Allah as the Opener or Judge) and a quote from Chapter 2 of the Holy Qur'an (Al-Baqarah), Verse 197: 'and the best provision is Al-Taqwa (piety, righteousness)'.

Below, four roundels with the names of the rightly guided caliphs surround the imperial Ottoman emblem or *tughra* of the Sultan Abd al-Majid (1839–1861), who commissioned this curtain. Like his predecessors, he employed the most accomplished calligraphers, among them Kadi Asker Mustafa Izzet (1801–1876), to provide designs for important religious textiles.

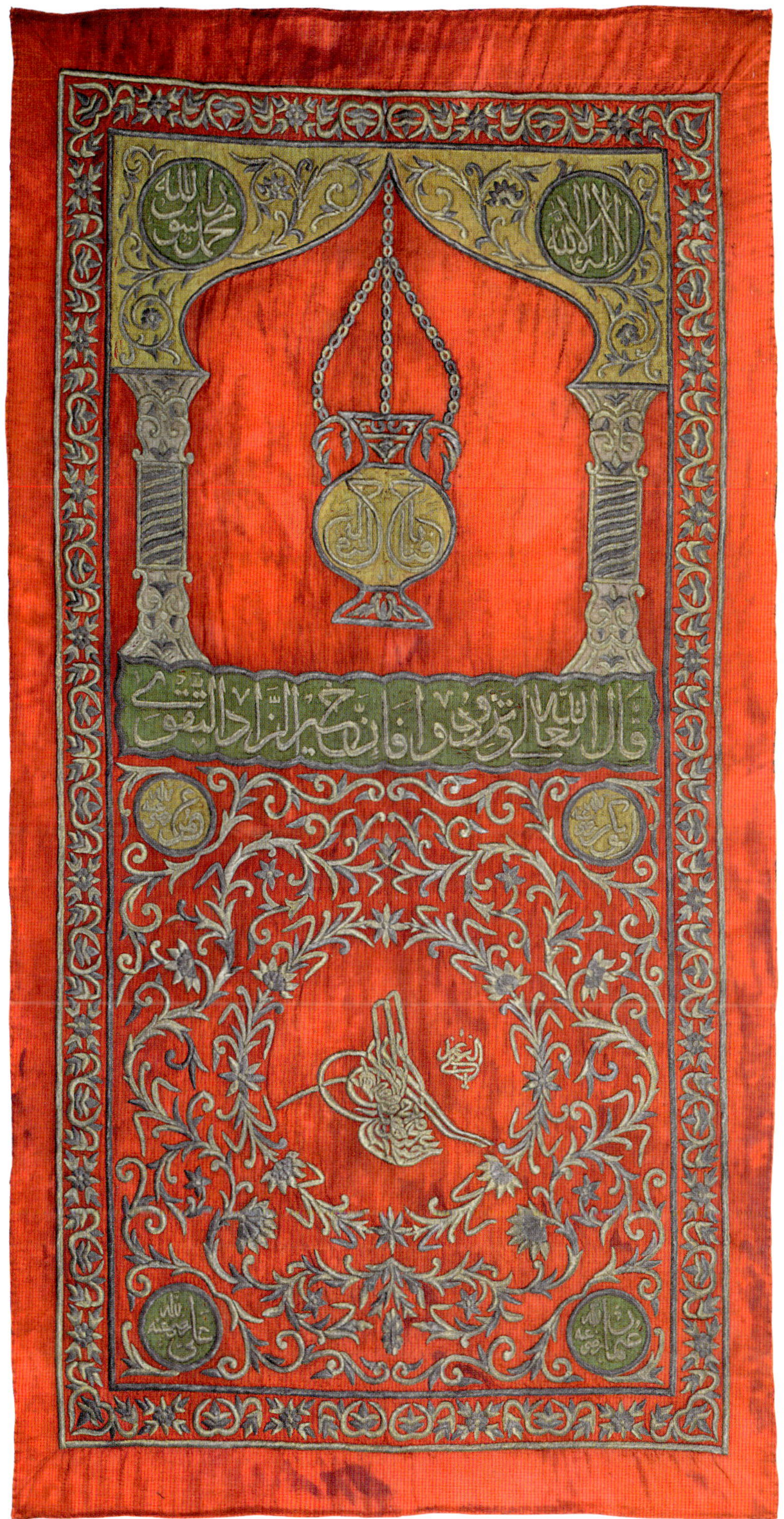

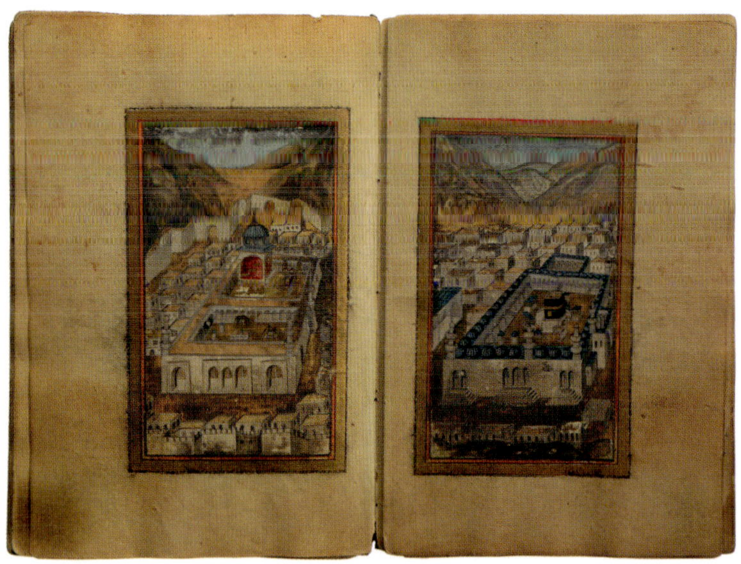

Throughout Islamic history, an extensive and culturally diverse body of religious literature evolved to support Muslims in their quest to live in accordance with the Holy Qur'an. This manuscript relates to the Hajj and its two most important sites, the Holy Mosque in Makkah and the Prophet's Mosque in Madinah. It also contains a compilation of prayers for the Prophet Muhammad (pbuh) and other faith-related information. After its publication in the 15th century, this prayer book became popular throughout the Muslim world and particularly in the Ottoman world. This copy is illustrated with images of the two sanctuaries. On the right, the Ka'ba appears dressed with the Kiswah, its black ceremonial cover, enhanced by a *hizam* (golden belt) above and a *sitara* or *burqu'* (golden door curtain). On the left, the tombs of the Prophet (pbuh) and the first caliphs Abu Bakr and Umar appear draped in golden covers — perhaps a reference to the precious gold- and silver-embroidered textiles that were spread over the tombs in Ottoman times.

Dala'il al-Khayrat (Guidelines to Blessings)

by Abu Abdallah Muhammad ibn Sulayman al-Jazuli
Ottoman Turkey, 19th century
paper (polished), black ink, opaque pigments, leather, gold, written in Al Naskh script
168 x 115 mm (closed)
Sharjah Museum of Islamic Civilization, Sharjah Museums Authority, SM2006-2181

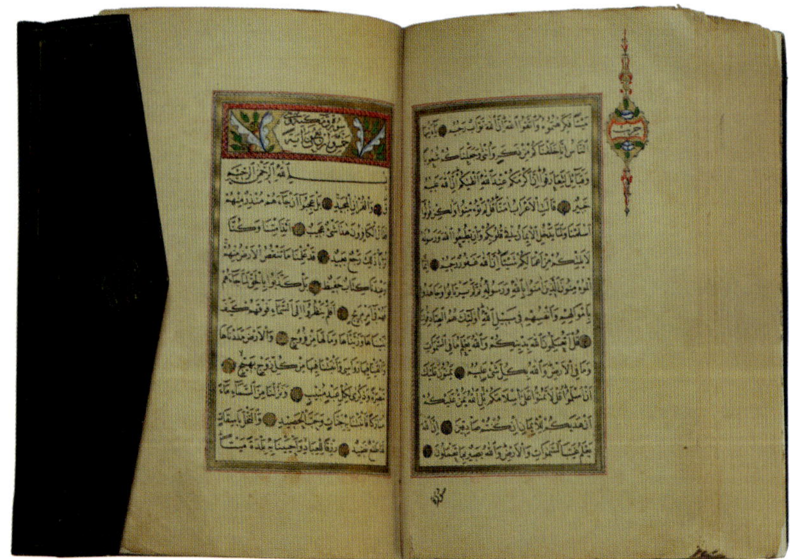

Lithographed Qur'an

original calligraphy by Shukr Zadeh (died 1753)
Ottoman Turkey, 1850
paper, coloured and gold inks, leather, gilding, silk, written in the Naskh script
200 x 295 mm (open); 200 x 132 mm (closed)
Sharjah Museum of Islamic Civilization,
Sharjah Museums Authority, SM2006-1467

Qur'ans like this were commissioned by the Ottoman Sultan Abdulaziz in the late 19th century as special gifts from the Ministry of Education Press in Istanbul. They are precise reproductions of the calligraphed and illuminated original. This copy is open at the *sura* (chapter) that is at the heart of this exhibition. In Chapter 49 (Al-Hujurat), Verse 13, Allah tells us the value of respect and human equality despite individual differences:

> *O mankind, we created you from male and female, and made you into Nations and tribes, that you may know each other (Not that ye may despise each other). Verily the most honoured of you in the sight of Allah is the most righteous of you. And, Allah has full knowledge and is well acquainted (with all things).*

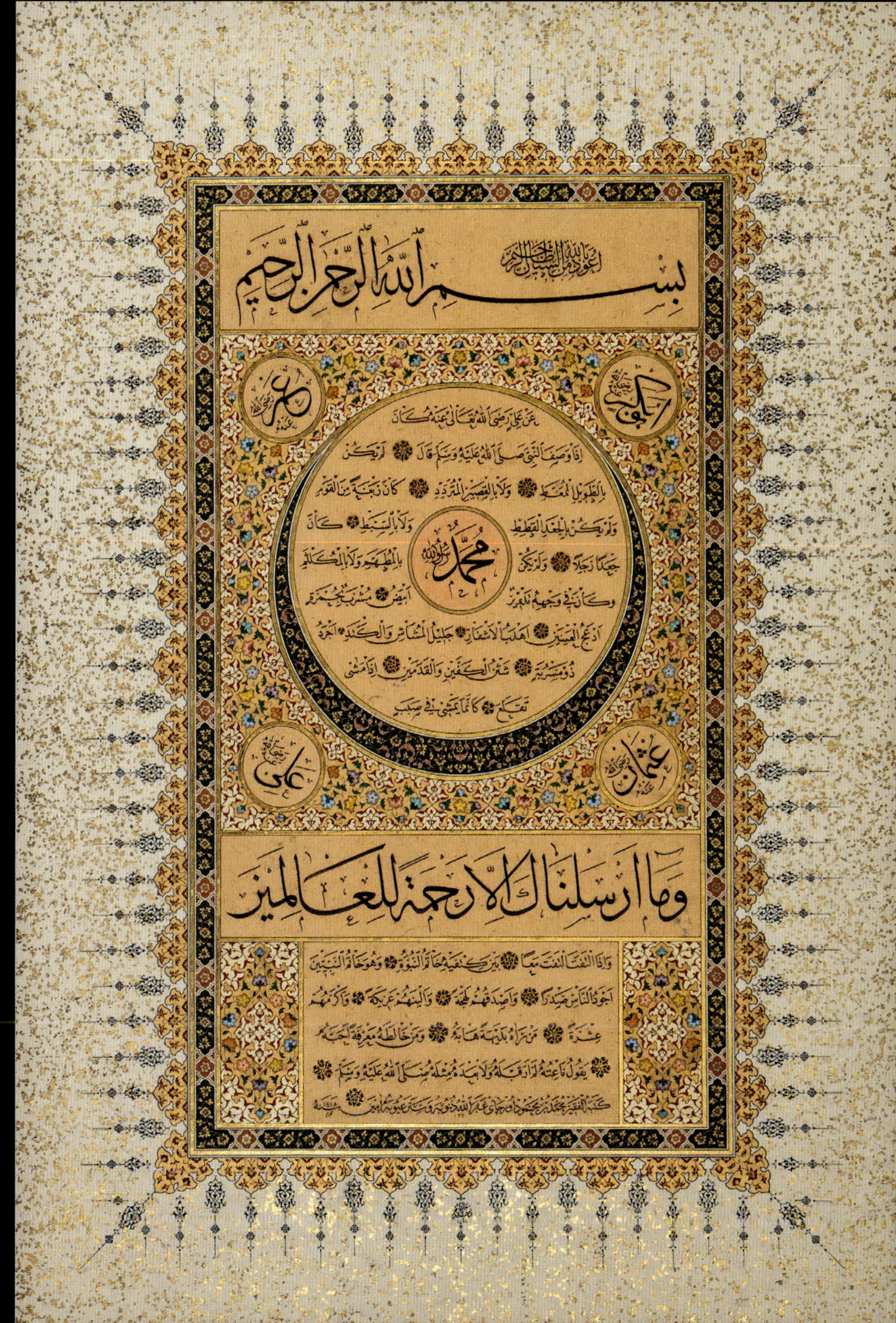

Al-Hilya Al-Sharifa (calligraphic description of the noble qualities of the Prophet Muhammad)
calligraphy by Mohamed Ozgay
Turkey, 1998
paper, inks
470 x 285 mm (closed)
Sharjah Calligraphy Museum,
Sharjah Museums Authority, SM2006-69

Imagery is not permissible in Islamic religious art. Instead, compositions of Islamic calligraphy — typically taken from the Holy Qur'an and religious tradition — abound. The Hilya (or Hilye) first originated as a genre of classical Ottoman calligraphy in 17th-century Istanbul. It includes traditions recounting the physical and spiritual attributes of the Prophet Muhammad (pbuh), as well as blessings and prayers, laid out in the unique way shown here and generally embellished with rich illumination. Its popularity over centuries was closely linked with the deep loyalty and affection Muslims all over the world feel for the Messenger of God (pbuh).

This Al-Hilya Al-Sharifa contains several different scripts: Al Thuluth, Al Jaly, Al Naskh and Al Diwani. The ornamentation is in the Turkish style, which uses different size pens, coloured inks and gold.

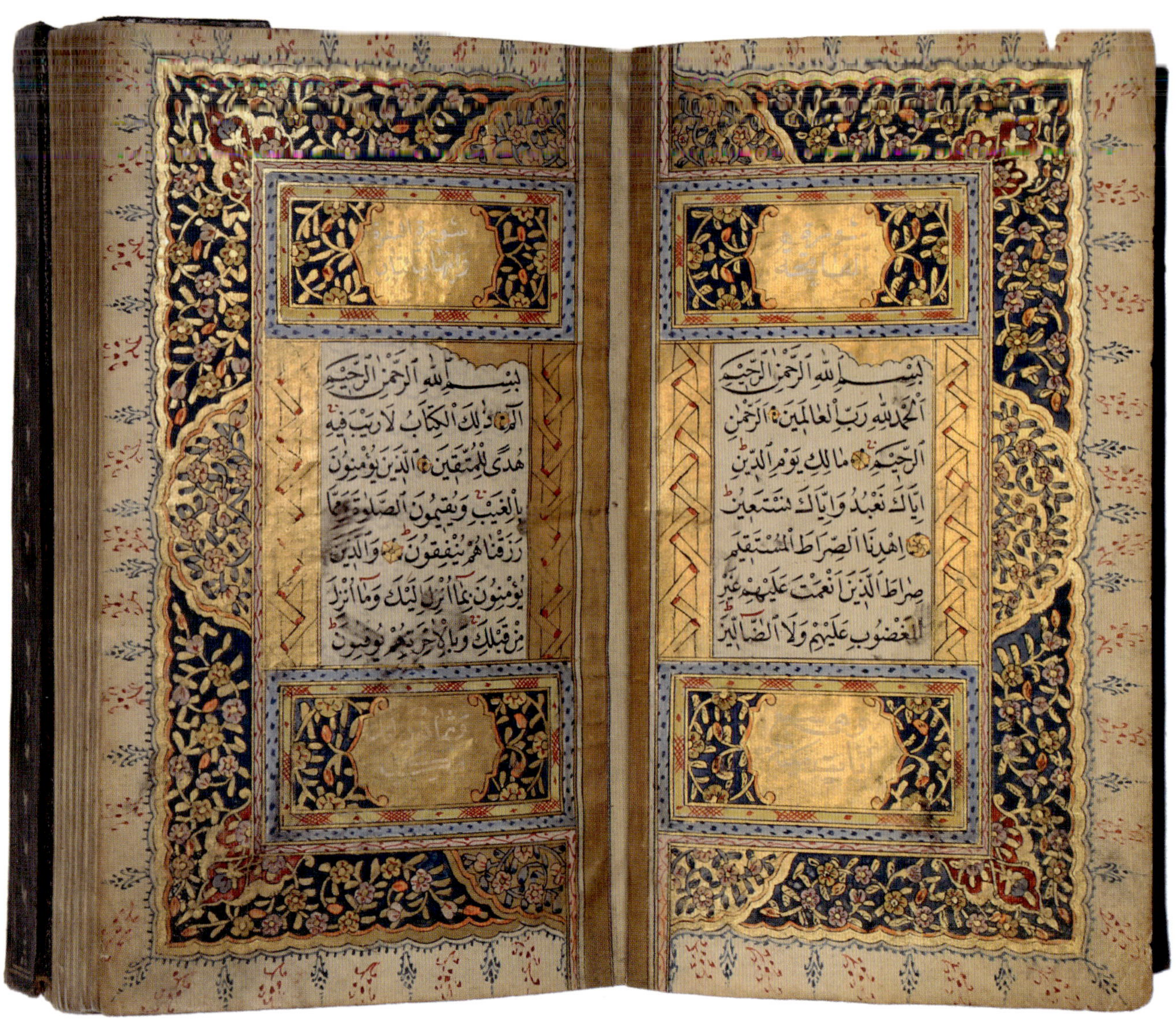

Illuminated Qur'an manuscript

calligraphy by Hussayn al-Hilmi, a student of Muhammad Amin, known as Izzi
Ottoman Turkey, 1823
paper, black ink, pigments, gilding, pasteboard, leather, in the Naskh script
185 x 230 mm (open), 185 x 115 mm (closed)
Sharjah Museum of Islamic Civilization, Sharjah Museums Authority, SM2006-1446

To Muslims, the Holy Qur'an is the sacred Word of God as revealed to the Prophet Muhammad (pbuh) in Arabic through the Archangel Gabriel between 609 and 632. Initially, the revelations were mainly memorised and transmitted in spoken form. They were first brought together in a standard edition under the Prophet's third successor, the Caliph Uthman bin Affan (644–656). That text became the authoritative version from which copies were made and distributed throughout the Muslim world. Consisting of 114 *suras* or chapters, the Holy Qur'an asserts the oneness and omnipotence of Allah without equals, and enjoins Muslims to believe in Him alone, Muhammad (pbuh) as his messenger, the monotheistic prophets, from Adam to Jesus, their revealed scriptures, the angels as helpers of God, the Day of Judgement, the Resurrection and Divine Predestination. It is central to every aspect of a Muslim's life. Further guidance is derived from the Sunnah (the practice and example of the Prophet (pbuh)) and the Hadith (reports of what the Prophet (pbuh) said or approved of).

Merfa'a (Qur'an stand)

Middle East, late 19th – early 20th century
hardwood, ebony, bone, horn, mother-of-pearl
523 x 640 x 263 mm (open)
Sharjah Museum of Islamic Civilization, Sharjah Museums Authority, SM1996-42

For Muslims everywhere, the Holy Qur'an represents the materialisation of the Word of God, initially transmitted orally to the Prophet Muhammad (pbuh) through the Archangel Gabriel. Touching, handling or reciting from it requires particular reverence, respect and ritual physical purity achieved through *wudhu'* (formal ablutions). The Holy Qur'an itself states that only those who are clean and pure should touch the sacred text (56:77–79). The Qur'an stand is designed to minimise touching and contact with unclean surfaces. In the United Arab Emirates a Qur'an stand is called a *merfa'a* but the classical Arabic name is *rihal*.

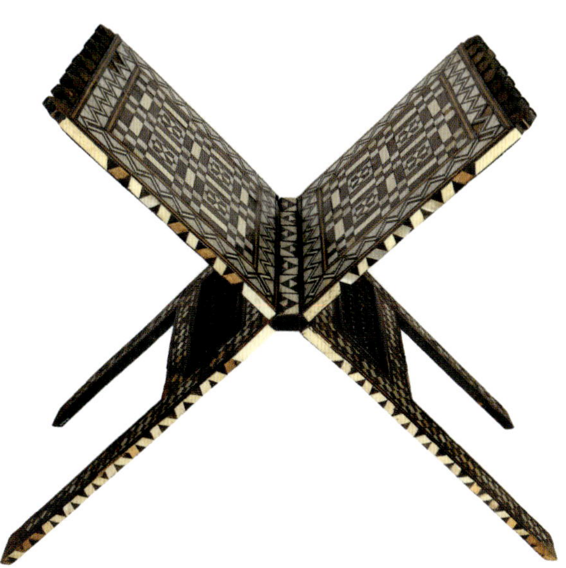

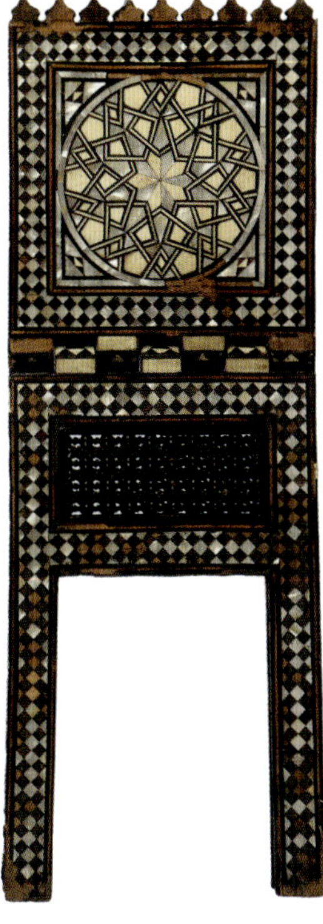

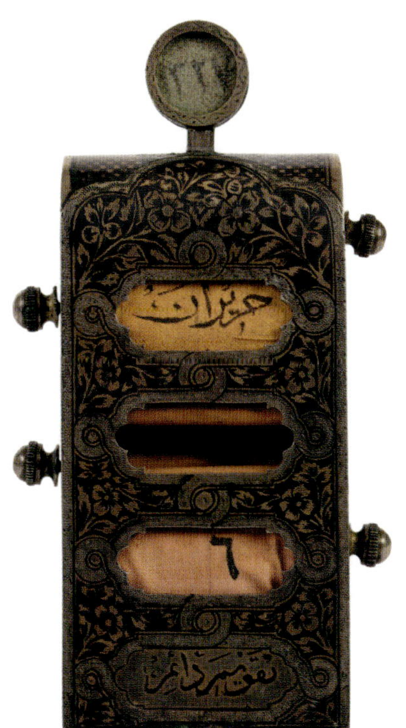

Perpetual calendar

Ottoman Turkey, 1909
silver, niello (engraving powder), printed paper and fabric
130 x 70 x 33 mm
Sharjah Museum of Islamic Civilization, Sharjah Museums Authority, SM1996-237

Traditionally, Muslims follow the lunar Islamic calendar, counted from the year 622 CE, when the Prophet Muhammad (pbuh) emigrated from Makkah to Madinah with his followers and established the first Islamic community. In the 19th century, the influx of Western cultural ideas into the Middle East led to the gradual adaptation of the Western-style Gregorian calendar alongside the Islamic one. The fusion of cultural ideas is also represented by the stylistic elements of this perpetual calendar, which combines Ottoman, Armenian and Russian influences.

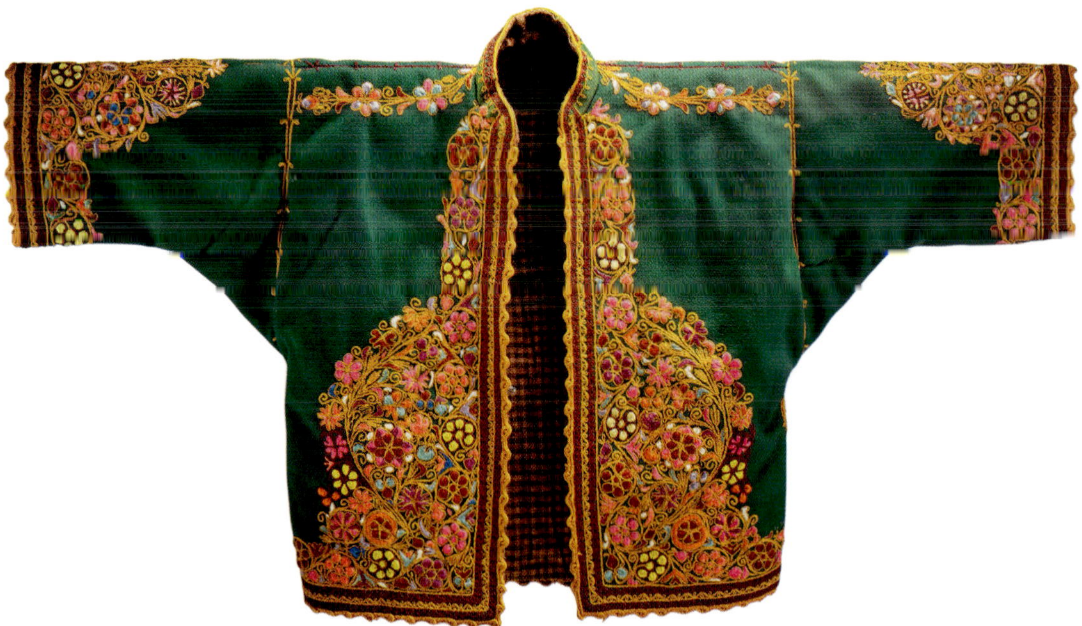

Taqsireh (lady's festive jacket)

Bethlehem area, Palestine, late 19th – early 20th century
green felted woollen broadcloth, silk- and metal-thread embroidery, cotton lining
510 x 1010 mm
Vatican *Anima Mundi* Museum, inv. 112314

The women of the Bethlehem area are said to have taken their inspiration for this distinctive style of jacket from the uniform jackets of Ottoman and, later, British officials and officers. Due to its rapid success, the *taqsireh* was soon made commercially, using European textiles and local as well as imported embroidery threads. Soon one of the key items in a Palestinian woman's *kisweh* (trousseau) all over the Jerusalem area and the southern Palestinian hills, it was worn over a richly decorated *malak* (festive dress), its voluminous pointed sleeves pulled through the jacket's short sleeves.

Taqsireh (lady's festive jacket)

Bethlehem area, Palestine, first half of the 20th century
mukhmal (velvet), golden yellow silk cord, cotton lining
490 x 920 mm
Vatican *Anima Mundi* Museum, inv. 112312

This short-sleeved *taqsireh* is made from dark-coloured velvet imported into Palestine from Germany and France from the 1920s onwards. Richly embroidered velvet jackets made in Bethlehem and the surrounding areas gradually replaced the older, much more colourful jackets the area had been famous for.

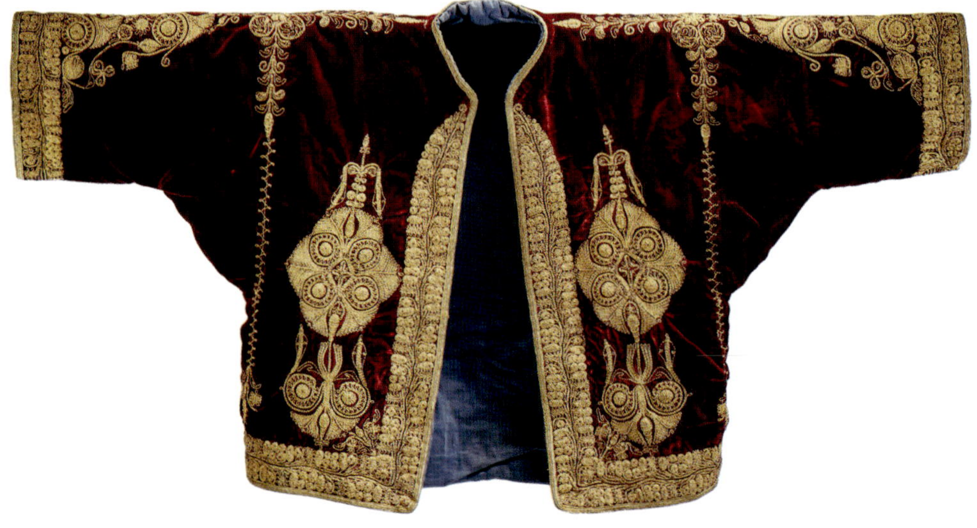

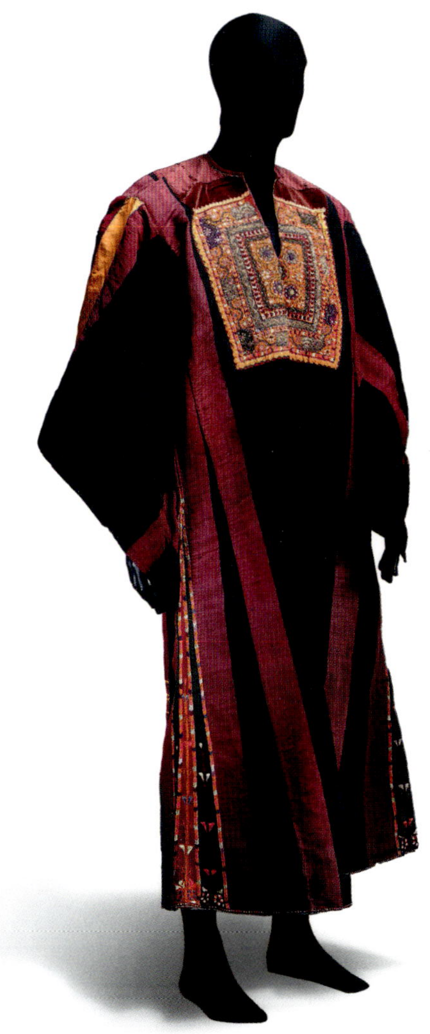

Malak/Thob ikhdari (lady's festive gown)

Bethlehem/Jerusalem area, Palestine, late 19th - early 20th century
locally woven linen, silk, silk- and metal-thread couching and embroidery
1445 x 147 mm
Vatican *Anima Mundi* Museum, inv. 112419

Until 1948, Palestine was famous for its rich and diverse embroidery traditions. Young girls learnt to embroider the garments for their wedding trousseaus. Fabrics, colours, designs and embroidery styles were specific to a particular village, district or town and reflected the owner's economic and social status as well as her identity and beliefs. The distinctive square *qabbeh* (chest panel) on this dress was intended to protect and bless the wearer. After 1948, the individual local styles were replaced by pan-Palestinian, red, green, black and white designs, embroidered by women in refugee camps and in exile to reassert and keep alive their Palestinian identity.

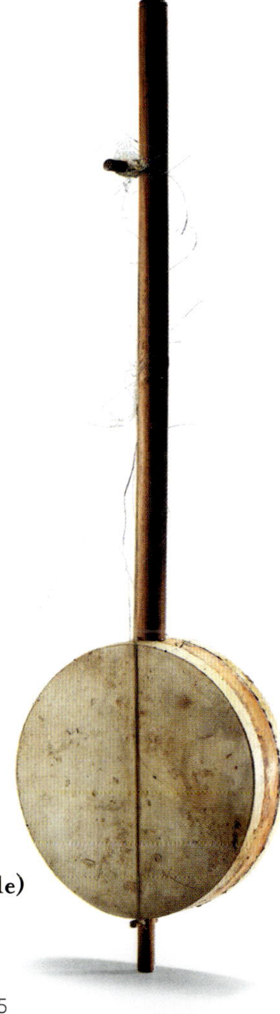

Mijwiz (single-reed double pipe)

collected in Lebanon, early 20th century
bamboo, plant fibre, metal
310 x 40 x 15 mm
Vatican *Anima Mundi* Museum, inv. 112376

Despite having been collected in Lebanon in the 1920s, the *mijwiz* is one of the traditional wind instruments popular all over the lands reaching from Egypt to Iraq. It is used traditionally in folk music and to accompany the *dabkah*, the characteristic line dance of the Levant.

Rebab (single-string spike fiddle)

collected in Lebanon, early 20th century
wood, animal skin, string
860 x 240 x 70 mm
Vatican *Anima Mundi* Museum, inv. 112355

Popular all over the Middle East, the *rebab* is characterised by its round sound box with a spike below, long thin neck and peg to tighten its single string. It is usually played placed on the knee, with a strongly curved bow, which this instrument has lost. Traditionally, the *rebab* has been most popular among the Arab Bedouin, who appreciate its melancholic sound as an accompaniment to their poetic recitations and epic songs of desert life, valour, victory and heroic times past.

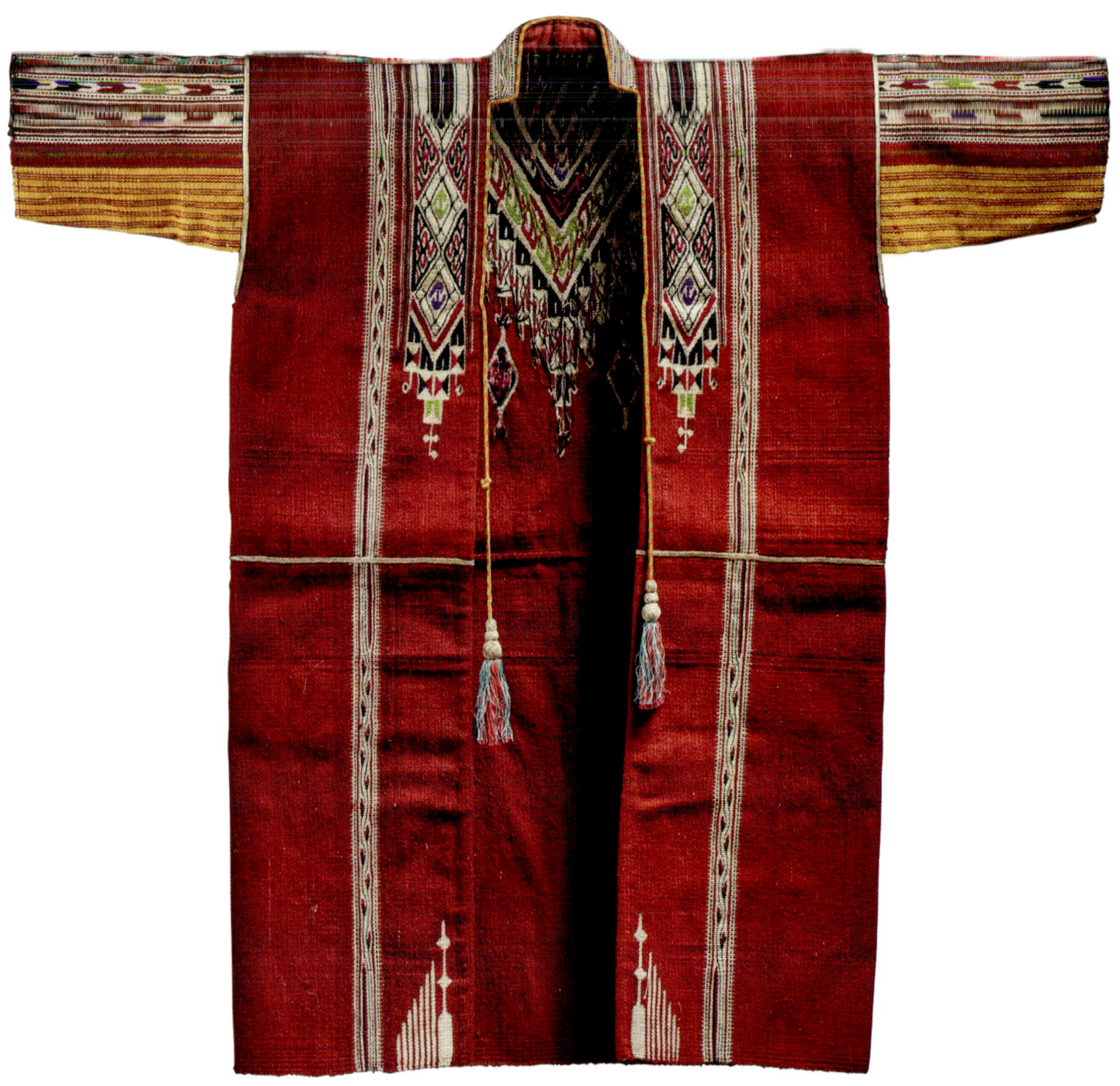

***Meshla* (overcoat)**

Syria, Damascus or Aleppo, 19th century
tapestry-woven wool, silk and metal thread brocading
850 x 960 mm
Vatican *Anima Mundi* Museum, inv. 112279

Meshla were produced mainly in Syria, most notably in Damascus and Aleppo. They could be worn by both men and women. Many were decorated with simple, broad white, brown- or black-and-white stripes, but the most elegant ones could be brightly coloured, with intricate geometric designs. Because of their excellent quality, woollen *meshla* were not only popular in the areas they were produced but were also exported.

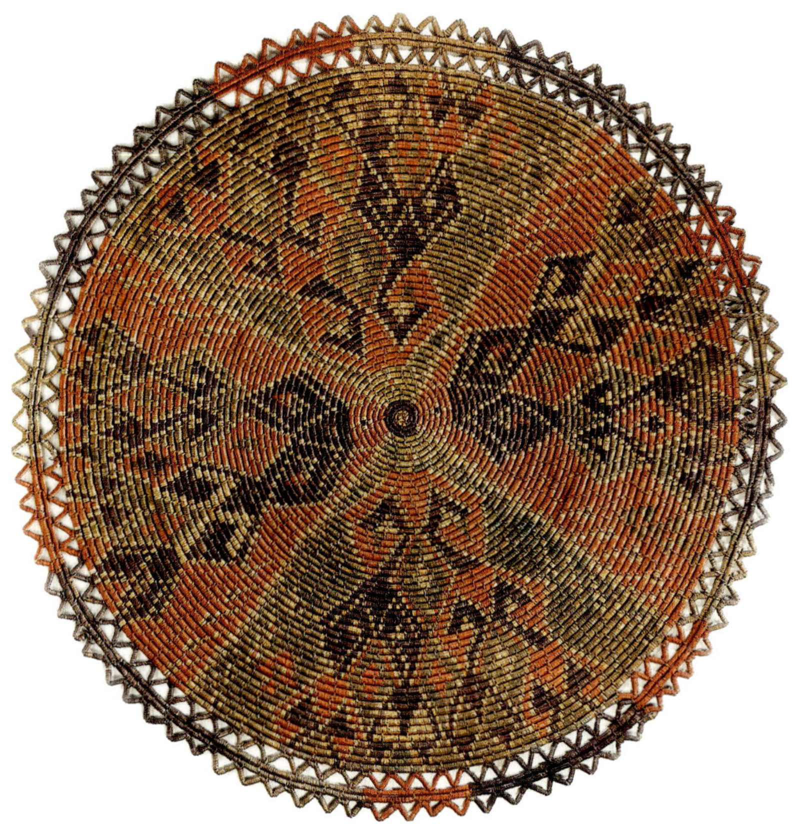

Hand-woven basketry mat

Palestine or Greater Syria, late 19th – early 20th century
plant fibres, natural pigments
10 x 1000 mm (diameter)
Vatican *Anima Mundi* Museum, inv. 112169

Mats like this one were traditionally made in rural areas after the end of the harvest season. Before the introduction of European-style furniture in the 19th century, mats were used for communal, ceremonial and celebratory meals with people seated on the ground around them. At other times, they decorated the walls of village houses. Similar mats, made of palm fronds, continue to be made and used in the Gulf region to this day.

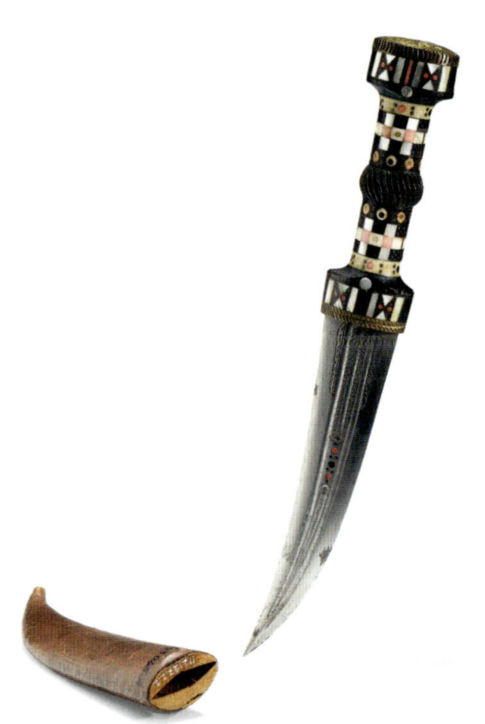

Dagger and scabbard

Magdal Shams, Golan Heights, Syria, late 19th – early 20th century
metal, wood, mother-of-pearl, bone, leather
313 x 55 x 33 mm
Vatican *Anima Mundi* Museum, inv. 112127

This type of dagger was traditionally made by Druze artisans in the village of Magdal Shams in the Golan Heights. Most characteristic is the style of its handle, with its colourful, geometric designs made from tiny squares of horn, bone, mother-of-pearl and brass.

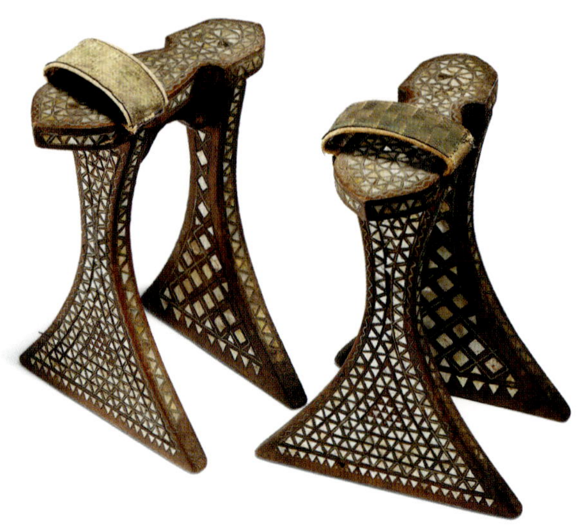

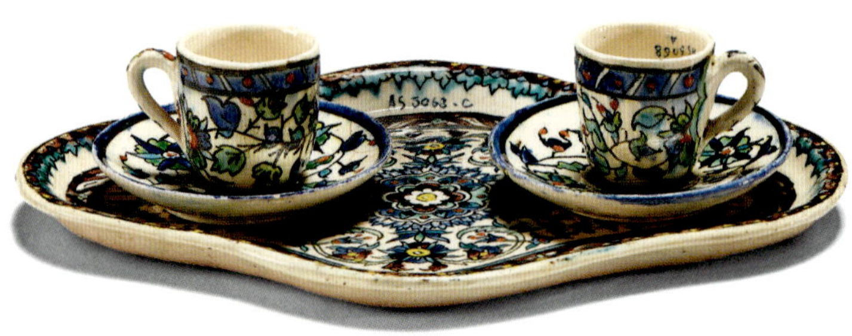

Qabqab (sandals on stilts for use in the bathhouse)

Syria, late 19th – early 20th century
wood, mother-of-pearl, fabric with silver wire, leather, metal
310 x 235 x 210 mm
Vatican *Anima Mundi* Museum, inv. 111980

Although the original museum records state that these sandals were intended 'for a young Turkish bride', such footwear was commonly used throughout the Ottoman Empire. Attached to the feet with ribbons or leather strips, they were worn mainly in the *hammam* (bathhouse), where the high support ensured feet stayed clean, dry and well away from hot and slippery floors. The name '*qabqab*' may refer to the distinct sound the sandals make when walking.

Ceramic coffee set

Kütahya, Turkey, early 20th century
stone-paste, polychrome underglaze pigments, clear glaze
305 x 223 x 20 mm (tray); 60 x 110 mm (cup with saucer overall)
Vatican *Anima Mundi* Museum, inv. 102439; 102440.2; 102441.2

The small Anatolian town of Kütahya has been a prolific pottery-making centre since the 15th century. Its artisans were traditionally Armenian Christians. The designs on their ceramics combined Ottoman-Islamic influences with others from China, India and, later, Europe. Coffee cups and saucers have been among the most popular Kütahya exports since the craze for coffee and coffee houses first began in the 16th century.

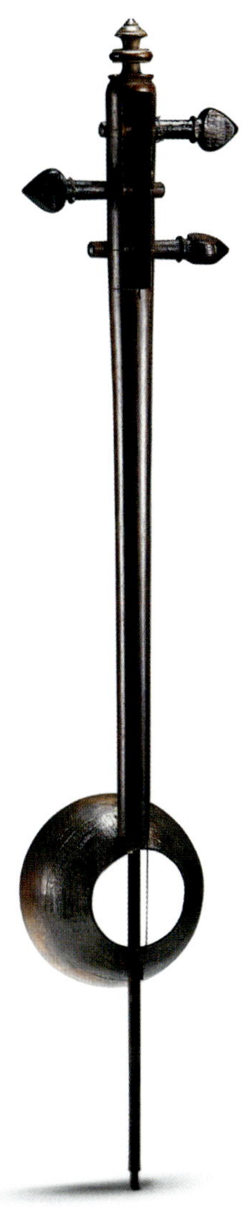

Joze or *kemanche* (bowed spike fiddle)

Baghdad, Iraq, late 19th – early 20th century
wood, copper
650 x 110 x 60 mm
Vatican *Anima Mundi* Museum, inv. 112358

The names for this instrument reflect its appearance. '*Kemanche*' means 'small violin' (from Farsi '*keman*' for 'violin', '*che*' for 'small'), while '*joze*' refers to its sound box, which was often made from a coconut (Arabic '*joz*'). In Iraq, the *joze* plays an important role in its unique *maqaam* tradition, in which a fixed repertoire of classic songs is accompanied by a small musical ensemble, the Chalghi al-Baghdadi. Up to the early 1950s, the performance of *maqaam* was the speciality of Jewish musicians, who performed mainly in coffee houses, with concerts often lasting all night.

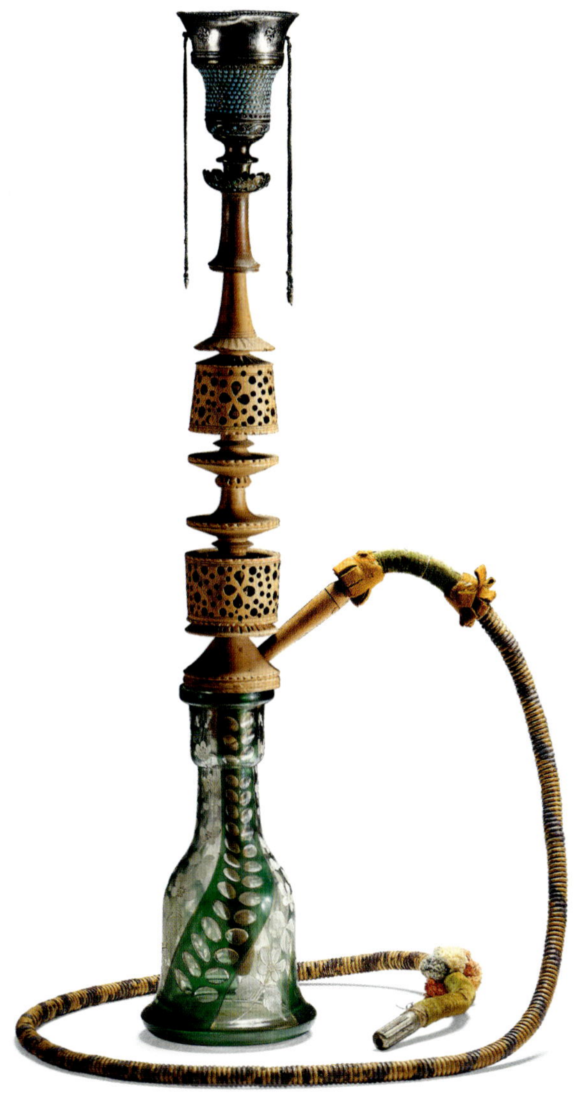

Hookah or *nargileh* (water pipe)

attributed to Iraq, late 19th – early 20th century
crystal, wood, metal, glass paste, paper, cloth, wool
240 x 300 x 740 mm
Vatican *Anima Mundi* Museum, inv. 112550

From 16th-century Iran and India, the *hookah* spread all over the Middle East. It remains a central part of popular culture today, most commonly found in coffee and tea shops, where people come together to socialise and relax. In the 19th century, the component pieces of a *hookah* could come from different places. Cut-glass bases were often imported from Europe. The best turned and carved wooden *hookah* necks came from Syria and Iran, which also produced the turquoise-inlaid tops.

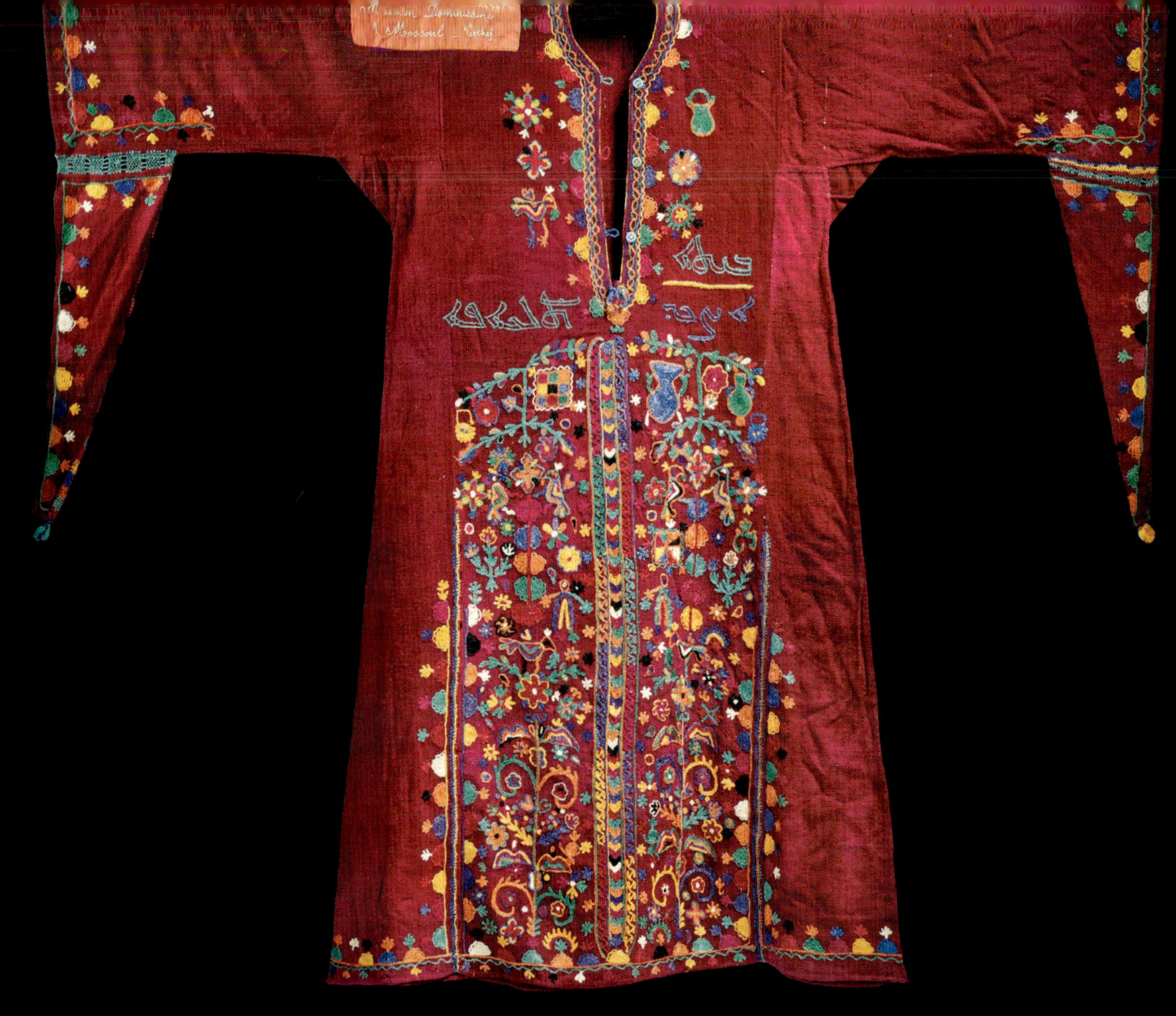

Girl's dress

Tel Kaif, Northern Iraq, early 20th century
cotton fabric, polychrome cotton embroidery threads
1210 x 1110 mm
Vatican *Anima Mundi* Museum, inv. 112265

The area around Mosul in Northern Iraq is an ancient, kaleidoscopic tapestry of different ethnic groups, languages, religions and customs. It has been the heartland of Iraqi Christians since the second century. In the 18th and 19th centuries, Dominican monks and nuns were sent by the Vatican to serve local Christian communities. Some established hospitals and schools, while others went to villages like Tel Kaif to teach, including teaching sewing and embroidery to girls. This dress, embroidered in the community's ancient Syriac script, is a result of their efforts.

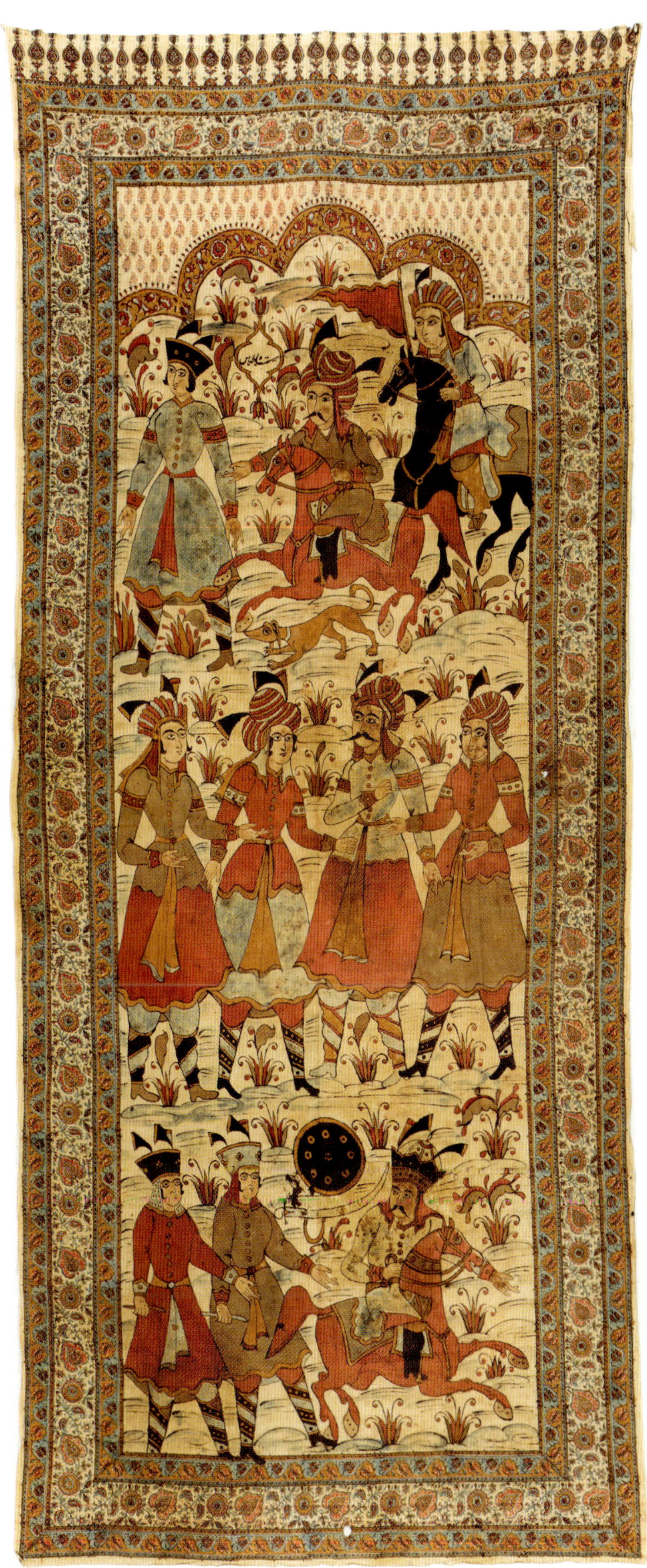

Block-printed and painted hanging

Iran, Isfahan, early 20th century
cotton, synthetic dyes
2800 x 1200 mm
Vatican *Anima Mundi* Museum, inv. 112546

The technique of block printing and painting cotton textiles probably came to Iran from India in the 17th century during the reign of Shah Abbas I, shown with a formidable moustache in the upper centre of this textile. Isfahan became the most important centre for this art, known as '*kalamkar*' (from Farsi, 'pen work'). After a ban on the import of foreign textiles in 1923, the Iranian *kalamkar* industry produced a wide variety of colourful textiles like this one, often used in tea houses as backdrops for storytellers relating tales of legendary kings and heroes.

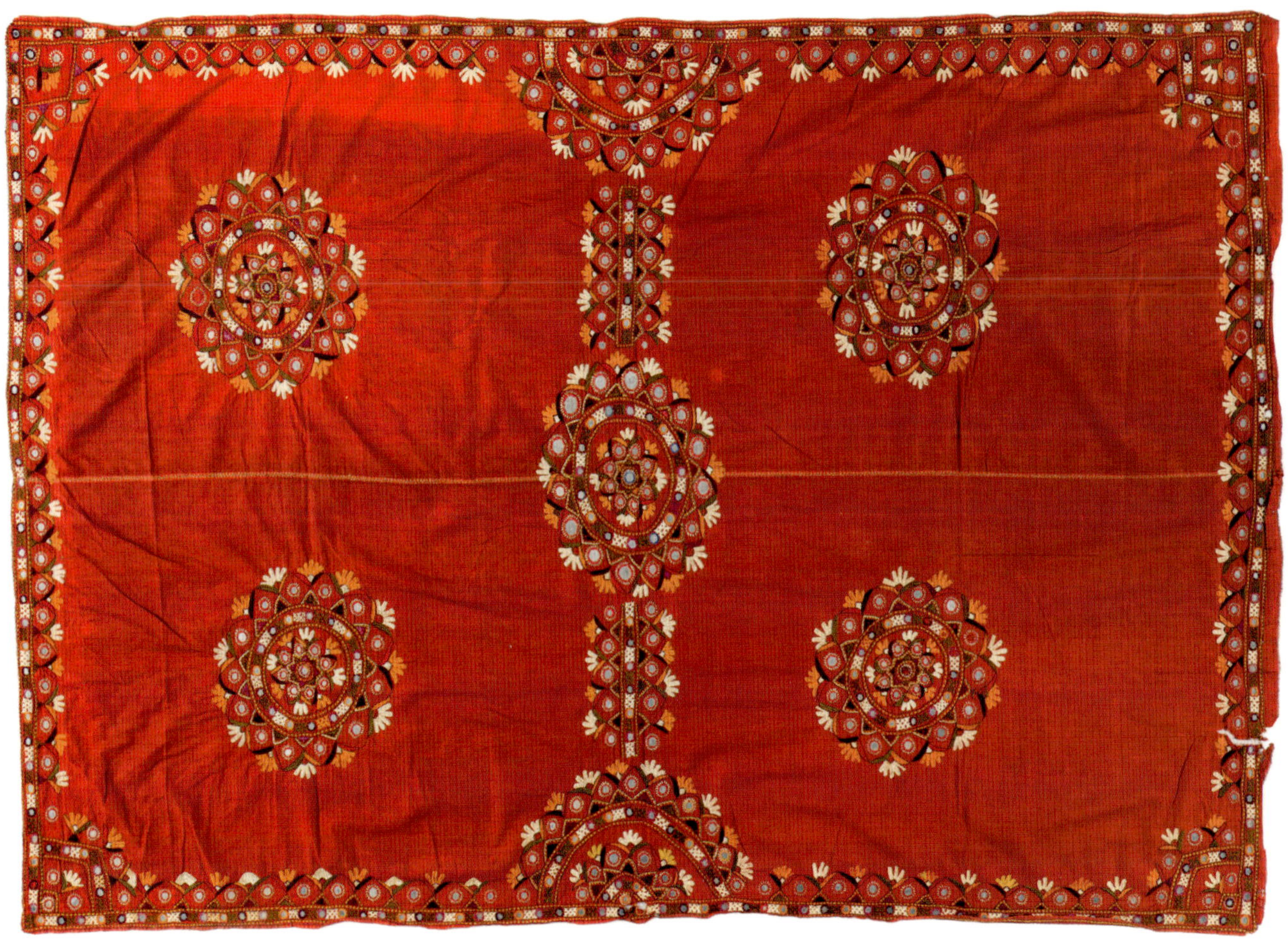

Embroidered wedding shawl

Thar Parkar, Sindh, Pakistan or Kutch area, Gujarat, north-western India, late 19th – early 20th century
cotton, silk, multicoloured silk threads, mirror work
1310 x 2130 mm
Vatican *Anima Mundi* Museum, donated in 1929 by Signora Maria Brarda, the widow of Abelardo Barberini, inv. 112406

The dense embroidery on this wedding shawl is called '*pakko*' or 'permanent' embroidery as it is so hard-wearing. Associated with the Muslim Memon people who inhabit the Thar Desert areas of Sindh and the region around Kutch in Gujarat, embroideries like this one were made as dowry pieces and to adorn the bride and bridegroom on their wedding day.

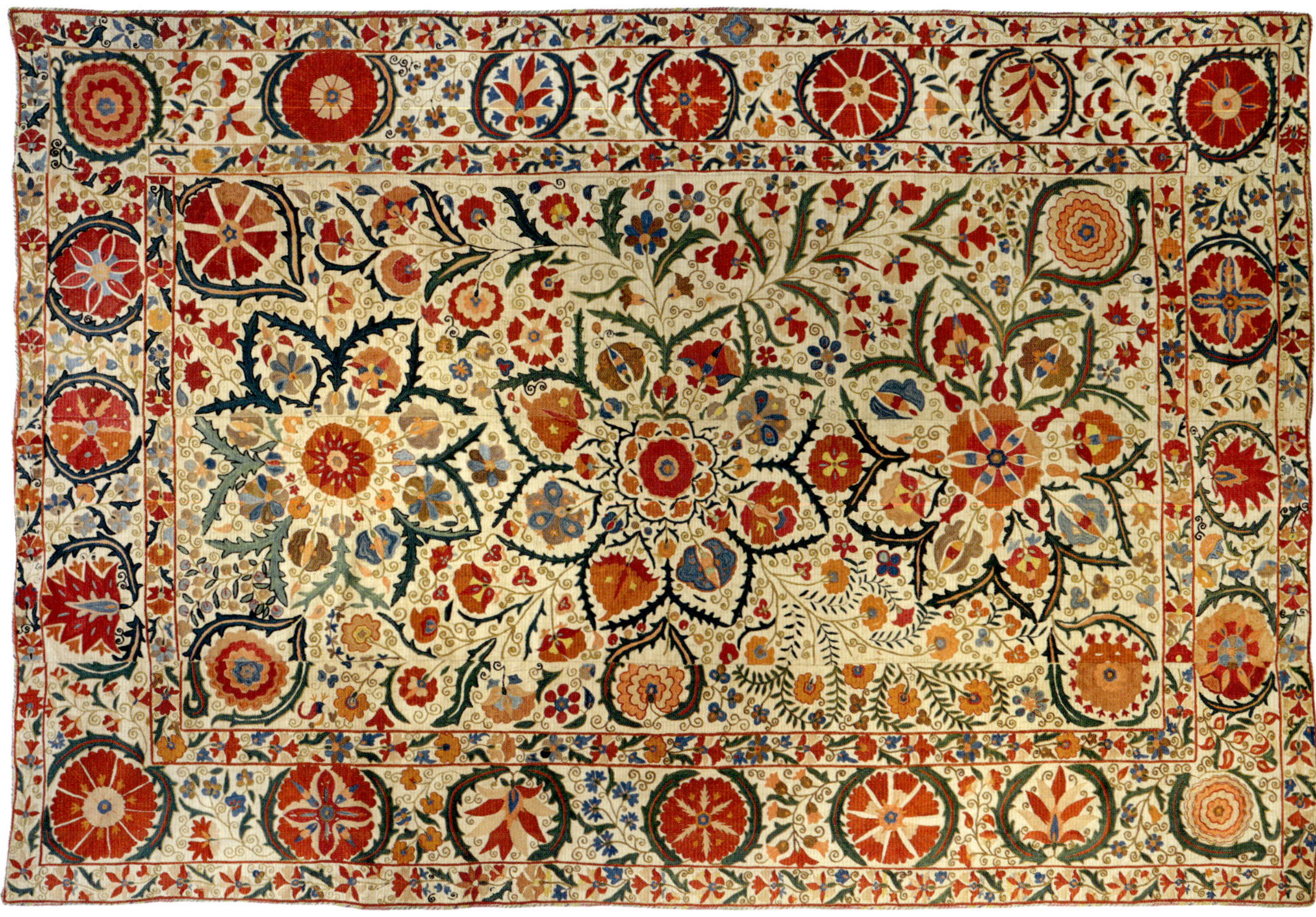

***Suzani* (embroidered textile hanging)**

Bukhara, Uzbekistan, late 19th century
cotton, multicoloured silk threads, silk edging
1710 x 2600 mm
Vatican *Anima Mundi* Museum, inv. 112536

Suzani (from Farsi 'needle, needlework') embroideries are among the most characteristic traditional textiles of Uzbekistan. First, narrow strips of cotton cloth were sewn together for the design to be drawn out. The pieces were then separated again, embroidered by different embroiderers and eventually resewn together to make up the final piece. Several centres in and around Bukhara made *suzani* — their bold flowers, scrolls and diverse ornamental motifs all chosen to promote good luck, prosperity and fertility. The pieces were part of a bride's dowry and used as hangings or bedcovers.

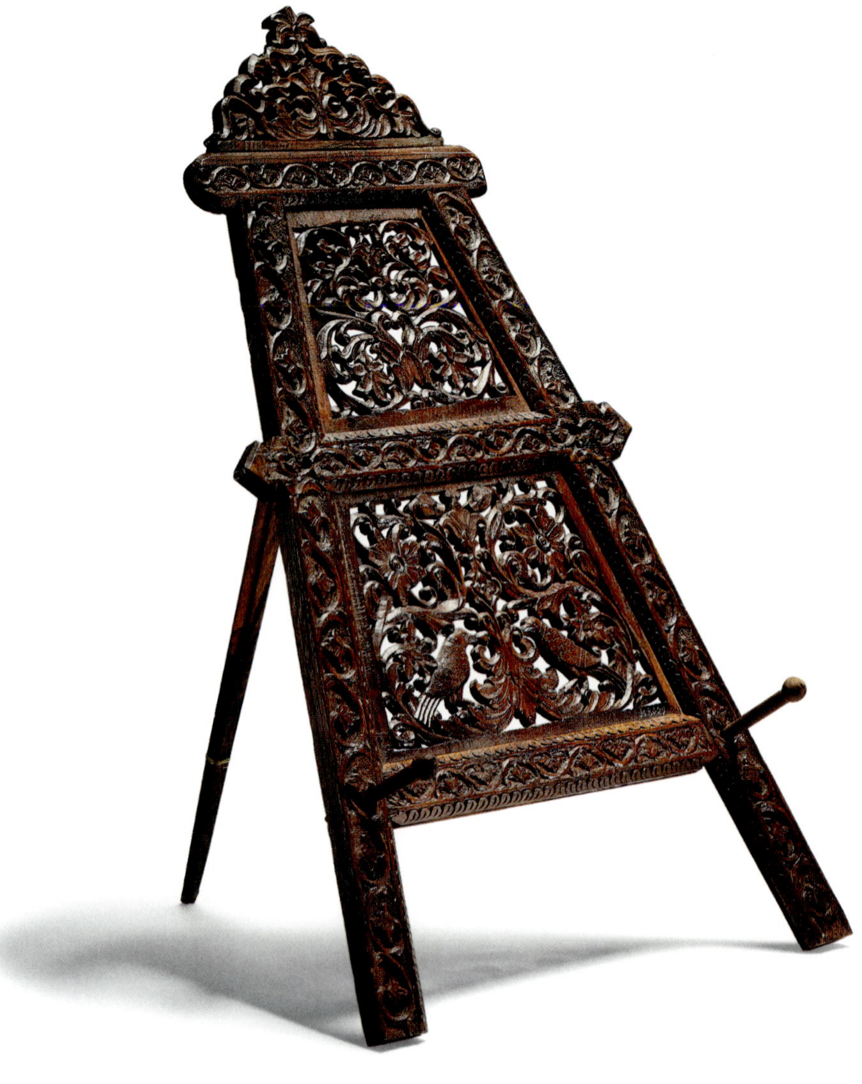

Lectern

Mumbai, India, late 19th - early 20th century
blackwood
775 x 460 x 525 mm
Vatican *Anima Mundi* Museum, inv. 122030

Although recorded as 'sent from Agra' in the museum records, this lectern was probably made in Bombay (Mumbai), at the time famous for the production of Western-style 'Bombay blackwood' furniture. This typically featured carved and pierced designs of foliage, floral scrolling, mythical beasts and animals. Workers from Ahmedabad and Surat executed the designs, which can be strikingly similar to those that reached Zanzibar from India and appear there on its famous doors carved around the same time.

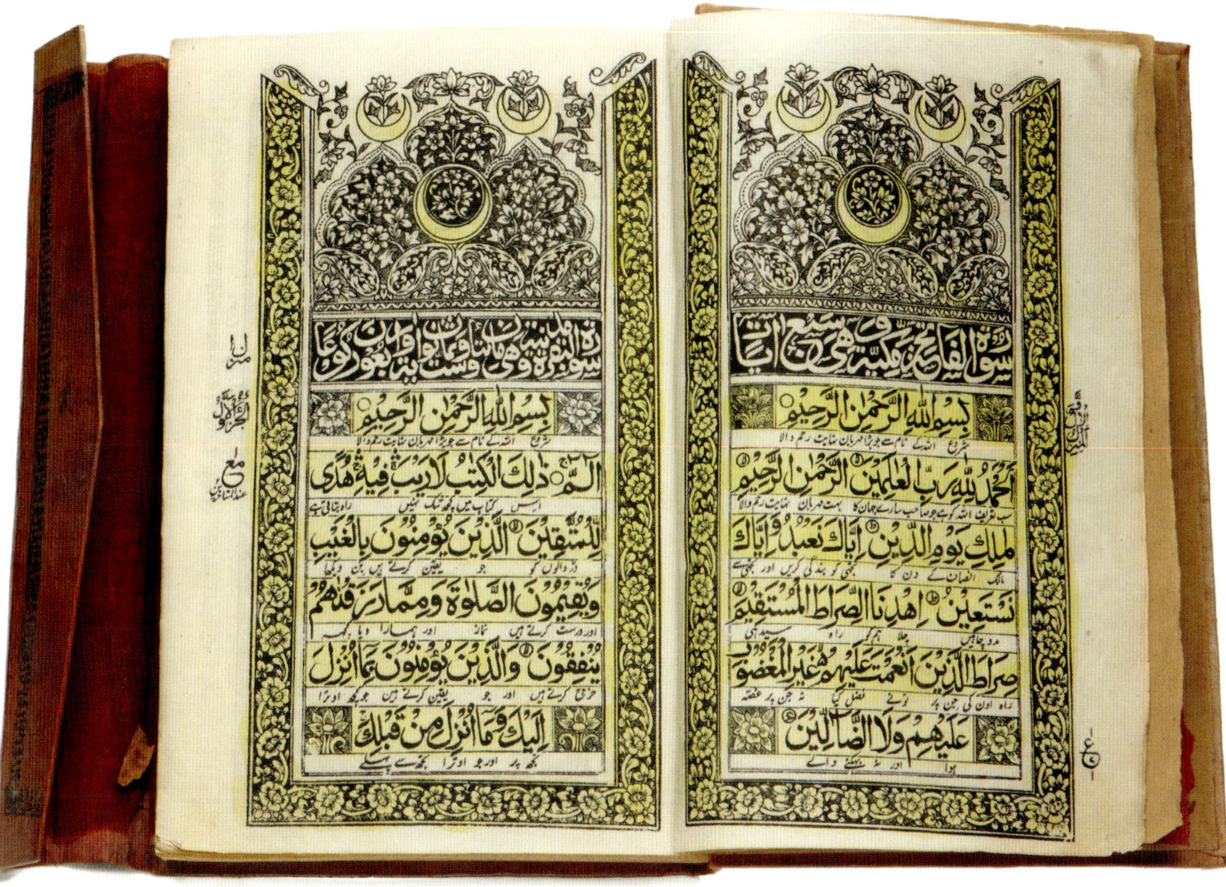

Lithographed Qur'an with Urdu translation

Agra, Uttar Pradesh, India, late 19th century
lithographed and part-coloured paper, leather
280 x 185 x 55 mm
Vatican *Anima Mundi* Museum, inv. 122029

Within the Muslim world, the Holy Qur'an was not printed until the 19th century. Only the precise art of calligraphy was considered authentic and reliable enough to materialise the Word of God. As the advantages of printing Qur'ans were gradually realised, India emerged as a major hub for its production, and lithographic printing houses in Lucknow, Bombay and Delhi started mass-producing Qur'ans and other theological books in Urdu, Persian and Arabic. This volume was published by the printing house of Abu'l 'Ala'i in Agra near Delhi.

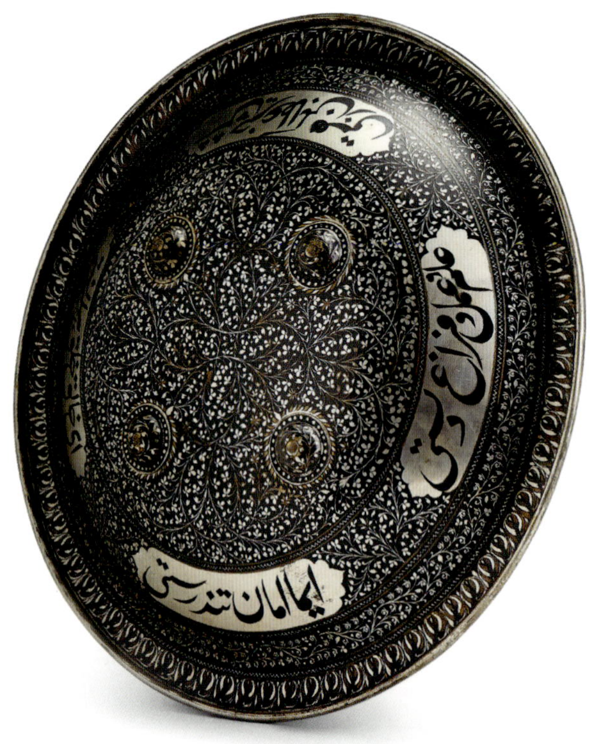

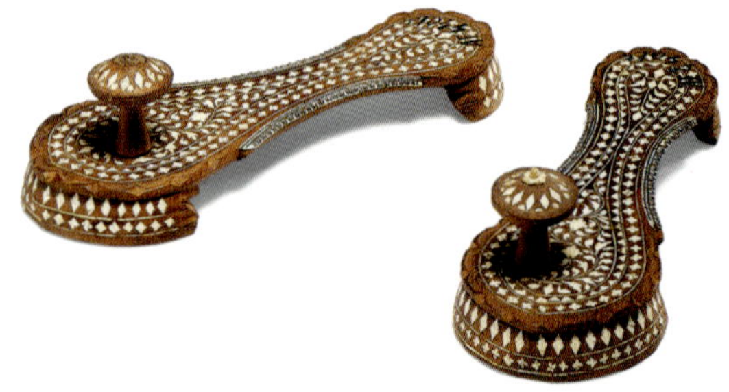

Bidri shield with Farsi poem

India, late 19th century
cast zinc alloy, silver and brass inlay, velvet
372 x 55 mm
Vatican *Anima Mundi* Museum, inv. 122028

The Bidri metalwork technique first became popular around the early 17th century. Ever since, it has been practised by mainly Muslim craftsmen in centres like Murshidabad, Lucknow, Purnea, Hyderabad and Bidar, from which it takes its name. Much Bidri ware, like this shield, was made for ceremonial use or display.

The poem translates: 'Oh Creator of creations, all high [and] low, grant from existence six things: knowledge, [good] deeds, generosity, faith, safety and good health'.

Our gratitude to Tariq Ahsan, Ahsan Qadir and Dr Saqib Baburai (SOAS) for helping with the translation and transcription of this poem.

Paduka **(pair of toe-knob sandals)***

probably Hoshiapur, Punjab, Northern India, late 19th century
shisham wood (rosewood), ivory
253 x 95 x 80 mm
Vatican *Anima Mundi* Museum, inv. 111998.2

This pair of toe-knob sandals belongs to a distinct and popular type of Indian footwear known as *paduka*. Its design is extremely minimalist, but perfectly suited to a hot climate, as the sole of the foot is raised from a hot, wet or dusty ground. More elaborate versions like the pair shown here might have been used in a wealthy household, perhaps in the *hammam* (bathhouse). Interestingly, its characteristic style of ivory inlay (*dant ka kam*) is inspired by Islamic arts, but its inlayers tended to be Hindus.

*Object not exhibited in Australia

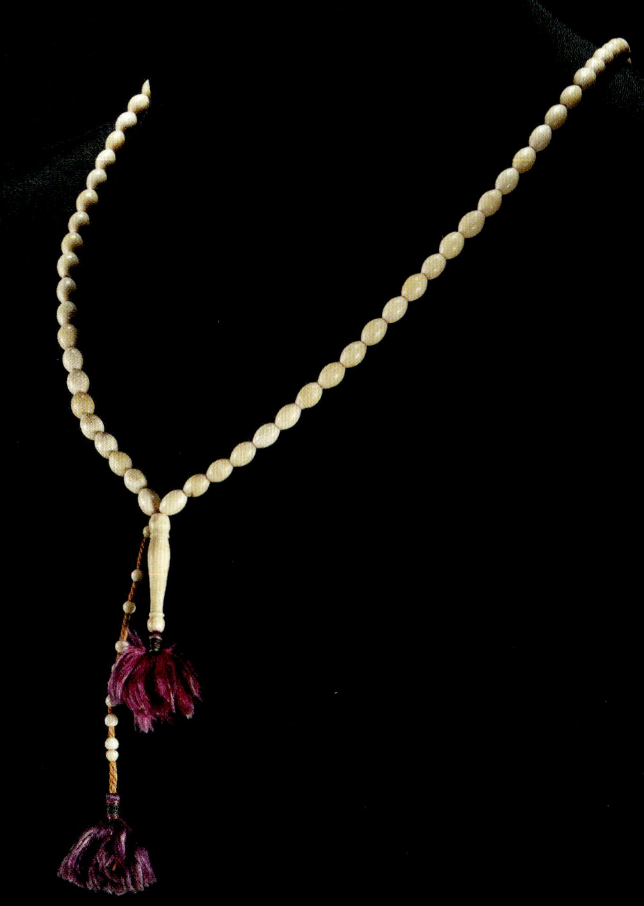

Misbaha (ivory prayer beads)*

Agra, Uttar Pradesh, India, late 19th – early 20th century
ivory, cotton, silk
600 x 15 mm
Vatican *Anima Mundi* Museum, inv. 126093

In Muslim cultures throughout the world, the misbaha is used for the meditative remembrance and glorification of Allah. The beads are moved along while repeating in succession the three phrases 'Subhan Allah' (Glory be to Allah), 'Al Hamdulillah' (Praise be to Allah) and 'Allahu Akbar' (Allah is the Greatest). Islamic traditions vary slightly with regard to the number of times each phrase should be repeated. Most advocate 33 times each, but some prayer beads like this reflect the opinion in some places that 'Allahu Akbar' should be repeated 34 times.

*Object not exhibited in Australia

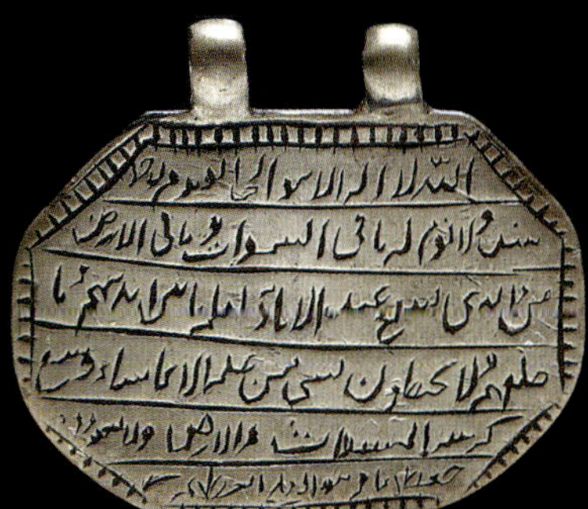

Ta'wiz (eight-sided amulet pendant with Qur'anic inscriptions)

India, late 19th century
silver
30 x 34 x 4 mm
Vatican *Anima Mundi* Museum, inv. 122035

The surface of this pendant shows Verse 255 (Ayat al-Kursi) from Chapter 2, 'Al-Baqarah', of the Holy Qur'an. Throughout the history of Muslim cultures, the so-called 'Throne verse' was believed to have particularly strong, beneficial and protective qualities. According to Islamic tradition, the Prophet (pbuh) himself is said to have considered this verse as the most exalted in the Holy Qur'an and encouraged Muslims to recite it to call upon Allah's protection and in their quest to attain paradise.

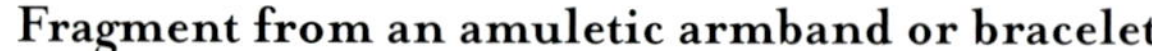

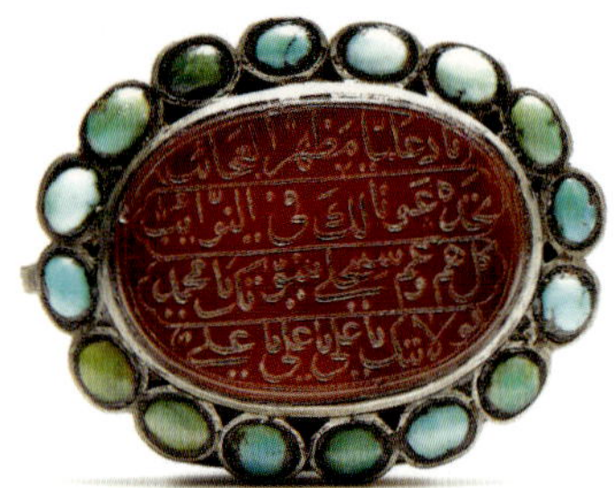

Fragment from an amuletic armband or bracelet

probably Northern India, late 19th century
base silver, carnelian, turquoise
45 x 34 x 17 mm
Vatican *Anima Mundi* Museum, inv. 122051

Islamic prayers and words of thanksgiving to the Prophet Muhammad (pbuh) and Ali, his cousin, son-in-law and one of the first four rightly guided caliphs in the history of the Islamic community, are inscribed onto this amulet. Pieces like this could be worn openly, or more often — for maximum benefit and to avoid pollution — beneath the wearer's clothing, either around the neck, arm and wrist or within turbans and other clothing accessories.

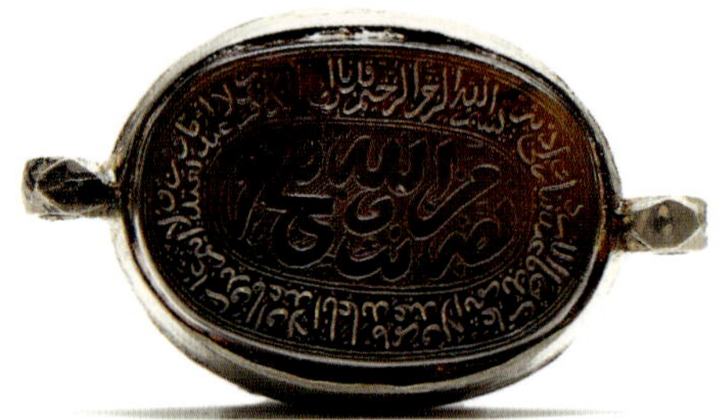

Fragment from an amuletic armband or bracelet

Northern India, late 19th - early 20th century
black semiprecious stone, silver
50 x 30 x 15 mm
Vatican *Anima Mundi* Museum, inv. 122058

The central Qur'anic inscription of this amulet is taken from Chapter 61 (Al-Saff), Verse 13: 'Help from Allah [against your enemies] and a near victory'. Around the edge runs Chapter 109 (Al-Kafiroun):

> *In the Name of Allah, the Most Gracious, the Most Merciful. Say 'Oh Al-Kafirun (disbelievers in Allah, in His Oneness, in His Angels, in His Books, in His Messengers, in the Day of Resurrection, and in predestination)! I worship not that which you worship. Nor will you worship that which I worship. And I shall not worship that which you are worshipping. Nor will you worship that which I worship. To you be your religion, and to me my religion.*

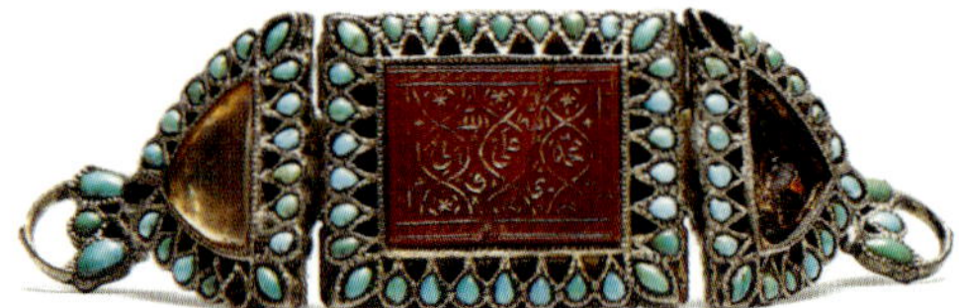

Amuletic jewellery element

probably Northern India, late 19th century
silver, agate, turquoise, crystal or glass
30 x 110 x 11 mm
Vatican *Anima Mundi* Museum, inv. 122049

This beautifully designed piece of jewellery may have come from an armlet, secured to the upper arm with a string or band. Within the interlacing central design, the names of Allah, the Prophet Muhammad (pbuh) and Ali appear. Agates, particularly carnelian, and turquoise stones were used for amulets and talismans in many Muslim cultures as they were believed to have particularly strong, protective qualities.

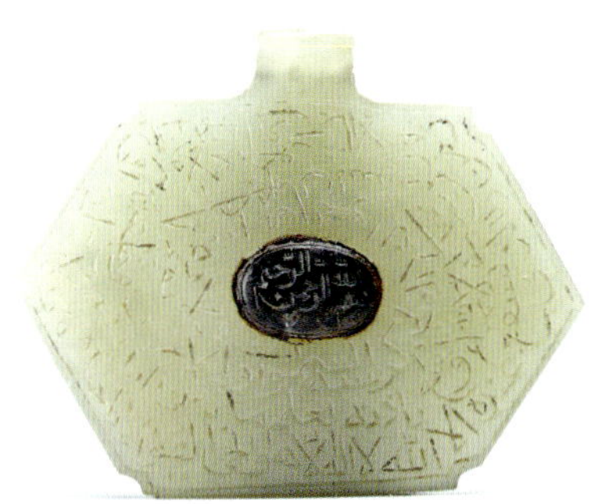

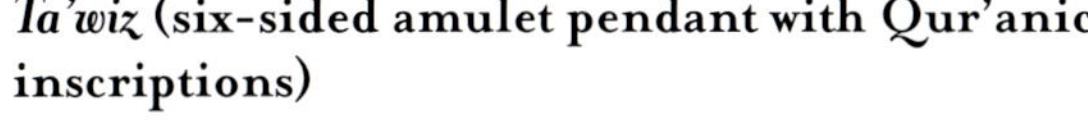

Ta'wiz (six-sided amulet pendant with Qur'anic inscriptions)

probably Northern India, 1843
jade, rock crystal
47 x 53 x 6 mm
Vatican *Anima Mundi* Museum, inv. 122041

This pendant shows the Bismillah — 'In the Name of Allah, the Most Gracious, the Most Merciful' — under the central rock crystal. The remaining text presents Verse 255 from Chapter 2 (Al-Baqarah), known as the 'Throne verse' (Ayat al-Kursi). Qur'anic amulets have been popular in many Muslim cultures across the centuries. Their quotations were carefully chosen to pray for God's blessings and protection. The choice of material was also significant. Jade and rock crystal were associated with preserving good health and purity.

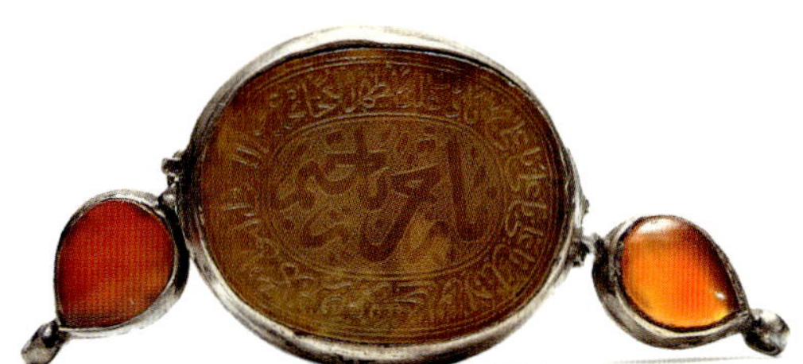

Fragment from an amuletic armband or bracelet

probably Northern India, 19th century
silver, agate, chalcedony
75 x 28 x 7 mm
Vatican *Anima Mundi* Museum, inv. 122054

This amulet carries Islamic prayers and words of thanksgiving to the Prophet Muhammad (pbuh) and Ali. The engravers of amulets like this one were highly skilled artists who had to be versed in all the classical calligraphic styles as well as the precise mastery of the incredibly fine cutting tools needed to transfer them onto the stone.

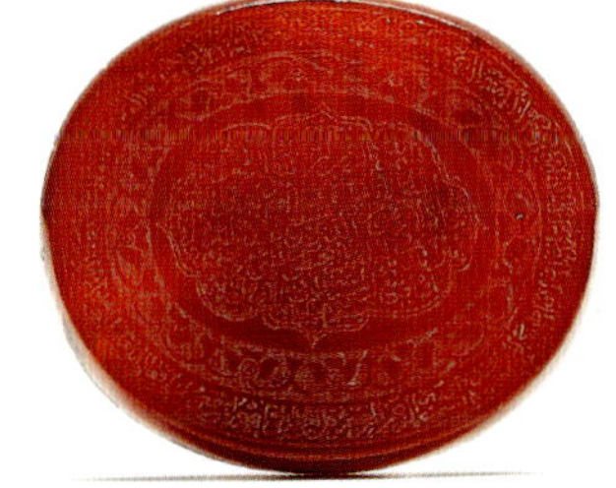

Ta'wiz (carnelian amulet with Qur'anic inscriptions)

Northern India, 1748
28 x 22 x 4 mm
Vatican *Anima Mundi* Museum, inv. 122045

This extremely delicate and elegantly engraved, oval carnelian stone shows the Bismillah and Verse 225 from Chapter 2 (Al-Baqarah) of the Holy Qur'an. The border around the edge contains the stone's date and Chapter 112 (Al-Ikhlas), which powerfully affirms the oneness and omnipotence of Allah.

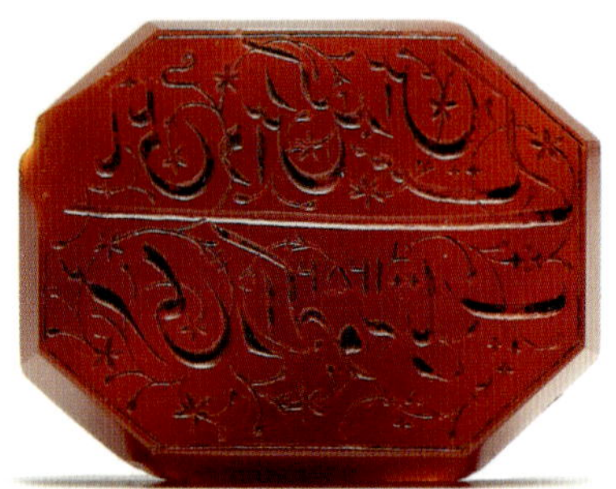

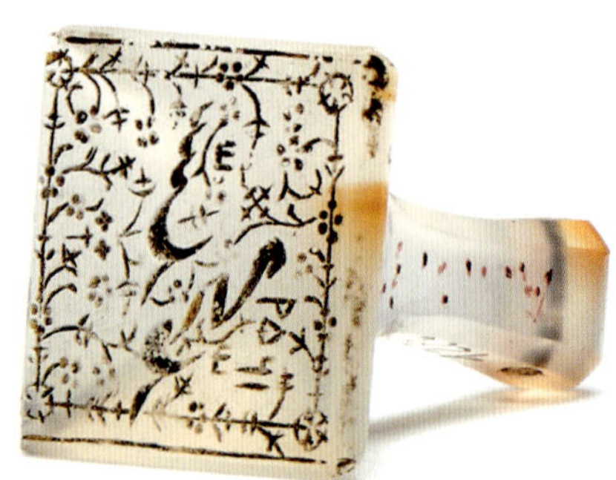

Seal stone

India, 1836–37
carnelian
30 x 40 x 7 mm
Vatican *Anima Mundi* Museum, inv. 122043

A fascinatingly deceptive example of interfaith and intercultural fusion, this seal with its elegant *nasta'liq* inscription appears to give the name of a Hindu dignitary, His Eminence Rāghav-Pratāp, Bānke-dās the fosterling (?) of Kabi-dās, who lived during the very last years of the Mughal Empire.

سری راگھو پرتاپ بانکے داس رست کبداس کے ٩٥٢٥

srī rāghav pratāp [b]ānke dās rust kabi-dās ke 1252

Our gratitude to Dr Saqib Baburai (SOAS) for helping with the translation and transcription of the inscription on this item.

Personal seal

probably Northern India, 1835
white agate
35 x 20 x 20 mm
Vatican *Anima Mundi* Museum, inv. 122047

Not an amulet but a personal seal, this elegant little artefact would have been used to mark personal correspondence. The name of the owner, Sayyid Mohammad, executed in delicate *nasta'liq* script, and the date are set against a background of extremely fine, vegetal scrolling. Agates were well suited for seals as the sealing wax did not stick to them. At the same time, they were believed to promote prosperity and good health.

We are grateful to Dr Saqib Baburi (SOAS) for the transcription of this item.

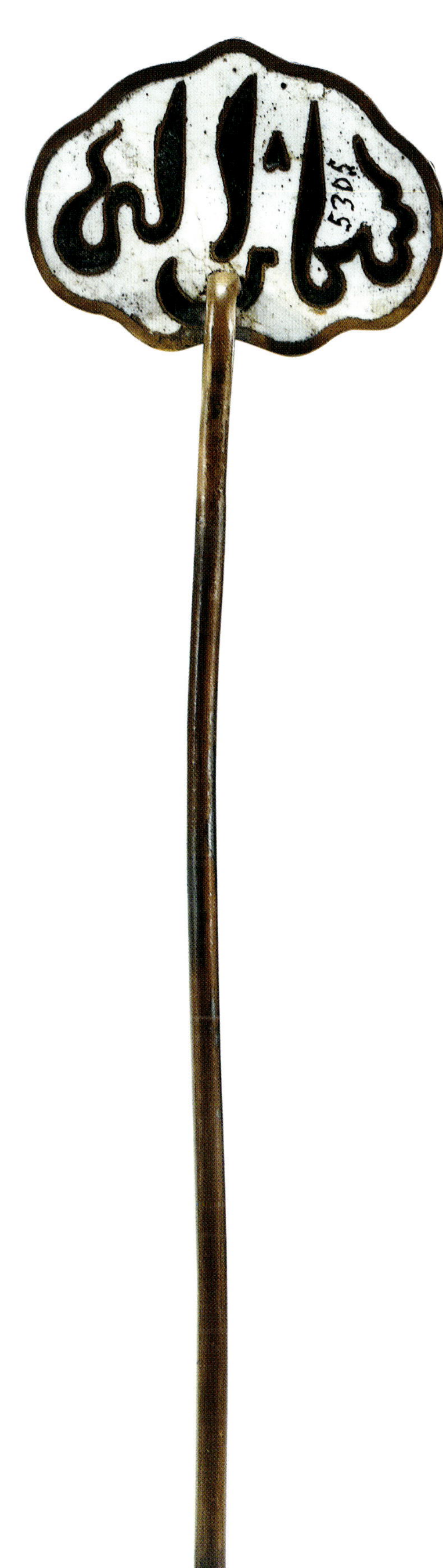

Sceptre or standard with Islamic inscription

China, Qing Dynasty, early 18th century
brass, black-and-white cloisonné enamels
202 x 58 mm (overall width); 4 mm (diameter)
Vatican *Anima Mundi* Museum, inv. 120603

'Subhan Allah' (God is glorious) is written on the lobed finial of this long staff. Its style appears to be a fusion of a traditional, ceremonial staff common in China and an Islamic staff. The *ruyi* (Chinese 如意 'according to your wishes') sceptre symbolised longevity and good fortune and was used during auspicious occasions and celebrations. Certain types of Islamic standards and staffs were used in religious ceremonies or by Islamic mystics, particularly in Iran and South Asia.

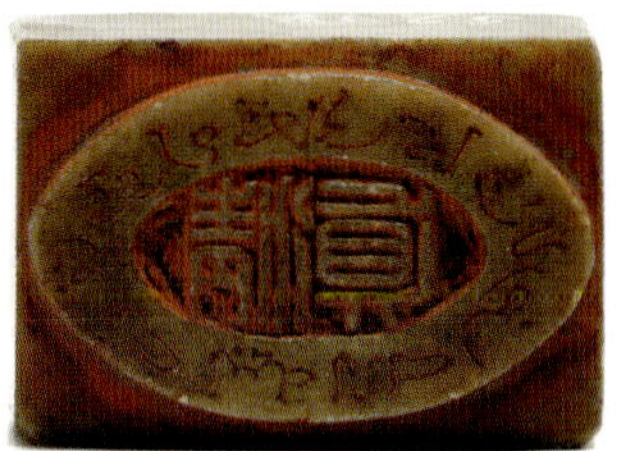

Red-dyed jade seal with Arabic and Chinese inscriptions

China, Qing Dynasty, 18th century
43 x 30 x 22 mm
Vatican *Anima Mundi* Museum, inv. 120597

Though minute in shape, this jade seal reveals a fascinating intercultural and interfaith fusion of Chinese and Islamic elements. The Chinese characters in the centre read 'Qing Zhen' ('Muslim/Islam'). The Arabic inscription quotes a part of Verse 168 from Chapter 2 (Al-Baqarah) of the Holy Qur'an: 'of that which is lawful and good on the earth' followed by the Arabic word '*haqeeq*' ('worthy, fit'). The combination of this term with a Qur'anic quotation from a verse calling upon Muslims to eat what is lawful, suggests that this seal was once used to certify a food item as 'halal', i.e. permitted for consumption by Muslims.

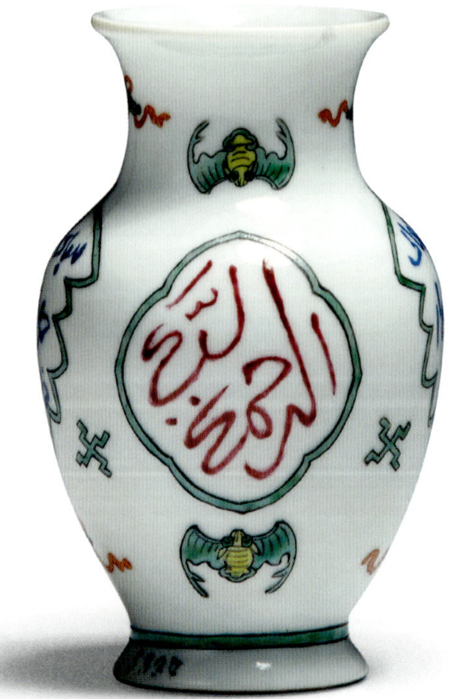

Vase with Islamic inscriptions and Buddhist symbols

China, Qing Dynasty, 18th–19th century
underglaze-painted porcelain
125 x 80 mm (diameter)
Vatican *Anima Mundi* Museum, inv. 120613

This vase combines Islamic inscriptions with auspicious Chinese and Buddhist symbols. The cursive blue inscriptions are taken from the Holy Qur'an. One cartouche contains Verse 22 from Chapter 83 (Al-Mutaffifeen): 'Verily, Al-Abraar (the pious and righteous) will be in Delight (Paradise)'. The second one shows the first sentence of Verse 185 from Chapter 3 (Al-'Imraan): 'Everyone shall taste death'. The red inscriptions praise the omnipotence and mercy of Allah. The small Buddhist symbols — the colourful pearl decorated with ribbons (not seen), the swastika and the ribboned hat (not seen) — evoke longevity, justice and perfection. The bat stands for happiness, as it shares its homophone with the Chinese character FU, which denotes this sentiment.

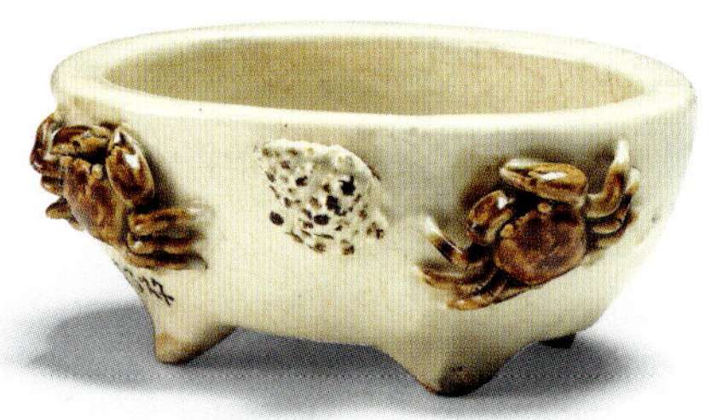

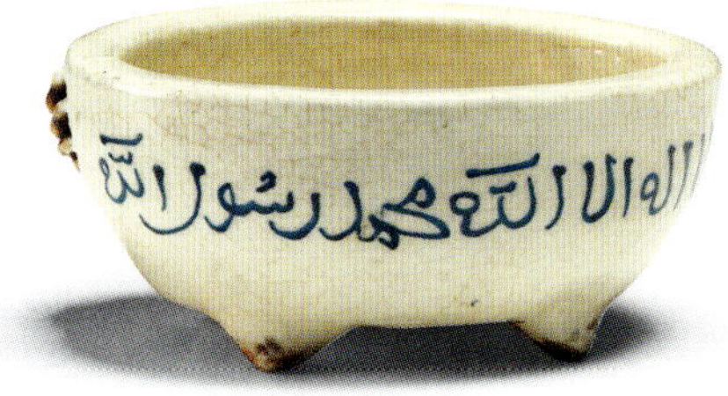

Bowl used for cleaning calligraphy brushes

China, Qing Dynasty, late 18th – early 19th century
white porcelain, underglaze cobalt pigment, clear and coloured glazes
47 x 11 x 91 mm
Vatican *Anima Mundi* Museum, inv. 120607

This small bowl combines traditional Chinese with Islamic influences. One side shows the Islamic Profession of Faith (*shahada*), which states: 'There is no god but Allah, Mohammad is the Messenger of Allah'. The crabs on the other side symbolise harmony in Chinese Buddhist culture, while the conch shells represent purity.

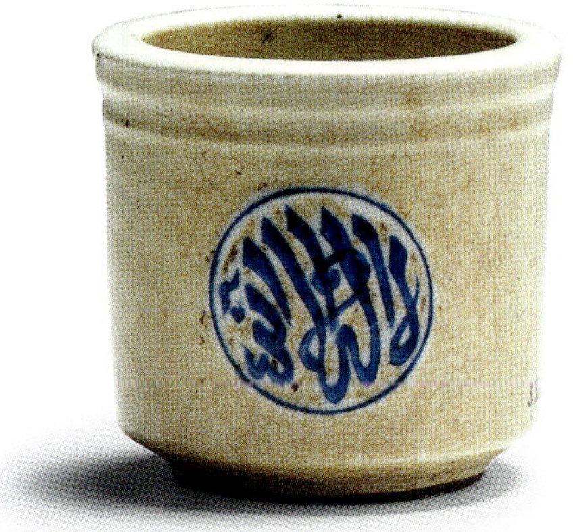

Shahada **(censer with the Islamic Profession of Faith)**

China, Qing Dynasty, 18th century
underglaze-painted porcelain with crackled glaze
119 x 111 mm
Vatican *Anima Mundi* Museum, inv. 120606

Originally part of an incense-burning set traditionally used in a Chinese mosque, this vessel is decorated with three roundels containing raised Islamic inscriptions in the so-called Sini (Chinese) style. The inscriptions read: 'The most virtuous remembrance of Allah Is', 'There Is no god but Allah' and 'Mohammad is the Messenger of Allah'.

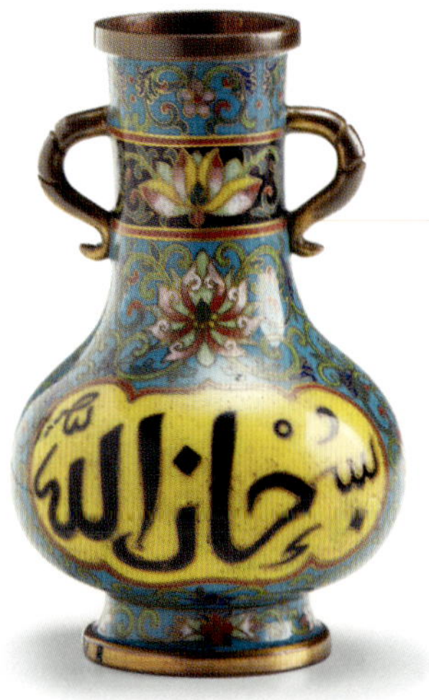

Cloisonné vase with Islamic inscriptions

China, Qing Dynasty, early 18th century
brass, polychrome enamels
143 x 43 mm (diameter of mouth)
Vatican *Anima Mundi* Museum, inv. 120592

Together with an incense box and burner, this vase once formed part of an incense set used in a mosque. It is inscribed with the words 'Praise be to Allah' and 'Glory be to Allah'. The vase, together with the other Chinese enamel and porcelain in the exhibition, belongs to a collection of around 40 artefacts sent to the Vatican in 1925 by Cav. Ufficiale Giuseppe Ros, who worked at the Italian Consulate in Shanghai and had assembled a significant collection of Chinese Islamic items.

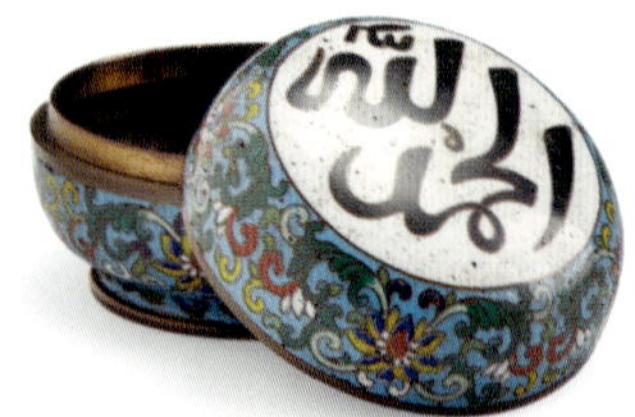

Cloisonné incense box with Islamic inscription

China, Qing Dynasty, early 18th century
brass, polychrome enamels
100 x 109 mm (diameter)
Vatican *Anima Mundi* Museum, inv. 120601

This lidded enamel box, inscribed 'Praise be to Allah', once formed part of a set of implements used for the burning of incense in a Chinese mosque. The cloisonné technique came to China in the 14th century from Byzantium, perhaps introduced by Muslims, who subsequently seem to have specialised in its execution. The decoration was achieved by gluing extremely fine strips of metal (French '*cloisons*') onto the surface. The resulting compartments were filled with coloured enamel pastes, and the object fired to fuse the enamel to the metal.

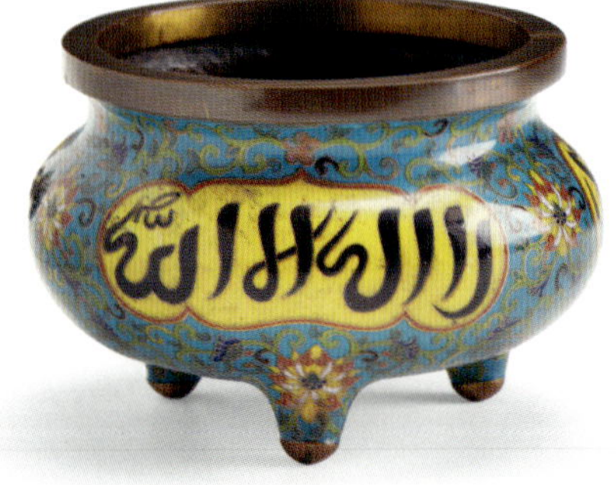

Cloisonné incense burner with Islamic inscriptions

China, Qing Dynasty, early 18th century
brass, polychrome enamels
107 x 143 mm (diameter of mouth)
Vatican *Anima Mundi* Museum, inv. 120623

Originally combined with a vase and incense box to serve in a Chinese mosque, this vessel is decorated with three cartouches with inscriptions in the Sini (Chinese) style: 'The most virtuous remembrance of Allah is', 'There is no god but Allah' and 'Mohammad is the Messenger of Allah'.

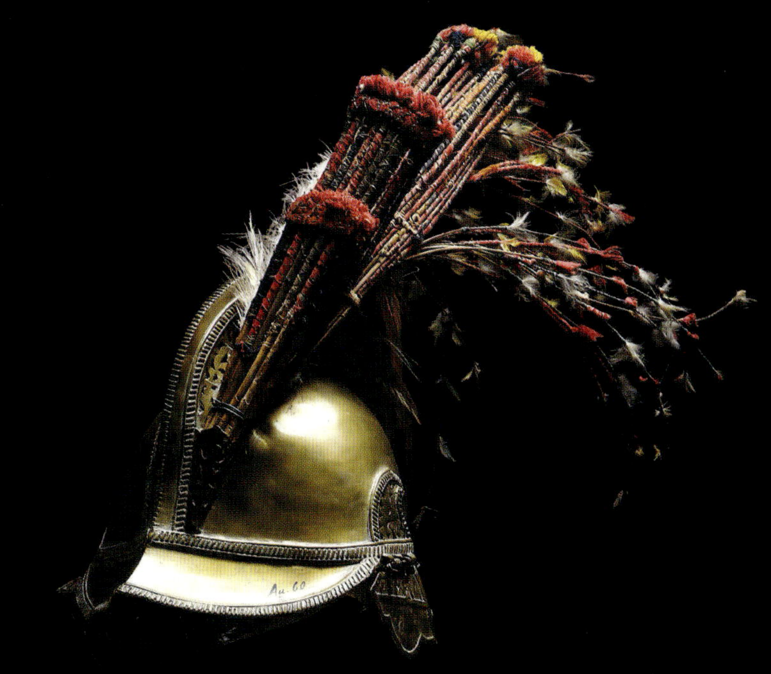

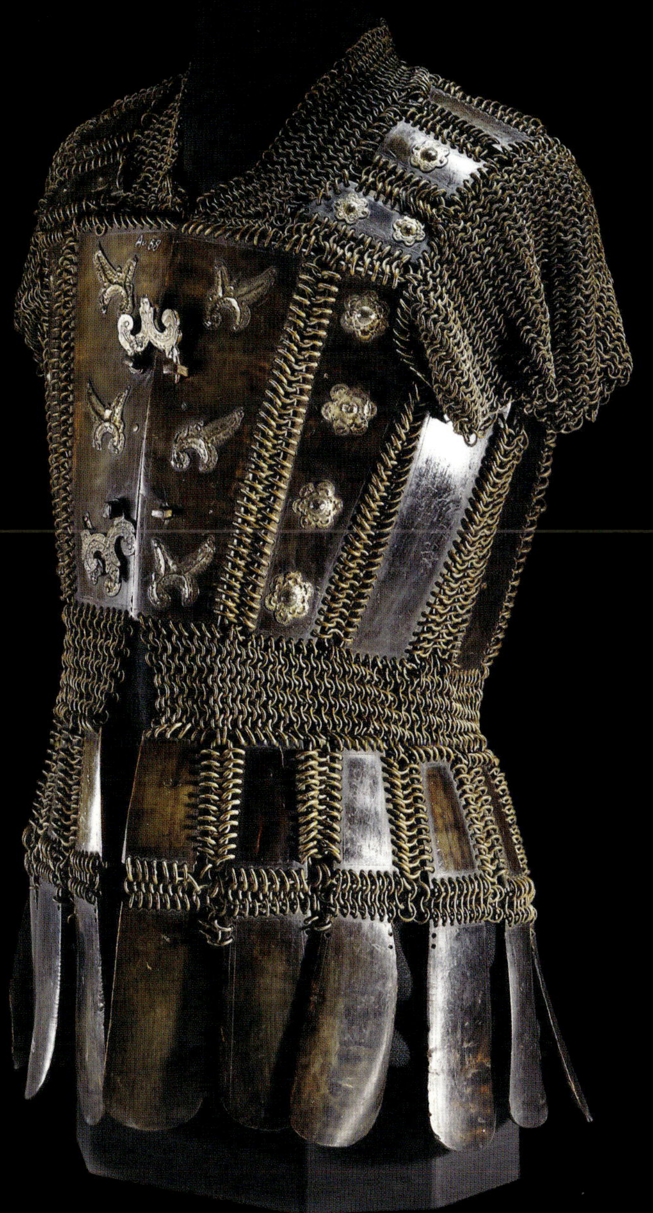

Kurab-a-kulang marano (Moro war armour) and helmet

Jolo Island, Sulu Archipelago, Mindanao, Philippines,
18th – 19th century
brass, brass chain mail, carabao (buffalo) horn (armour);
brass, feathers, plant fibre, wood (helmet)
670 x 450 x 250 mm (armour); 470 x 280 x 322 mm (helmet)
Vatican *Anima Mundi* Museum, inv. 123358; 123514

The Moros (or Bangsamoro) form the Indigenous Muslim population of the Southern Philippines, based mainly in Mindanao and Sulu. They received their name from the Spanish, who colonised the Philippines in the 16th century and incorporated them into their empire for the next 300 years. This armour and helmet clearly copy Spanish prototypes and would have been used in the Moros' ongoing struggle for freedom and independence.

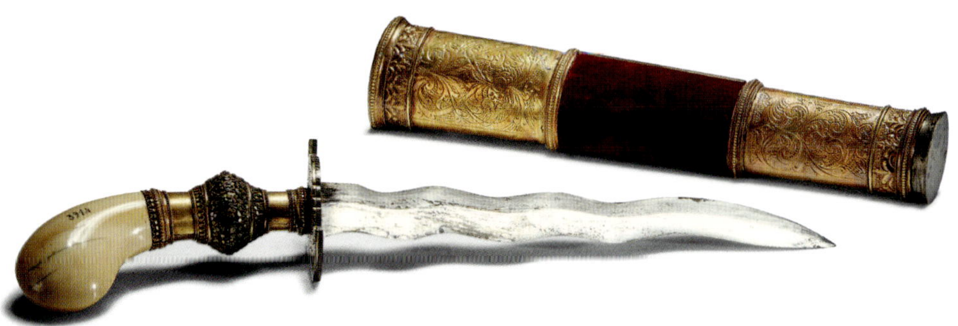

Kalis (dagger with wavy blade and sheath)*

collected in Lanao Province, Mindanao, Philippines, 19th century
iron, gilt copper alloy, gold, ivory, velvet, wood, silver
325 x 85 mm (dagger); 244 x 47 mm (sheath)
Vatican *Anima Mundi* Museum, inv. 101275.2

*Object not exhibited in Australia

Given to Pope Pius XI in April 1934 by the Apostolic Delegation of the Philippine Islands, this dagger — according to museum records — once belonged to a senior member of the Muslim aristocracy ruling the Lanao province of Mindanao Island. The sultanate of Lanao was founded in the 16th century following the arrival of Muslim missionaries and traders from the Middle East, India and Malaya, who peacefully propagated Islam in the region. The dagger's last Indigenous owner, Datu Tapuki Pualas, is reported to have inherited the weapon from his father, Sultan Sa Pualas. Handed down through the generations, the *kalis* was a powerful symbol of authority, status and divine protection.

Moro ornamental bracelets and buttons

Western Palawan, Southern Philippines, late 19th - early 20th century
copper alloy, gilt silver, semiprecious stones, glass
80 x 34 mm, 60 x 38 mm (bracelets); approx. 20 mm (button diameter)
Vatican *Anima Mundi* Museum, inv. 100143; 100145; 100154.2

These intricate items of jewellery reflect the multicultural artistic influences that came together in the arts of the island cultures of the Philippines. Indian, Indonesian, Chinese, Arab and European elements combine in their designs, which copy gold and silver prototypes.

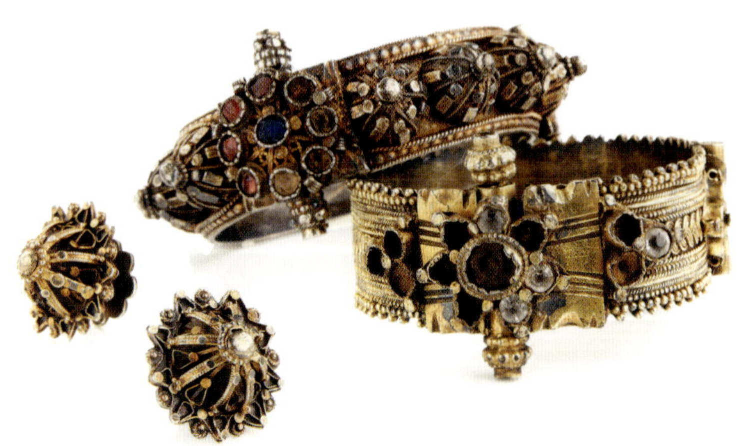

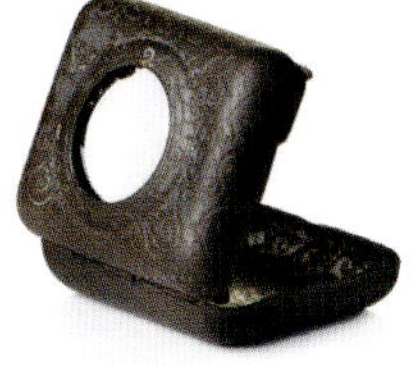

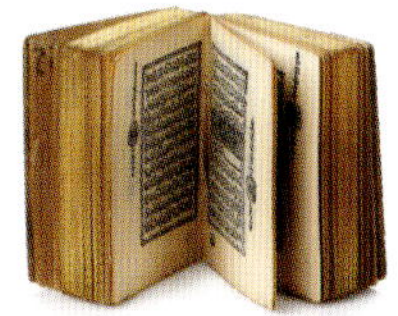

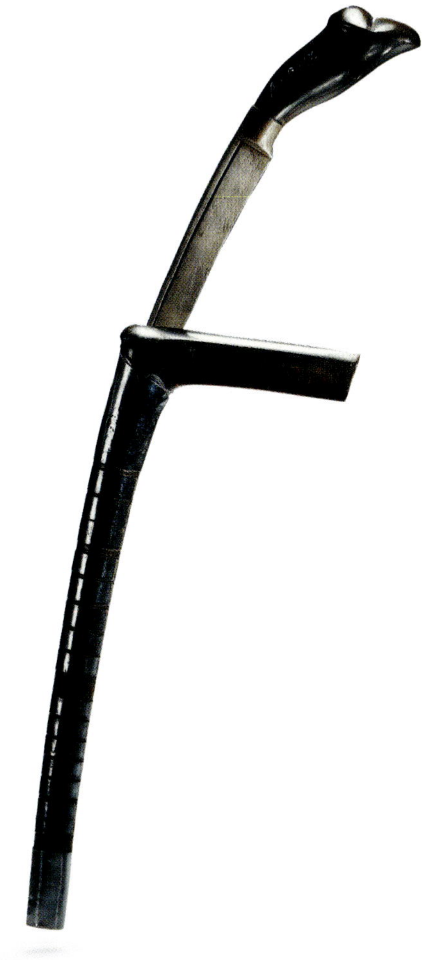

Locket with printed miniature Qur'an

collected in Indonesia, early 20th century
paper, base metal, glass
35 x 28 x 13 mm
Vatican *Anima Mundi* Museum, inv. 100131.2

The miniature Qur'an of this locket, once worn for blessing and divine protection, was first printed in Glasgow in about 1900 by publisher David Bryce (1845–1923). Bryce had developed successful techniques to transform ordinary books into tiny, yet still perfectly legible, miniature versions. Many, like this Qur'an, were housed in metal lockets with a small, central magnifying glass. Similar Qur'an lockets were issued to Muslim soldiers fighting in the First World War. Perhaps this locket reached Indonesia during that time.

Sword with scabbard

Minangkabau, West Sumatra, Indonesia, 18th century
wood, dark horn, iron, white metal
245 x 47 mm
Vatican *Anima Mundi* Museum, inv. 124782.2

Said to have formed part of the 18th-century collections of Cardinal Stefano Borgia, this dagger was once used by the indigenous people of the Minangkabau highlands of West Sumatra in Indonesia. The Minangkabau are Muslims with a proud history and rich culture, famous for traditional textile, jewellery and metal arts. More than 60 per cent — about one billion — of the world's Muslims live in South and South-East Asia, with Indonesia as a major hub.

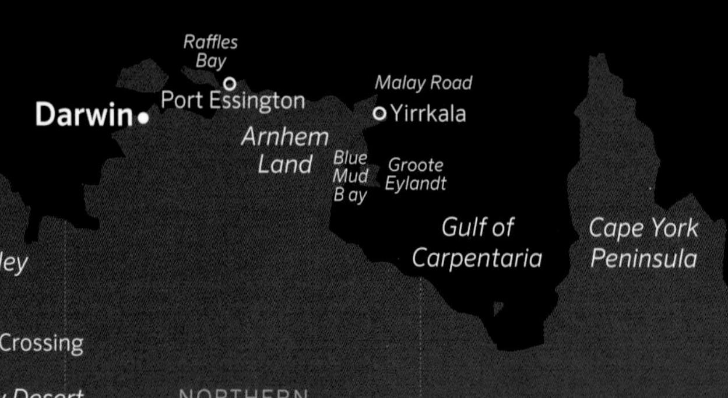
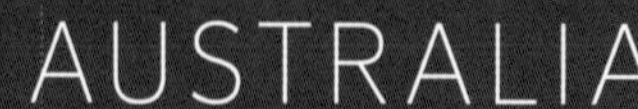
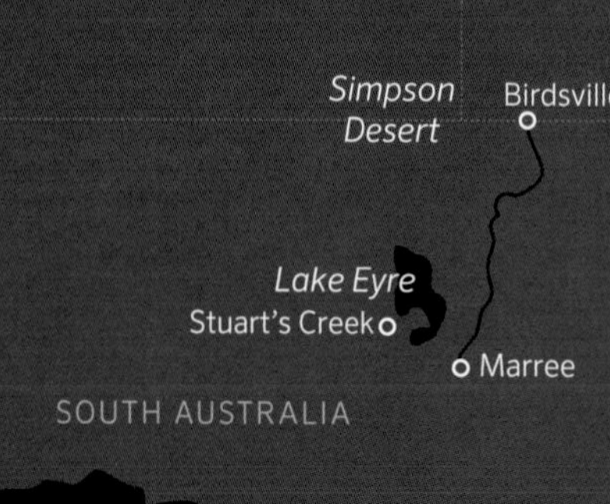
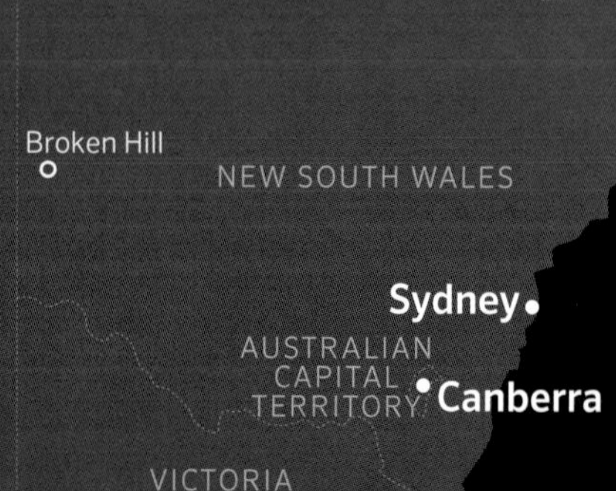
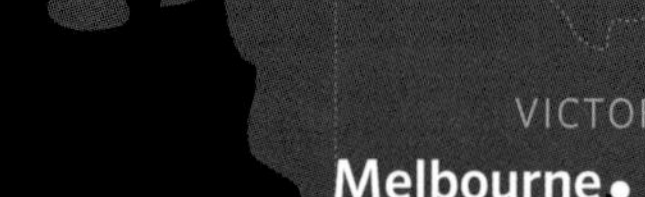
Sulawesi
Makassar
Bone
INDONESIA
Raffles Bay
Port Essington
Darwin
Malay Road
Yirrkala
Arnhem Land
Blue Mud Bay
Groote Eylandt
Gulf of Carpentaria
Cape York Peninsula
Kimberley
Fitzroy River
Fitzroy Crossing
Great Sandy Desert
NORTHERN TERRITORY
AUSTRALIA
QUEENSLAND
Bejah Hill
Simpson Desert
Birdsville
Lindsay Gordon Lagoon
Lake Way township
Brisbane
Geraldton
WESTERN AUSTRALIA
Lake Eyre
Stuart's Creek
Marree
SOUTH AUSTRALIA
Perth
Fremantle
Broken Hill
NEW SOUTH WALES
Port Augusta
Sydney
Adelaide
AUSTRALIAN CAPITAL TERRITORY
Canberra
VICTORIA
Melbourne
TASMANIA
Hobart

Islam in Australia

From the 18th to the early 20th centuries, the period during which most of the objects in this exhibition were created and used, people of Islamic faith made unique contributions to Australian history. The Makasar traders from Sulawesi were the first of these people to arrive on Australian shores. For nearly two centuries, their trading fleets rode the annual monsoonal winds southwards in search of trepang (sea cucumber or bêche de mer), an item prized in China for its culinary and medical uses. These visitors developed mutually beneficial trading and working relationships with local Aboriginal people along the coasts of Northern Australia. The exhibition traces the earliest recorded evidence of this cross-cultural encounter, and explores the economic enterprise that sustained it.

The second group of Muslims to arrive in Australia were the cameleers, known as 'Afghans' or 'Ghans', who came from parts of India and present-day Pakistan (then British India and Afghanistan). Sponsored to assist with the exploration and development of Central Australia, they were well-equipped to navigate and survive in its vast and inhospitable desert country. The exhibition highlights the legendary figure of Bejah Dervish, perhaps the most famous Muslim cameleer. Today, descendants of the Muslim cameleers who remained in Australia are justifiably proud of their ancestors' incredible feats of endurance and fortitude.

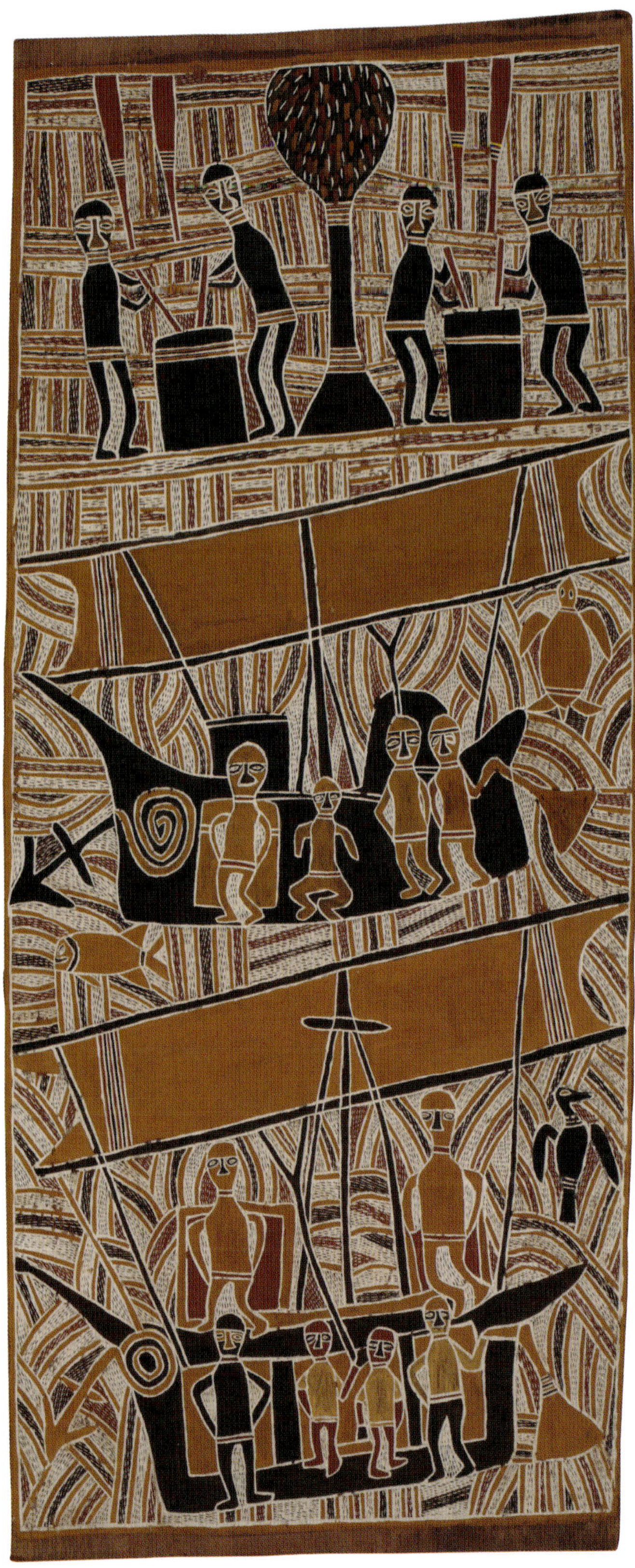

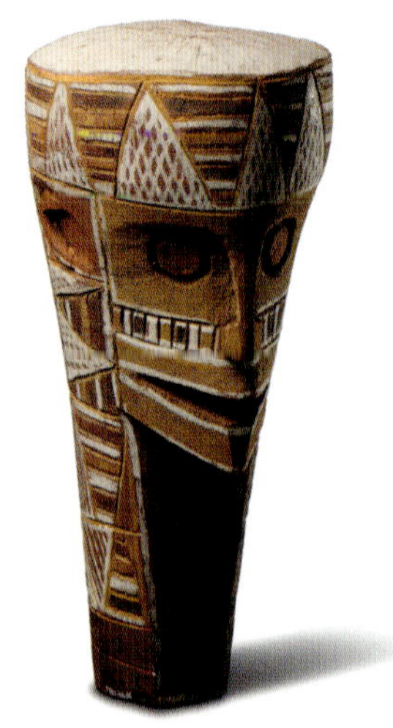

Head of a Makasar

by Munggurrawuy Yunupingu (about 1907–1978), Gumatj clan, Yolngu people
collected by Professor Ronald Berndt at Yirrkala, Arnhem Land, Northern Territory, about 1946
wood, natural pigments, adhesive
310 x 140 x 140 mm
National Museum of Australia, 1985.0083.0038

Yolngu artist Munggurrawuy Yunupingu was a significant bark painter and wood carver. He was also a leader in the Yolngu fight for land in the 1960s and 1970s. In 1935, he was one of the first artists to produce barks for sale at the Yirrkala mission. In the mid-20th century, Munggurrawuy and other artists at Yirrkala extended their range of subjects to carving the heads of historical and traditional characters.

Makasar Boiling Down Trepang

by Mathaman Marika (1920–1970), Rirratjingu clan, Yolngu people
collected by JA Davidson at Yirrkala, Arnhem Land, Northern Territory, 1964
bark, natural pigments
1350 x 575 mm
National Museum of Australia, 1985.0259.0095

The upper scene of this painting depicts a typical trepang processing site, with black-painted Aboriginal men boiling the trepang in large metal cauldrons under a stylised mangrove tree. In the two lower scenes, the yellow-painted Makasar fishermen are shown commanding their distinctive *prau* with its individual cabins, sails, paddles and anchors.

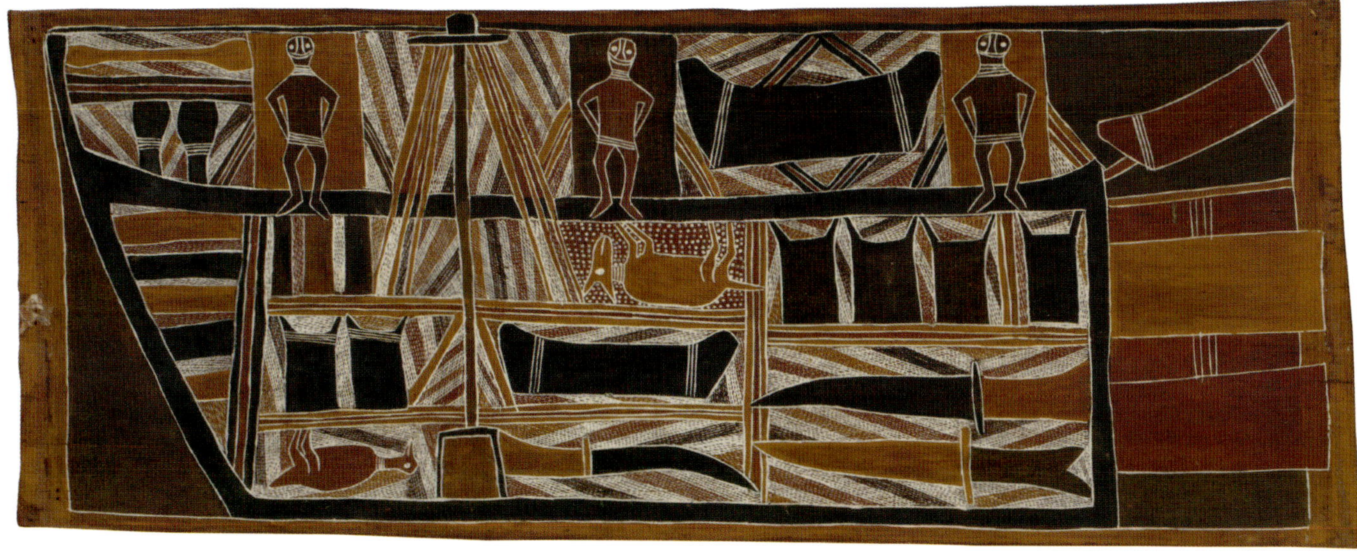

Makasar Prau

by Mawalan Marika (1908–1967), Rirratjingu clan, Yolngu people
collected by Dorothy Bennett at Yirrkala, Arnhem Land, Northern Territory, 1964
bark, natural pigments
530 x 1320 mm
National Museum of Australia, 1985.0246.0002

This painting reveals an internal view of a *prau*, and shows the new technologies introduced by the Makasar, together with the exotic goods they brought with them. We can see the tripod mast, rudders and the captain's and crew's cabins. Details include several canoes, a yellow goat, a red rooster, black rice sacks and three types of steel knives.

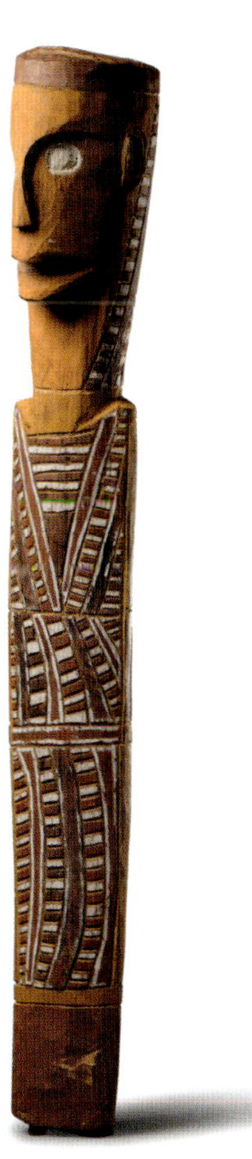

Makasar Wuramu Figure

by Munggurrawuy Yunupingu (about 1907–1978), Gumatj clan, Yolngu people
collected by Professor Ronald Berndt at Yirrkala, Arnhem Land, Northern Territory, about 1946
wood, natural pigments, adhesive
575 x 80 x 80 mm
National Museum of Australia, 1985.0083.0034

Munggurrawuy made these sculptures, known as *wuramu* figures, for anthropologist Ronald Berndt in the 1940s. *Wuramu* figures were derived from rituals relating to Makasar burials and incorporated into Yolngu mythology and ceremony. *Wuramu* figures are usually depicted with a *songkok*, or Muslim cap, which can be clearly seen in this carving.

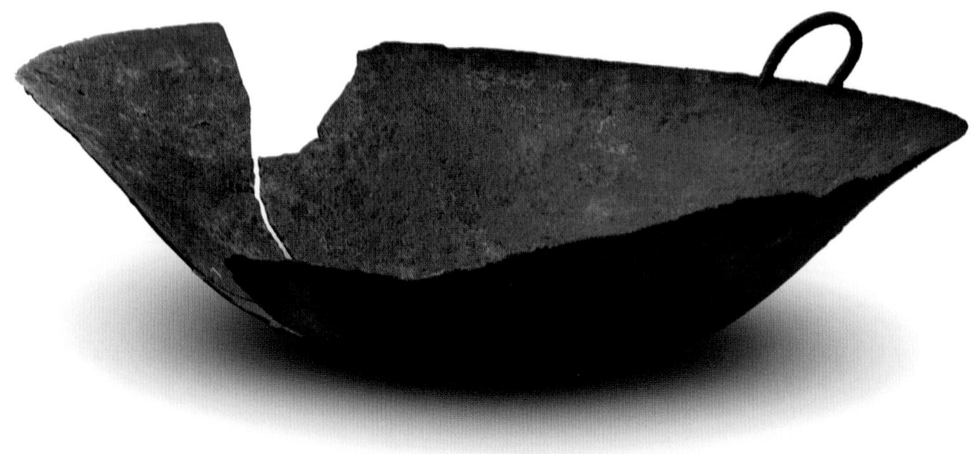

***Kawa* (cauldron)**

Record Point, Port Essington, Cobourg Peninsula, Northern Territory, 19th century
cast iron
225 x 920mm (diameter at widest point)
Museum and Art Gallery of the Northern Territory, Gift of Cedric Petterson, TH93/018.1, TH93/018.2

Kawa (Makasar for 'cauldron'), used for boiling the trepang in salt water, were the most valuable items on a trepang-processing site. Made from heavy-gauge iron, they were set into rows of stone fireplaces and carried from camp to camp. This rusting and fragile vessel, recovered from a Northern Territory beach in 1909, remains the only complete example to have survived in Australia.

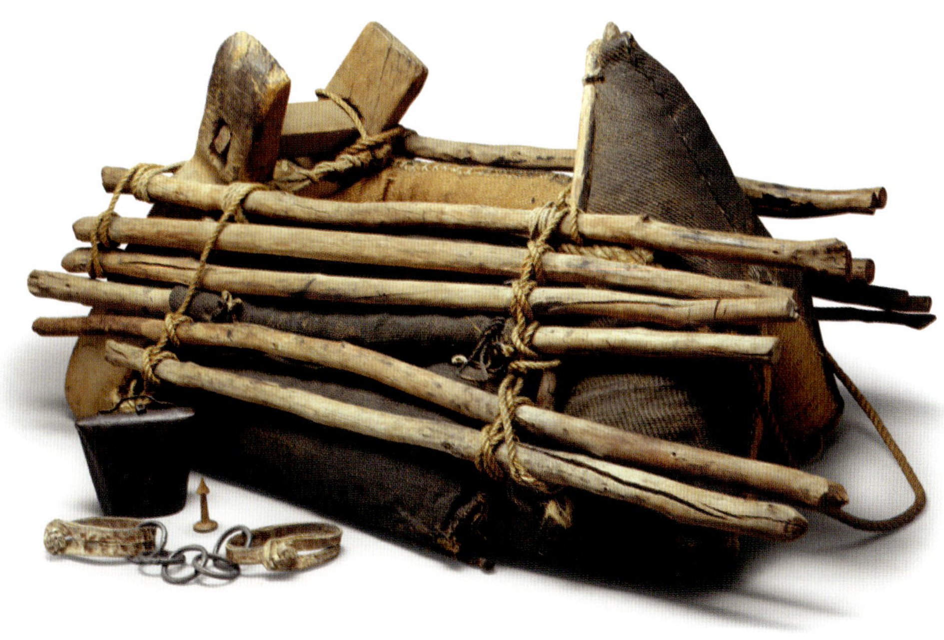

Nosepeg, bell and hobbles

South Australia, about 1870–1900
wood, metal, leather
Museum of Applied Arts and Science, Sydney, H6926

These objects assisted in the control and management of working camels. The timber nosepeg, inserted into the camel's nostril, allowed them to be safely led, while the metal bell, worn by all camels, ensured the herd stayed together at night. The rawhide hobbles prevented camels from moving swiftly, while still allowing them the freedom to graze.

Camel packsaddle

South Australia, about 1870–1900
wood, hessian, straw, rope, timber cross-sticks
630 x 700 mm
Museum of Applied Arts and Science, Sydney, purchased 1962, H6926

This saddle and the other camel handling objects were retrieved from a northern South Australian station by Inland explorer Michael Terry in 1961. The saddle is the only known surviving example of hundreds of similar saddles, made to the same simple but efficient design by Muslim cameleers. It comprises a timber framed hessian packsaddle covered with straw. The saddle protected the camel's back and hump from chaffing, and if properly fitted and carefully maintained, allowed camels to comfortably carry heavy loads for extended periods.

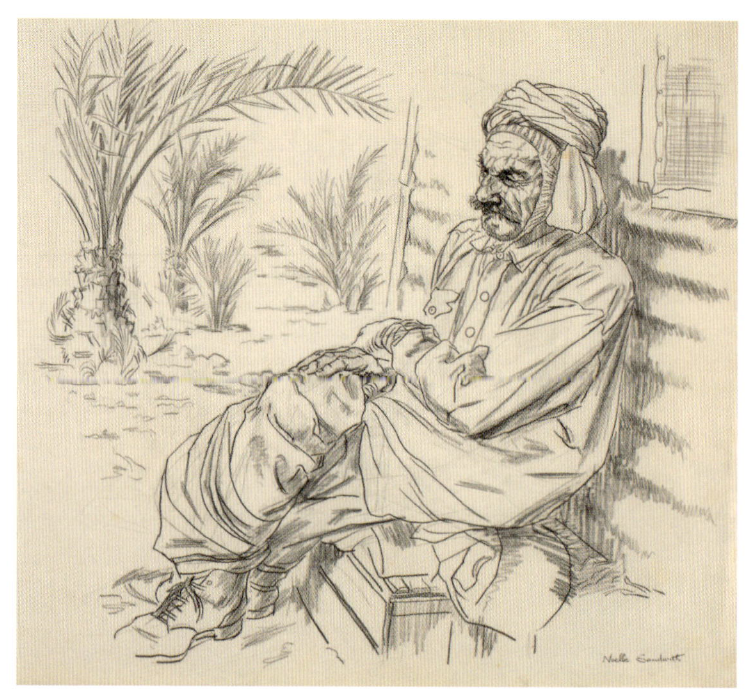

Said Goolamadeen, Retired Camel Driver

by Noelle Sandwith
Marree, South Australia, 1953
graphite, paper
561 x 764 mm
National Museum of Australia, 1993.0100.0042

Said Goolamadeen was born in Baluchistan in 1870 and came to Australia in 1901 to work with camels. He settled near Broken Hill, in far western New South Wales, before moving to Marree, where he died in the early 1960s. Noelle Sandwith, who sketched his portrait in 1953, calls him 'the last survivor of the so called "Afghans"', and describes him as always wearing his 'national dress, his turban [which] crowned a Balaclava helmet'.

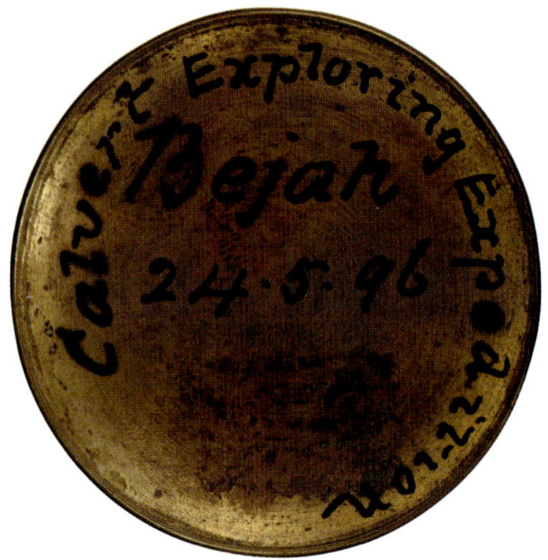

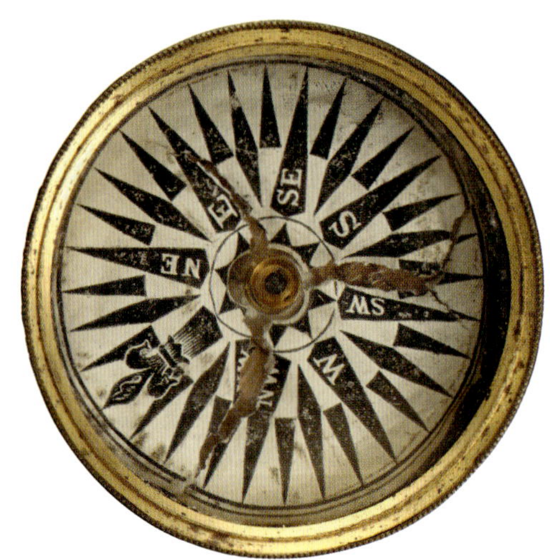

Compass given to Bejah Dervish by Calvert Exploring Expedition leader, LA Wells, on 24 May 1896

brass, paper, glass, inked inscription
19 x 50 mm (diameter)
South Australian Museum, donated by William Bejah, 2007A79472

Bejah Dervish was tremendously proud of the Calvert expedition compass that was later engraved and presented to him at a reception at Government House, Adelaide, in 1897. Inscribed with his name and the Calvert expedition details, the compass is recognition of both his role as an extraordinary cameleer, and the courage, enterprise and endurance that he had sustained throughout the journey. Sandwith describes Bejah's 'dark old eyes gleaming' as he showed her his 'sacred object of brass'.

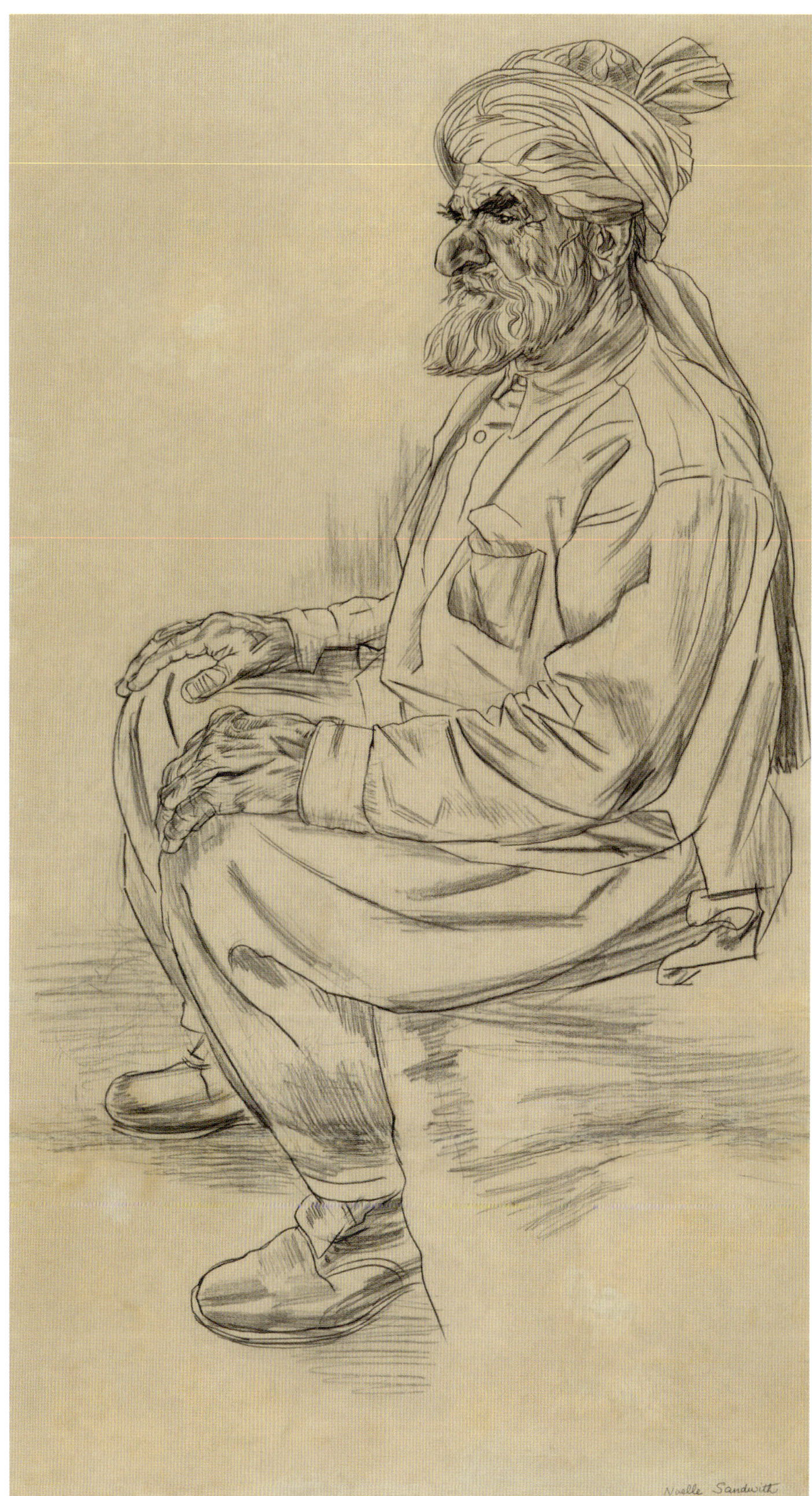

Bejah Dervish, Cameleer
by Noelle Sandwith
Marree, South Australia, 1953
graphite, paper
1050 x 590 mm
National Museum of Australia, 1993.0100.0044

Twenty-five-year-old English artist Noelle Sandwith was inspired to create 'something out of the ordinary' when she travelled 'down the track' from Birdsville to Marree in 1953. Keen to meet legendary camel driver, Bejah Dervish, she gives a lively account of their encounter, after gaining permission to sketch him. She describes 'his aristocratic profile', and his incredibly expressive eyes, reaching into 'the depths of his consciousness'.